D0231292

CL 1240744 5

Michael ELPHICK

Michael ELPHICK

The Great Pretender

Kate Elphick & Nigel Denison

The History Press

First published 2013

The History Press
The Mill, Brimscombe Port
Stroud, Gloucestershire, GL5 2QG
www.thehistorypress.co.uk

British Library Cataloguing in Publication Data.
A catalogue record for this book is available from the British
Library.

ISBN 978 0 7524 9147 9

Typesetting and origination by The History Press
Printed in Great Britain

Contents

Foreword

by Neil Morrissey

I remember the very first time that I met Michael. The producer of *Boon* at the time was Esta Charkham and she called me in. She had championed me at drama school, and had auditioned me for *Robin of Sherwood*, and then this part had come up. The character was described as being 'all dressed up in leathers with a helmet on', but when he took his helmet off, he had this long flowing hair and a puppy-dog face; Esta thought that I would be perfect for the role. She auditioned me and I got the part, but I still had to meet Michael to get approval for this new character on a show that by now was massive. I can't remember where we met now, but I sat down and we started chatting; I don't know who was with us or what we talked about, I was just nervous about meeting such a huge star but we did talk together for about half-an-hour and it went really well. You see I was nervous but I wasn't shy, which made a great difference. So he said, 'Well that's that, then. Let's go to the pub.' So to the pub we went and a very good job we were being driven around by Central TV at the time – there was no way I could have got on a bike or driven a car after that first session. I am sure that he realised then that he'd found another like-minded soul for socialising. He later said, 'You can drink in my company, but don't try and drink with me,' because he knew that he could out-drink any person on the planet.

What I had found was a great mentor in every sense. When he was on the set he was never 'starry' and visiting guest stars discovered that they couldn't be 'starry', either. You couldn't do that sort of thing in front of Michael, because he wouldn't wear it. He always came out of his camper without paper. He'd have his words learnt already, no bits of paper, so it would be kind of embarrassing if any actors were on set trying to learn their lines, which happened a few times. For him, it was first of all a matter of pride; secondly, he wanted to be ready to help those, like me, less equipped, who might be floundering a bit. He was amazing: he taught me how to hit marks. It was very important in those days, when they were using film, to get to the right position exactly and not be an inch out for close-ups. There's more latitude these days with digital cameras because you can shoot, reshoot and reshoot again and more. In film, it was the maximum three takes a shot. There was a game we used to play which taught me everything you needed to know about cameras and lenses and shots and apertures. Michael was technically amazing; wherever the camera was, we were allowed to ask what was the size of the frame. So, we then had to guess what was the distance from the lens, and what was the size of the aperture, and the nearest won a fiver; he took so much money off me, the bastard. But, basically, that game taught me all the technicalities of filming, knowing the size of the lens meant that you knew how to play to the lens. Occasionally I beat him and I was so pleased. So now, when-ever I'm on a film set, I'll always ask the size of the frame and I can pretty much gauge the lens size and when the stops are going to be. These days, of course, we rarely shoot on film so the techniques are very different.

He was such a quiet mentor: no question of telling you off. He just wanted you to maximise everything that was going on in that frame. He was always good friends with the crew. When guest actors turned up, they could see clearly how we were so in tune with the crew, the props guys, and certainly the lighting guys, 'the sparks'. He'd say, 'They're the most powerful union in the business, and if you've pissed off "the sparks", you're going to look ugly! They're not going to bother lighting you correctly – they just want to get on with their job and get home.' He was very friendly with all the technical staff as well. We'd go out drinking with the props and the lighting guys, and the occasional guest star joined us. I didn't understand how any hierarchy worked, so for safety's sake Michael said I should call everyone 'sir'. He said it was important that you had the right respect for everybody. Certainly he did for the DOP and the camera-operator – it was always 'sir'.

'Michael, could you ...'

'Yes, sir, no problem, sir.'

And it was that respect and discipline that I'd also learnt from this guy, Brian Hadley, in my youth theatre days. It always makes your job a lot easier. Michael said that you should always be on time. You don't wait until there's a knock, knock on your camper door. Whereas these days you might get people turning up late on set, you would never find Michael doing that. In fact, if anyone was late turning up, he'd go and knock on their door and say, 'Come on now, we've got a job to do. We all like sitting around doing nothing, but we can do that at the end of a day's work, after this job's done.'

So what I learnt from him was respect. I never hang round my camper; I'm always first out. I like to be on the set and get the job done. I've had that attitude bred into me during all those nine years of filming with Michael. I'd like to tell him how professional I've turned out to be as a result of that early discipline. I don't think that he was ever quite aware of what he was giving me. He was a teacher, not a preacher. It was always like a pat on the back. It would be, 'Well done, how about we do it like this', and there would be a little tweak, like planing a bit of wood smooth. He was a great listener as well; if you came in with new information, he'd store it. I expect that, when I was in my early twenties, which is what I was when I worked with him, I'd over-boast, you know, full of ideas, wanting to impress and he never told me to shut it; he might just go, 'Rocky, shh ...' I am sure he'd have had a sense of pride in me, the way I advanced. He was around for *Men Behaving Badly* and would have seen me getting better during the series at delivering comedy lines and things like that. His timing was brilliant; I learned by watching him, by observing, in the same way as learning the technical stuff that he had turned into a game. If he was around now, I'd like to say to him, that on my behalf, he doesn't have to be guilty: quite the opposite, in fact. He always used to say that he would probably die of guilt. He was full of guilt the whole time. It was guilt that came up in those late-night pre-bed conversations. He felt terrible about the neglect of his family, neglect of this person or that. He'd say, 'I must get in touch with ...' and make notes. So, I'd like to say to him, 'I'm proud of you. I'm thankful to you for giving me so much in my early days when I needed it. Otherwise I might have been an arrogant shit, or some starry arsehole because that wasn't your style at all. Thank you for taking me under your wing, and without making me feel useless, giving me a brilliant apprenticeship.'

Preface

by Kate Elphick

Over the years, Dad and I often discussed him writing his autobiography. Some days he'd be enthusiastic about the idea: We'd talk about travelling by train around West Sussex with a dictaphone and stopping off at all the places from his childhood, recording his memories together. Other days, he'd say he wouldn't want to write an autobiography, in case people thought it self-indulgent or vain. I think this view stemmed from the fact that the drink had taken a hold, and he couldn't see a happy ending. After Dad died, it suddenly became very important to me that I should write his biography, to record such an amazing catalogue of work, and as a tribute to both my dead parents: a way for my children to know a bit about the people that they were, my beautiful, brave, calm and optimistic mum, and my hilarious, fun-loving, gentle and inspirational dad. I love you both.

For me, I think what has been beneficial is reliving the years when my parents were alive, and understanding, as an adult and as a parent myself, the situations we went through as a family. Fame, alcoholism, cancer and relationship problems were all issues that I dealt with then, but I can understand them differently now, as I view them from an adult perspective.

The words of *The Great Pretender* were handwritten in a little frame above my father's bed. It is the song that I have always associated with him. I remember hearing him singing it from when I was very little. He even made a recording of him singing it, which I cherish to this day. So, not only was it his own, personal anthem, but also, I think, a fitting title for this book, describing as it does an incredibly talented actor – *The Great Pretender*:

> Oh-oh, yes I'm the great pretender
> Pretending that I'm doing well
> My need is such I pretend too much
> I'm lonely but no-one can tell
>
> Oh-oh, yes I'm the great pretender
> Adrift in a world of my own
> I've played the game but to my real shame
> You've left me to grieve all alone
> Too real is this feeling of make-believe
> Too real when I feel what my heart can't conceal
>
> Yes, I'm the great pretender
> Just laughin' and gay like a clown.
> I seem to be what I'm not, you see
> I'm wearing my heart like a crown
> Pretending that you're still around

Preface

by Nigel Denison

This has been one of the strangest, but most rewarding experiences of my life, despite getting off to such an inauspicious start. Kate first approached me about six years ago to help her write her parents' biography. Whether it was the inertia of the newly retired or a genuine feeling of being unequal to the task, I'm not sure, but it was definitely one for the 'back burner'. Kate didn't press me, but I gathered that she had been disappointed before when the project had failed to get off the ground. She never dwelt on how the loss of both her parents had affected her. I knew she wished that her children could have had access to Julia, and Michael, particularly when he was well. She, herself, had been robbed of a mature relationship with them and she felt that any that her parents may have had with each other had been blighted by all the adverse press coverage that they had had to endure. I suppose I felt that it was going to be just a bit presumptuous for me to be the one going into that psychological hinterland. So I did nothing.

I think, perhaps, for me, it was the rash of funerals that we come across at a certain age that hastened the project's re-emergence. I know that Kate was delighted when we agreed to proceed with our publisher. She wanted to provide a family history of both parents, how they met and their careers prior to her birth, plus everything that happened thereafter. I knew Julia's parents and Mike's Mum, and both of them, more or less from the time that they met, but for both Kate and I, there were many more gaps to fill than words to fill them. I had the benefit of retirement time, while Kate was employed full-time with a young family, living in Portugal. We decided that I could be the research foot-soldier in the UK, and that we would both be writing. It was an odd notion, but we felt it best if we wrote jointly in Kate's voice: that anything we learnt along the way would be as Kate discovered it. We had the best of two worlds: people could perhaps be franker with me than they might be with a friend's daughter, but they could be more familiar sometimes with Kate than they might be with a stranger.

What I had not expected was how frank Kate herself might be. She proved more than equal to the task of objective biographer. It was established fairly early on that there would be no hiding from Mike's alcoholism. We felt that if his relationships with women were part of a narrative development, we would refer to them, otherwise we would pass over them. We would quote his stories as he told or wrote them, knowing sometimes there might be a little exaggeration. Granny Joan, Mike's mother, has been one of our greatest aids, being an indefatigable collector of cuttings about her son. Sadly, in most cases, her scissors removed all reference to provenance: the date and name of publications and authors, for which we have to apologise. Kate Robbins, who has been an unofficial biographer of Mike, over the years, was also very helpful.

We have tried to indicate with some of our chapter headings Mike's love of songs, many shared intimately and exclusively with certain individuals. 'Be Lucky' is what he wrote with his signature as an autograph.

People use the word 'journey', employed un-geographically nowadays, very loosely, but it would be the *mot juste* for where Kate and I have been and the people that we have met in assembling this book. Throughout, there has been an understandable request to protect her parents' reputations, to honour her father's supreme acting skills and a huge celebration of his larger-than-life contribution to so many lives. Kenneth Cranham said that Mike should have lived in another age, that he stepped out of a Henry Fielding book; that he was actually too big for the age that he had arrived in. It has been a privilege to work with Kate to bring the story to a wider public.

1

The End

It was a Saturday, the day Dad died, Saturday 7 September 2002.

He had been in and out of casualty during the time preceding his death with a series of drink related problems ... At this time he was hardly recognisable as the good-looking, rugged, leather-clad biker Boon. His body was now struggling, badly bloated and weak. He looked ill, his face puffy and eyes discoloured and watery. He was suffering with diabetes and his body was straining now, seriously, with the effects of years of alcohol abuse and neglect. Above all, at this time, to me he looked sad: so sad, and lost. It broke my heart every day.

He would get up, not late, each morning, pull on his old, blue soft towelling dressing-gown and meander from the kitchen to the garden for a fag, finally settling for a while on the sofa in front of the morning news. Sometimes I would catch him (as I peeked around the door, having quietly come to bring him a coffee and to say 'Hi') sitting forlorn with his head in his hands. I knew that he hated being a slave to the drink, hated what it had done to him and to the rest of us ...

We had divided the two floors of our beautiful Edwardian home so that my little daughter Jasmine and I lived upstairs, converting one of the four bedrooms into our living room, whilst Dad had turned what was once his study into his bedroom. It was a lovely, spacious room at the front of the house with the huge bay window facing out to the front garden and the road. When I was little, my dad's study had a piano that I would go in and play – *Chopsticks* mostly; he had wanted me to learn, as he wished that he had learned to play the piano himself ... and to tap dance! The room always smelt of him – a mixture of his aftershave, tobacco and his own scent. I remember so well that smell I loved. Now his bedroom, the walls were still terracotta and covered with pictures: some framed posters of plays and pantos he had performed in, memorabilia from *Boon*, and even a framed silver disc of 'Hi Ho Silver', the theme tune from the series. There was a signed Francis Bacon amongst other prints and various paintings, and also a cork board of photos and children's drawings and cards from Jasmine, and even mine from the past. The ceiling-to-floor dark-green curtains were always closed to allow him his privacy and I think that he liked the dark, safe, cosy effect with the soft lighting. The mahogany desk and piano were now replaced with a double bed and bedroom furniture.

We shared the kitchen, the focal point of most houses. It was where our paths would cross throughout the day: a beautiful, big country kitchen that reminded us both of Mum. We would share some time there in the morning before Dad headed out. The smart, original black-and-white chequered tiles of the huge hallway would give way here to polished floorboards, on which stood a big pine table, breakfast bar and an old pine dresser, displaying Mum's collection of country plates and jugs picked up from different antique shops and fairs. Opposite the door, above the sink was a huge window, filling the room with light; to the right, as you faced it, were stable doors leading through to the utility room, Dad's shower room and the back door to the garden. Dad had chosen the colour of the walls – 'primrose yellow' he had wanted.

I would cherish that morning-time, alcohol-free, when we would chit-chat about nothing, relaxed in each other's company. After a while Dad would chuck on his shabby, dark tracksuit bottoms, squeeze his (now unkempt) feet and overgrown toenails into black trainers or slip-on shoes, find a t-shirt, and walk up to the top of our tree-lined road, onto the grubby, bustling Willesden High Road. Around the corner was the bar, 'Sparkles' as we locals called it (even though, I think, its actual name at this time had changed to 'The Isobar'). It wasn't one of your traditional pubs, far from it, being what I always described as 'a bit of a dive'. It was a converted shop in a parade with constantly sticky floors and stinking toilets. However, during the day it was quiet, and Dad knew all the regulars. He would sit by the glass front, so that he could watch the world go by, with a script or *The Guardian*. He had got to know the manager Zaman Bader well and occasionally relied on him for a lift home.

Some weeks before he died, Dad had spent a short spell in the Central Middlesex Hospital, where he had been admitted after collapsing in our road on the way back home from the bar. Since then, he had seemed to be noticeably more concerned about his condition: not that this, as far as I could tell, had been reflected in his need to drink. He had got into the habit of calling up ambulances whenever he felt slightly unwell, but then swiftly discharging himself when he felt a little better. That is exactly what happened the night before he died.

On the Friday afternoon he had again had to call an ambulance; this time to pick him up from 'Sparkles'. To my mind, the whole thing was getting ridiculous: he called me about six o'clock in the evening, asking me to come and get him, with a change of clothes, as he was going to discharge himself. I was absolutely furious. We then had the same disagreement we'd been having daily for months: 'You need treatment ... You have to stay in ... They say *you must stay in* ... You can't keep discharging yourself'.

I was so fed up. I had become totally exhausted from the constant worry: calls from the hospital to say that he was there, or visits from the neighbours to say he had collapsed. Then, within a day, he had discharged himself and the whole sorry process would begin all over again. I called my boyfriend, Luke – reluctantly, as we hadn't been together that long (less than a year). I needed a lift, and some moral support, but felt nervous about exposing him to too much of our family drama, for fear of scaring him off. However, he was great. We had lived on the same road through our school years and even walked there together as kids, as his older sister was in my year (we had reconnected through her earlier in the year). We took Jasmine to a friend living nearby and set off for the hospital. The light was now fading and Luke was quiet during the journey as we sat in the usual London traffic, sensing my anger at the situation. And my fear. I think he knew there were no words to console me.

We arrived at the hospital and were swiftly ushered into a room to meet a couple of doctors who were obviously concerned. Their advice was very straightforward: I had to tell Dad that the best course of action was for him to be admitted. They said that he was in serious need of medical attention.

I felt as if a huge scream was welling up inside me shrieking, 'Yes, I do know! I do live with him!' It was a scream that had been fed for more than ten years by Dad's concerned friends telling me that I really should try and get my dad to stop drinking. It was as if they thought that the idea had never occurred to me, as if I had never tried. 'You know,' they would say, 'he should get help; maybe a move abroad would improve his chances?' or 'He probably needs a hobby; has he ever tried golf?' Only the family of an aloholic can tell you that it's pretty difficult to convince them that golf can be a substitute for vodka or that it's best to live where booze is even cheaper.

We left the hospital in silence. I gave Dad that look that indicated I was too angry even to speak to him. I marched tight-lipped and stony-faced to the car. Dad trundled on behind, looking like a guilty child awaiting his fate. But it was so hard to stay cross with him for long. He was such a gentle man and so vulnerable in these circumstances. He lowered himself into the passenger side of Luke's new Mercedes C200 Sport with a cheery, 'Nice motor, mate!' and as we moved off they both began discussing cars. Soon he had us both laughing over some story or other – I wasn't really taking on board the substance. The stress of the previous few hours had begun to take its toll.

With some relief I leant my head against the window in the back of the car, listening to the murmur of the two men chatting in the front. It felt like an out-of-body experience, as I watched the rest of the world go about its business outside the bubble of Luke's car. It was a warm night, around nine by now, and the 'Friday Nighters' were on the move as we drove through Willesden Green; girls clattered by, dolled up for drinking and clubbing later; local lads began to collect in groups outside the fried chicken and kebab shops; a tired driver was taking the 260 bus back to the depot. Like on most Friday nights, litter was beginning to build up across the pavements and the street benches were moving to full occupancy as even the poor and needy were settling in for the weekend.

I was beginning to doze. The colours from the different lights in the road were reflected in the window ahead, as we turned past the tube station, into our road. What happened next was as shocking as it was predictable. When we look back, Luke and I find ourselves as saddened as we are amused by it. 'Typical!' is what everyone would say.

Luke slowed the car to turn the corner. 'Hang on!' Dad cried, catching us unawares as he had already opened the passenger door to make good his escape, 'Got to see a man about a dog,' he grinned. The car never actually stopped before he had shot out the door. He turned to give us a wave and quick thumbs up as he headed off to Sparkles. Luke pulled the car up by the pavement; he was completely taken aback: 'Has he actually gone to the bar? God, Kate, I really don't think you should let him go – he's just got out of hospital!'

I looked at him. 'What do I do?' I asked quietly. 'Go in there and make a scene? Demand that he leaves? Drag him out? Even if I do that, he'll just go and buy a bottle to drink at home.' So there he was: a man who had experienced his fair share of salubrious drinking holes, back in Sparkles in Willesden Green. 'Come on, Luke,' I said, 'I've got to get back and pick up Jasmine.'

It's strange but I'm really glad now that I didn't try to intervene with Dad's progress to the bar. He usually came home well before eleven on a Friday, before the DJ started his routine and the bar began to fill with youngsters. However, I heard him get in at about one-thirty, so I knew he had had a good night. Apparently, all his friends had been in and Zaman's brother had dropped him off and he'd seemed fine. So I am glad that his last night alive wasn't spent rowing with me or sitting drinking alone.

During the early hours of Saturday morning – it was about 5 a.m., I think – I was woken by a terrible noise; the sort of noise that wakes you up instantly and completely. All senses alert, I was sitting up in bed before I was aware that I had been woken. Then I heard it again and I felt sick: 'AAAAAArrgh!' Dad was shouting out in agony. I rushed downstairs into his room. He was lying on his side, his face screwed up, contorted in pain. I watched as he struggled to move his great bulk, looking for a position that might bring him some relief from the pain. Each movement seemed to hurt him more and he held his arm weakly to his chest.

I helped him (as best I could) to sit up and told him that I was going to call an ambulance; the phone was in the hall just outside his room, so I could see him as I dialled. There was a very gentle female voice at the end of the line asking me questions; as she asked, I was reminded of a first-aid class I'd attended and a video we'd watched of a man having a heart attack. The operator's voice was calm and I was calm. There was no way that I could actually be feeling calm, but I did seem to be responding in a very calm way. I told her everything that was happening and prepared myself for any instructions that I might be given to administer first aid.

Perhaps through shock, the memory of events is now a little erratic. After I put the phone down I went back into the bedroom. Dad was now sitting on the edge of the bed. Under my breath I know I was thanking God for letting him live a little longer. I think subconsciously I had been preparing myself to go back into that room and watch him die. We put his dressing-gown on him and waited together for the ambulance. Jasmine was asleep upstairs, so when it came, I told Dad that I would meet him at the hospital, once I had sorted out somewhere for her to stay.

He seemed a little better now and certainly more relaxed. The paramedics were really sweet, a young girl and guy, gentle and caring. The lad turned to Dad and said something along the lines of: 'You know we can't keep coming out to get you, if you won't stay in? You mustn't keep discharging yourself!' I hoped to God that he'd pay heed to the advice this time. The three of them left, Dad leaning heavily on them for support. His head was bowed as they slowly made their way down the path towards the flashing lights of the ambulance in the road.

Having seen him play so many parts, this seemed like yet another – except now he wasn't framed by the edges of a TV screen, and I could feel the cool, intrusive night air on my face. The ambulance drew away. After a while I shut the door and called his partner, Liz.

By the time that I had organised myself and Jas, and got to the hospital, it was about nine o'clock and Liz was already there. Dad was in casualty, sitting up on a hospital bed, a gurney, waiting for a ward bed to become available. The doctors had told him his heart was struggling to survive, as were most of his organs. On hearing this he had agreed to stay in for treatment. I was totally elated that at long last he'd seen reason. He told me it was going to mean a long spell in hospital and giving up booze for good, but that he didn't want to die. He realised that he had to go through with it. He had agreed to everything the doctors had planned for him and he meant it. I couldn't believe my ears; I could tell that he meant every word.

We waited in casualty, as you do, waiting for a bed, reading newspapers and drinking endless cups of not-very-nice tea. Late in the morning Dad said I might as well get back to Jas: there was no point in hanging about all day. It was my friend Amber's birthday and she was having a barbecue. I said that I'd pop in there and be back later that evening. Liz was going to stay with him. I felt as if a huge weight had suddenly been lifted. Dad was staying here – away from the bar – safe.

As I bent to kiss him goodbye, he put a hand round my waist and gave the low of my back a little rub. The papery skin of his hands felt rough but his touch gentle and reassuring. I remember feeling very conscious of that tiny action, almost as if I were hyper-sensitised. I can recall it perfectly even now. It was the last time I would ever see my dad or feel his touch again. He died early that evening from a massive heart attack.

2

When Michael Met Julia

When you are writing about your parents there is a large part of their story that is inevitably outside your experience because it precedes you. Here I have been reliant on some press interviews that Dad gave, and diaries, but mostly on the collective memories of their friends and our relations. What will always fascinate any child is where their parents met – in my case Chichester, or more specifically Chichester Theatre – the place that I have to thank for being brought into the world. Chichester was also Dad's home town, or city, rather, as the residents will be quick to remind you.

When you're excavating past times it's always good to remember how quickly places can change within a generation or two, and a lot was changing rapidly in post-war provincial England (something that my parents' contemporaries have been keen to emphasise).

My parents met in Chichester in the 1960s. It wasn't exactly a backwater but according to my mum's friend Ros Lemm, who grew up there (and was responsible for my parents' meeting each other) it had a slow, traditional pace of life – resistant to change and unimpressed with the rapidly exploding cultural scene of the capital, less than 70 miles away. It had been a relatively prosperous market town, now city, with a history of livestock farming. Dad's family had been cattle farmers.

Ros remembers a childhood of insufferable boredom. When she describes it, though, it seems to me idyllic. Children 'played out' – no one worried about them, they were independent, could go riding off on bikes, taking picnics, and not returning home till dark. My Uncle Robin remembers cycling to Bognor with a group of children – he was four. A sort of Enid Blyton freedom. But Ros says that nothing seemed to happen. Market day was a highlight. The 'pictures' provided entertainment and all children went unaccompanied on a Saturday morning. She remembers a neighbour getting the first television – to watch the Queen's coronation in 1953 – and being allowed to go in and watch during the short time each day when it broadcast a programme. In their own house they continued to gather round the 'wireless' before her father gave in to her (and her brother's) insistent clamours for a TV. But when they got one it came disguised as a sideboard with doors that closed firmly over the screen. Television gradually gained a hold of the local consciousness and cinemas began to close. As the new rock-and-roll phenomenon reached the south of England, one local band member recalls that it was slow to catch on in Chichester: 'there were ten times as many local dances in nearby Bognor.'

Every child was faced with the 11+ exam – the most divisive benchmark in the English education system, which, in effect, weeded out 80 per cent of children. Children who had played together through the primary years were suddenly separated. If you passed, you went on the bus, bedecked in brand-new uniform, far too big (so you could grow into it), to the grammar school. Everybody else attended the local secondary modern. People, to this day, talk about the stigma of failing the 11+. You probably remember John Prescott, Tony Blair's deputy prime minister, confessing that he never got over it. Ros passed. She got a new bike as a reward. My dad failed. Ros went to the Chichester Girls High School, and my dad to the Lancastrian Secondary Modern School. In 1971, the Lancastrian was to merge with Chichester Boys High as part of the government's comprehensive school plans, but in my dad's day, in shire England, class and education operated a highly successful apartheid system. The chances of the two of them meeting socially would be virtually zero. Their expected future pathways would be different too: hers, to pass exams and move to a campus far away; his, to leave school at the first available opportunity and get on with the real business of life. A view not shared by my grandparents at all.

My dad never got over failing the 11+. I wonder whether his determination to favour the underdog, his visible dislike of privilege – he was quick to challenge the sort of braying smugness of 'Hooray Henrys', to the shocked amusement of lookers on – was rooted in that?

School was really not for him – and teachers were exasperated (except for one). But he was no slouch when casual work was in the offing in the early days. Like many of his contemporaries he found that a good source of revenue was to be found in a newspaper round, although as a child he had always dreamed of running away and joining the circus. One used to come to Chichester every year and he was very cut up when the site for the circus, which was also the traditional site for the annual Chichester Sloe Fair, was later designated for council development. What he was to discover in time was that 'the development' was a car park for a brand new theatre.

His round took him close to where the foundations of the theatre were being laid, and he said that he used to pause every morning to see how far they had advanced since the day before. When he was much older, when he'd had his first starring role on television in a series called *Holding On*, he met the author of the original book, Mervyn Johns, at a reception. He was surprised at his greeting: 'You've come a long way since you delivered my papers!' the famous writer said to him.

In his early teenage years he was always on the lookout for a bit of paid work. He got a job at Goodwood Racecourse, picking up litter and tidying up after race meetings. There was also a little rowboat ferry that crossed Chichester harbour between Itchenor and Bosham. For the pedestrian it could save you a 13-mile round trip, but it was mostly used by mariners who wanted to be taken to their moored boats. Anyway, Dad – who by the age of thirteen had managed to grow a noticeable, if not luxuriant, moustache – became a part-time ferryman as well.

He also found ways to spend money. His best friend of those days, Bill Bray, remembers them both being members of the same youth club, St Georges. As Bill says of those days, 'So little happened then. You had to create your own excitement. So every Saturday night we hired a room at the back of the New Inn and brought a quarter of a bottle of gin, for 11 shillings each, for a ritual get-together.' Dad later went on record to say:

> I've always looked much older than I am. In fact, I had my first pub drink, a brown ale it was, when I was about thirteen. I got caught once. I was in the school athletics team. I took the Sussex record, for my age, for the 880 yards, and the local paper printed a picture of me together with my age. 'What's this mean?' said the landlord that evening. 'Printing mistake.' I said.

But what Bill remembers most about Dad in those years – and what brought Ros and him into the same ambit from different sides of the town – was the wonderful world of drama: a world neither he nor his best friend at the time realised was going to change his life.

Mr Stubbs was the one teacher who saw the germs of his talent. English lessons at that time often consisted of play readings. Dad was evidently good enough for his teacher to encourage him to join the Drama Club. He was in quite a few productions. Bill Bray remembers playing a servant to Dad's Madame Coupler, when he was dressed in a crinoline, in Sheridan's *A Trip to Scarborough*. According to the programme, Mr Stubbs was in charge of make-up for the production: he must have had his work cut out, transforming Dad into an eighteenth-century lady. Dad was also in school productions of *Noah* and *A Midsummer Night's Dream* and was Shylock in *The Merchant of Venice*.

But Mr Stubbs had more ambitious plans for young Elphick. In 1932 there had arrived in Chichester an optometrist, a businessman, called Leslie Evershed-Martin. He had been a committed member of amateur dramatic societies in other English towns in which he'd lived, and was astounded that no such organisation existed in his adoptive city. He decided to put this to rights and using the local newspaper, the *Chichester Observer*, as recruiting sergeant, organised a meeting: a large crowd attended and The Chichester Players were born in 1933. More of Mr Evershed-Martin as we progress but Mr Stubbs, nearly thirty years after The Players were instituted, was keen for his protégé to experience a broader theatrical experience: namely, The Players' production of *The Lady's Not For Burning* in The Assembly Rooms in Chichester. It wasn't a large part but it gave Michael a little bit more confidence to tread the boards outside the school environment.

It's not difficult to imagine how this young boy from the other side of the tracks regarded the polite society of The Chichester Players. He really wasn't going to hang around there. By chance, one of the young Players, Julia Goodman, had become involved in a new youth drama group. New organisations like this – just for the benefit of young people – were terribly *outré*. The new organisation was called The Attic Players. It was called this because one of its founders, Julian Sluggett, had a father who was a prominent accountant in Chichester, and who had a spare attic in the offices of his practice. Here the young people could rehearse whenever they wanted to (free of charge) prior to performing in whatever church hall or temperance club was available. Tom Chadbon, who has been a perennial performer over nearly five decades of television, was also a founder member. Later, as membership grew and productions got bigger, it moved to a room over a pub, with a fish-and-chip shop conveniently situated nearby.

Julian met my dad when they were fourteen, and he was the one who encouraged him to join The Attic Players. As his father was an old friend of Granddad Elphick, he must have realised that Dad had done some stage work. Anyway, as he remembers it:

> I was standing outside The Punch House, one Saturday afternoon with these two girls – I think one was Julia Goodman – talking about

finding another man to do the fourth Knight Templar in *Murder in the Cathedral*. It was always the same problem: you could find the women, but not the men. Suddenly, Mike appeared round the corner carrying a football. One of the girls said, 'Why not ask him?'

I did. He agreed and I said, 'You might as well get rid of that football. You're not going to have time for that in the future!' And, indeed, he didn't.

Ros Lemm joined The Attic Players and remembers appearing in a review they had written. The production of *Murder in the Cathedral* took place in Wick village church. Bill Bray was working backstage and out front with any lights that might have been available. In June of 1962 The Attic Players performed the play *Billy Liar* in Stockbridge Hall. Dad played Billy's father, Mr Fisher. It's such a sign of the times to read the review in the local paper:

> Members of Chichester's youthful Attic Theatre Company faced their most difficult task to date with the production last week of *Billy Liar* a satirical comedy set in the North Country. A play of this type is not easy to perform successfully even with a cast of experienced campaigners, and in all the circumstances, the standard of both acting and production reached a high level ... With a little more experience the Attic Theatre Company must surely go places ... lovers of amateur dramatics in Chichester can expect some worthwhile entertainment in the future. It was a spirited and bubbling performance by Tony Fabian in the title role. He obviously enjoyed himself in the part, and his enthusiasm and verve transferred itself to the audience. He received first class support from Michael Elphick as his grumbling, self-asserting father, a man who is sure he knows what is right and who is not afraid to call a spade a ... shovel – which he does perhaps too frequently in the play. Others who caught the eye were Patrick Hastings as his friend Arthur and Julia Goodman as his tarty girl friend Rita.

Apart from the subtext giving us a clue to the latent disapproval of such a play, it's interesting to note that 'the places' that some of the company would 'go' to were: Dad, Julia Goodman and Julian Sluggett,

The Central School of Speech and Drama; Tom Chadbon, RADA; Patrick Hastings, Oxford University Drama Society. But the appeal of The Attic Players was about to be superseded by an even more powerful influence on Dad's life.

My dad's first non-school acting experience had been with The Chichester Players, whose founder, Leslie Evershed-Martin, was going to have an even more profound effect on his life, indirectly, by being a television viewer. Mr Evershed-Martin, as well as being a successful Chichester businessman, was also a well-liked and able local councillor. He had risen to be mayor of the city and was thinking of retiring from this arena of public life.

One evening in January 1959 he sat down by the double glow of the fire and his black-and-white television set to watch the arts programme *Monitor*, presented by Huw Weldon. The subject was the building of a new theatre in Stratford, Ontario, in Canada; how it was following the design of the ancient amphitheatres, and how it was being built by public subscription. The leading protagonist was Sir Tyrone Guthrie, a theatrical force on both sides of the Atlantic. Mr Evershed-Martin turned to his wife and sons and said, 'If they can do that in Canada, why can't we do it here in Chichester?' He says that if the family had not been enthusiastic, he wouldn't have proceeded – a cautious approach he was to maintain at every stage of the project, from fundraising to design and administration. Through the *Monitor* programme he contacted Guthrie (at one point staying in his slanty-floored apartment in Stratford-upon-Avon, only a few miles from the slanty-floored hotel – 'The White Swan' at Henley – that my dad was later to own!). Tyrone Guthrie was very supportive. This meant that a number of important benefactors came on board, the great and the good of the county, as well as London theatre aficionados.

It was an uphill job, however: a complete outsider from the world of the Arts taking on the Herculean task of inspiring others to create a theatre with an international reputation in a small provincial city on the south coast of England. This at a time, of course, when theatre was slipping into the doldrums, like cinema, with the growing success of television. In terms of influencing the general public, the first founding fathers of the theatre cast their net far and wide. Julian

Sluggett recalls Mr Evershed-Martin unveiling a model of the theatre to a group of awestruck students, including himself, on a residential summer drama course in Pulborough.

Leslie Evershed-Martin was evidently a charismatic figure: he had been well-liked as a mayor; he had a streak of independence and hated the way party politics was beginning to impinge on local affairs. This independence seemed to be shared by many in the city, which made it less of a provincial backwater and more of a civic melting-pot.

Whether it was the persuasive talents of Mr Evershed-Martin, or other reasons, the appointment that sealed the fate of the theatre to the good, and that of my dad forever, was that of Theatrical Director. Sir Laurence Olivier was offered the job and accepted. He said at the time that he had, in recent years, worked with two theatres that had had to close down, and it would make a difference to be with one (and grow with it) from the very beginning. He had been making a lot of films and had spent a fairly exhausting time in the United States. He had a new bride, Joan Plowright, and was preparing to settle down in nearby Brighton. Many believed that running the Festival Theatre (the theatre would only operate during an extended summer season) was, for Olivier, the sort of experience that he required prior to taking on The National Theatre.

So McAlpines, the builders, started the early work of clearing the site in 1960. My dad was just 14, as his circus site was being destroyed, as he thought (it was merely being asphalted for car-parking and the fairs and circuses would continue to assemble there when the theatre season was over). As time passed he used to go down to the site to monitor the progress on a regular basis. Getting down to Itchenor and the ferry, or to the adjoining boatyards where he also picked up part-time jobs, was quite a bike-ride. The theatre site was nearer and local lads were being recruited for labouring jobs on a casual basis, 'I got a job on the site there navvying when I left school,' he later told a local reporter, 'I was then taken on as an apprentice electrician working on the lights.'

Partly true. But he was only fifteen when he got his first casual jobs on the site. He was still at school officially while working there, but as Bill Bray documents, was looking at least 18. So what started as weekend and holiday work gradually whittled away at his schooldays. The transition to electrician proved very beneficial. He and Bill Bray worked originally for the site electrical firm but then graduated to working for Bill Beauvoir, the stage lighting supremo. For Bill Bray it became a lifetime's occupation; for Dad it had wider implications: 'working on the lights is where I met Laurence Olivier. Olivier directed a lot of the early stuff so he did the lighting plots and, as I was working with the electrics crew, I got to know him more than the actors.'

The theatre was completed in May 1962. For most of the first season, which started in the July, Dad was little more than a 'powder monkey' on the great new ship. That year the season finished in early September so he could return to his studies at the Lancastrian without being missed. In fact, a lot of students were taken on for the summer season – school students, college students and those between the two. Ros became an usherette in the summer holidays, prior to her final year at school. The following summer she worked as an usherette again before going to college.

Her boyfriend was one of the founders of the Players, Bobby Clench. His daytime job at the time was working as a paint-sprayer in a boatyard, and as Ros says, 'This hardly made him the first choice of my father as my intended!'

As the end of her season of usheretting dawned, Ros received her 'A' Level results, which plainly lacked the levels for a university place but were sufficient to see her into The City of Birmingham Training College for Teachers, as it was known then. Similarly, my mum, Julia, was going through the same process and would arrive at the same place. They would not meet immediately, as friendship groups tended to be based on the hostels you occupied and theirs were a mile apart.

Ros said she opted for a college well away from home because that's what you did back then (with generous grants) to escape the suffocation of polite society. But it was not an easy call: unlike most of her contemporaries she was coming from this exciting city, with its new theatre and 'café society'. It had already caught a whiff of the 1960s phenomenon, so she didn't need the stimulus of a new environment. She was grateful, however, that Bobby could visit her without let or hindrance.

By the beginning of 1964 she had met Mum, mostly off-campus. There was a club called Fifth House, near Birmingham Uni, where an up-and-coming pop group called The Spencer Davis Group hung out, and they went there a few times. Clubs cost money, however, as did clothes and all the other necessities of young life. Holiday employment was a must and when Ros told Mum of the earnings available in Chichester, at the theatre, she needed little persuading. It was agreed they would both go down for the Easter holidays in 1964. Ros had discovered that the season was starting early because a contingent of actors was coming over from Stratford, Ontario, to perform a pre-season repertoire. She had also discovered that they could both get highly lucrative jobs waitressing in the theatre restaurant, rather than taking on those of the poorly paid usherette, which they duly did.

Dad, meanwhile, was having the time of his life. The atmosphere in the early days of the Festival Theatre was heady, to say the least. Budgets for productions were not exactly shoestring but directors were bound to think frugally. As a consequence, many of the backstage staff were encouraged to take walk-on parts. They would be non-speaking and probably used for crowd scenes. Of course, Dad had nothing to do with the backstage crew at this juncture, but his younger brother Robin did. He had been recruited as a general dogsbody in the costume department, and here it was that he heard the director of the new play was looking for a couple of well-built young men, who'd had some acting experience, to play walk-ons. Thus Dad's proper stage career began in the starry company of some of Britain's elite actors: Derek Jacobi, Robert Stephens, Frank Finlay and Ian McKellen, to name just a few.

He was coming to the end of his school career, such as it was. He had, according to his mother, had one occasion where school life met theatre life. The school had decided to use the brand-new theatre stage for its prize-giving ceremony. Needless to say, Dad was not going to be one of the happy recipients. However, he had his own ideas when it came to self-presentation. The rule was supposed to be for the tall boys to be at the back of the stage, standing almost invisibly. He disappeared from the line-up at the back only to re-emerge, using the trap-doors and passages he'd learned his way round so well, at the front, upstaging everybody. No wonder his headteacher said to him, somewhat acidly, at term's end: 'I suppose you still have stardust in your eyes?' Dad never got over his profound dislike of the headteacher at the Lancastrian and when he was later asked to preside at a school prize-giving, he ever-so-politely declined.

Dad passed just two School Cert exams. There could have been more if he'd turned up to take them. But this was the time of Chichester's great second season. Olivier had encouraged his new wife, Joan Plowright, to take the lead in Shaw's *St Joan*. As Dad said later, 'In *St Joan* I walked on as a guard and stood with her while that enormously long scene with the Inquisitor goes on. I had to stand absolutely still for twenty minutes.' The choice, then, was either rehearsing that role or doing your exams. A bit of a no-brainer for Dad! He reckoned that he first came to the attention of Olivier because his wife, Joan, complained that the young guard was handling her too convincingly and hurting her when he was shackling her for the Inquisition.

My grandfather was furious with Dad for throwing away his education, as he saw it. As he reminded him again and again, he himself had been the first in his family to have a proper education and felt that Dad was squandering his opportunity. He was also singularly unimpressed by the working environment his son had fallen into:

> One day my old man took a look at my pay packet – £80 a week was a fortune in those days – and he marched me up to the foreman to tell him it was obscene. The foreman explained that it was the night work that was bumping up the dosh. What neither my father nor the foreman knew, was that when I was clocked-on during the day I was mostly watching what was happening on the stage.

But as Bill Bray says, 'Life was pretty hard. We didn't see much of our bed. Mike was very good at his work. The job was hazardous up in the rafters hanging by our fingers, swinging from bar to bar, as there were no bridges or walkways.' Olivier, it seems, was Dad's inspiration.

Talk about work, I've never known anyone, before or since, work harder than dear old Sir Larry did on that job. He adored the place. So much so that he used to come in at night and work with us sparks on the lighting. He'd bring a bottle of whisky sometimes – so perhaps that's where I first got my taste of booze!

Bill Bray remembers a more eccentric Olivier: 'He was strange – he had the worst taste in the world and would wear black plasticky jeans with cotton stitching, with a sports jacket!' Dad, however, found him very approachable and was delighted to be informed on a number of occasions that his walk-on appearances merited further development. My Grandma, Joan, must have thought so too because she was very disappointed that, as Dad had no Equity card, he couldn't appear in the programme. Finally, he said:

I plucked up the courage to ask Sir Laurence about having a pop at it and he sent me home with two speeches to learn. One was a great big chunk of Bottom from *Midsummer Night's Dream* and the other was from a play called *Epitaph for George Dillon*, which was John Osborne's first play. It was all about a really screwed-up actor and he wrote it before he got round to writing about Jimmy Porter, the angry young man in *Look Back in Anger*.

When Dad returned to the great man with his renditions, he was truly impressed. He added two more for him to learn: the Introduction from *Under Milk Wood* and a speech from Shakespeare's *The Two Gentlemen of Verona*. He then sat down and wrote a letter of introduction on behalf of his new discovery to LAMDA, Rose Bruford, RADA and The Central School of Speech and Drama. Dad travelled up to London on subsequent days and auditioned for all four – and was accepted by all four. He chose Central as it had been Sir Laurence's Alma Mater.

But when my mum and dad met, this hadn't happened yet. She, of course, was waitressing in the newly opened Theatre Restaurant. He would have still been at school – just. As far as she was concerned he would have seemed to be one of the lighting crew of the theatre, possibly 19 years old instead of 16, with a readily available disposable income. At the end of a show, everyone, actors, backstage, usherettes and waitresses would descend on The Old Cross pub, which seemed to have a flexible licence in those days, particularly on a Saturday night/Sunday morning. As Ros says, 'It was a paradise for young people'. That Saturday night in The Old Cross everything was heaving. All the old Attic Theatre group would have been there. Ros introduced Julia to one or two; then she wouldn't have seen her for some time. They were walking home to Ros's house, 'Do you know someone called Michael who looks after all the lights in the theatre?' Mum asked her. Naturally she wasn't sure who her friend was talking about. The Easter holiday continued and was hard work for everyone, but the waitresses felt they earned their extra money – it was a long time to be on your feet.

Towards the end of her final night there, as exhausted as can be, she was serving the final guests, when one swivelled round in his chair and said: 'Remember me?' Mum nodded. 'I've got a free night tomorrow. How about you taking it off too?' Dad asked. 'I am taking it off,' said Mum, 'I'm going home to Bournemouth tomorrow morning ... and I'm going to bed early tonight!'

3

The Beginning

What drew my mum and dad together? Obviously looks played a part. Mum was tall, willowy, and strikingly beautiful, with green eyes and a wide, dazzling smile. She confided to a friend that she hated her teeth, and so was very reluctant to laugh. In reality, she had perfect teeth, but she would have preferred them to be smaller. Don't we waste a lot of time being self-conscious? Dad was dark, quite swarthy – handsome but not conventionally so. His eyes were full of humour – they really did twinkle – and his mouth was always set in a half smile, as if laughter was a second away.

There's a view, though, that other factors are involved. When we lock eyes across a crowded room we apparently rapidly and intuitively recognise in each other something of ourselves. Mum and Dad were quite different, as personalities. While Dad was outgoing, gregarious and expansive, Mum was quiet, reserved

– held something back. So I can imagine that they found each other intriguing. But they also had a lot in common. Both came from south coast towns. Both had dominant, controlling fathers who didn't tolerate dissent. Both had a clear idea of what they wanted.

My Aunty Sue, Mum's sister, says that all she ever talked about throughout her childhood was becoming a teacher. Likewise, Dad's mother Joan recalled that at the age of 4, while still at nursery school, her son 'liked to do puppet shows. He used to make puppets himself with toilet rolls and handkerchiefs. He loved to entertain!'

Both sides of Mum's family had originated from the Portsmouth area, again not far from Chichester. This is where her parents met, married and lived in their early days together. Granddad's job was based there. He worked for a company called Air Speed, a branch of de Havilland. Air Speed was the company that had been formed in the 1930s by a man called Nevil Shute Norway. After the war, the name Norway was dropped and he was to become the famous novelist of works like *On the Beach* and *A Town Like Alice*. Most of his novels bring sea or air travel in somewhere. In his autobiography *Slide Rule* we can read about his early days with de Havilland: he was chief mathematician on the R101 project. Working with him at the time, as the project's chief engineer, was Barnes Wallis, who went on to distinguish himself as the inventor of the 'bouncing bomb', featured in the 1955 film *The Dam Busters*. This was all a little before my grandad Fred Alexander's time at de Havilland, but he was well installed as an aeronautic engineer at the outbreak of war in 1939, and because of the nature of his work, it became a 'reserved occupation' – that is, one deemed too important for him to leave for call-up. So there he stayed throughout the war. Portsmouth was a really dangerous place to be for civilians because of night-time bombing, so Alma, my grandmother, with newly arrived baby James (later my Uncle Jim), moved to a flat on the Isle of Wight. Then they realised that wartime ferry schedules made access to the Isle of Wight no easy matter, so it was decided to move Alma and son much further down the coast, out of harm's way, but on the mainland: to Walkford, near Bournemouth, and then to a flat in nearby Highcliffe-on-Sea, where Susan was born in 1943 and Mum in 1944.

In the 1950s, de Havilland closed down their Portsmouth operation, as Portsmouth Airport no longer held the sway it once had, so Fred Alexander found a new job at C.F. Taylor, in Christchurch, another company specialising in aerospace projects, with premises much closer to home. The owner of their flat, Mrs Aylward, helped the young couple acquire a house nearby, and here they stayed for the rest of their life together.

It is strange to imagine, in times when families rove around the world, that the Alexanders and the Princes, both branches of my Mum's side, were very much Hampshire coastal people. Those who went away were quite different from the norm. My grandfather had three siblings who lived locally – a sister Dora and brother Bill, and a brother who was killed in action on board a submarine in the war. My grandmother had two sisters, one who stayed local, while the other went north because of her husband's work (although returned to the area after he had died).

When I think about what I have remembered of my grandparents' families, I am sure I have filtered out certain things, only leaving in my head those characteristics that I felt had some bearing on my own parents' lives. For example, my mum's father, Fred, had a military background; Fred's mother died when he was just 14; his father was a regular in the Royal Navy and never remarried. This certainly marked out Granddad's personality. My mother's mother, Alma, née Prince, had two sisters; Alma's father was a chauffeur/mechanic and her mother, sadly, had a bit of a drinking problem. The daughters were often despatched to the local to bring back a replenished jug! The couple spent a lot of time rowing, with the children taking refuge in their bedroom. This was to influence how Nanny behaved in later life.

My mum's and Aunty Sue's memory of life at home in Highcliffe was not exactly of a 'dry' house, but something close to it. Sue has a memory of only one occasion when Granddad became slightly intoxicated. This was when his great friend, Geoff Fish, was leaving the next day to emigrate to Canada. They had met at the petrochemical works at Fawley, in which Fred had latterly found employment. Fred was not a great socialiser and this friendship evidently meant a lot to him (so much so, that Mum and Sue would later go out to Canada to see the Fish family for a holiday).

The abiding memory of their father, of Mum and her siblings, however, was not of his abstinence, but of his moods. He not only brought a Victorian discipline and intransigence to the household, he also brought silence. Children being seen and not heard and, certainly, 'no talking at table' would be the order of the day; but Fred Alexander himself would sometimes not speak for days to his wife or his children over an issue that he found unpalatable. Sue says it could be weeks, and in one instance, months, where the only sounds he would emit would be simple instructions to his wife. He would bark out an edict to his children and expect it to be followed to the letter. As a consequence, his eldest, his son Jim, took the first opportunity to leave home and went and joined the Navy. Julia, the youngest, learnt to tolerate this silence, to accept it, and to cut herself off from its emotional impact. She learnt to live within herself and she found that getting deeply absorbed in books helped.

Sometimes I wonder if Granddad was truly happy in his work. During his working life he was a strong believer in communism, and for a time was an active member of the Communist Party, which could have been difficult, considering the nature of his occupation. Certainly Mum inherited his left-wing views and would espouse many of his anti-capitalist ideas in the future.

I was never aware of this moodiness because I never saw it. When his eyes fell on me he always seemed delighted and was relaxed and loving with his grandchildren. By the time all his children had left home and he had retired, he and his wife were enjoying a wonderful relationship, heading off to the Channel Islands for holidays, she with her paints and canvases to capture the scenes out there. He was obviously at his worst during my mum's teenage years.

Despite their closeness in years, Mum and Aunty Sue were very different. They both used to horse-ride as children at the local stables, but Sue was by far the more committed. Sue remembers that it wasn't just apathy that kept Julia from riding, but also very bad hay fever. In a way, she traces her sister's love of reading to days marooned in her bedroom with the affliction.

Julia wasn't just a reader, she was also 'brainy', according to Sue. She tells a terrible story of how, when they were both in the same primary school, her sister who was in the year below, was brought up into her classroom to demonstrate how to answer a problem that she, Sue, patently couldn't. Perhaps it was this humiliation of her sister that formulated in her head the need to teach – with a care for children of all abilities.

Fate had further plans for the Alexander sisters, as that great divider of society that damaged generations: the 11+, the scholarship – call it what you will – split up the siblings. The two girls were going to be well-advanced into adulthood to pick up the reins of strong friendship again because Sue failed and went to a secondary modern, while Julia passed and went to 'Brock' (Brockenhurst) College. Sue says she was initially pleased – while she could walk to school, Julia had to gallop off, toast in hand, to travel by bus to New Milton and then by train to Brockenhurst. It meant, however, that they had very different friendship groups and the divide was to get larger. By the time Julia was on her way to teacher training college, Sue was working, about to get married and contemplating starting a family.

My mum said years later that her college years were not her happiest. Her lack of confidence was deeply hidden – no one knew it at the time as, according to friends, she looked stunningly beautiful, serene and assured. And she must have enjoyed the attention. In a college that had originally been 'women only' and was in the process of becoming co-ed, but where the ratio was still two-thirds women to one-third men, her looks were a considerable asset. The co-author of this book, Nigel, was one of several who featured as an item in her college life.

The life of the college was greatly enhanced by the inclusion of a large number of 'mature' students who had worked in the great world outside before considering a teaching career. For a number, the nearest they would get to a teaching career was their three years at college! They were a mixed but stimulating bunch, whose future careers, whether teaching or not, would demonstrate a dynamism that one lecturer would celebrate as being 'almost red-brick university'.

A fortnight-long arts festival, in Mum's first year there, featured John Arden, the playwright, appearing courtesy of the drama society;

Ted Hughes for the literary society, and Paul Simon, who happened to be over from the States, for the folk club. Mum, whose principal subjects were English and Drama, appeared in the festival with a mature student, whose name was Roger Hume, in the play *Miss Julie*. Roger arrived as an actor and left to become one again: he is most famously known for playing the part of Bert Fry in *The Archers* until his early death at the age of 55. So, for Mum, the college was providing the excitement and buzz that she would never have experienced in slow-paced New Milton. It might even have prepared her, to some extent, for the the razmatazz of showbusiness that would face her in the future. And Ros, while she missed the chutzpah of the Festival Theatre, could take great pleasure in developing her skills in creating costumes for drama productions.

If I've given the impression that Mum was a bit of a shrinking violet when it came to a social life, I've been misleading. Nearby Bournemouth was a wonderful place for young people to find holiday jobs and she was no exception. With her friend Carol Skinner, she worked in most of the municipal cafés and restaurants in the area; Carol lived in Boscombe, close to work, so Mum stayed with her. In the summer she got to know the Irish students who poured over from Belfast, most of them from Queens University, also looking for work. They were a joyful and riotous assembly.

Stimulated by two terms in college, with her waitressing skills honed by two seasons of waitressing in Bournemouth, Mum was ready to be introduced to the polite society of Chichester. She duly set off that Easter holiday with her new-found friend Ros, to find waitressing work and, thereby, also Dad!

So perhaps I should give you something of the background of my dad at this point. The Elphicks had had a history of cattle rearing in the area for more than two generations; they had originated from Steyning and were known as prize bull breeders. Dad's grandfather, Frederick Elphick, was one of thirteen children, not all of whom went into the meat business; Dad's father, my Granddad Herbert didn't, and neither did his brother, Ray. Some became butchers, like Great-grandfather Frederick. Mention the name 'Elphick' to anyone born between the wars in Chichester and they would most likely say 'Sausages!' Yes, Elphick's Pork Sausages from Elphick's Pork Butchers Shop were justly famous. But this was not Frederick's shop – his was an 'all-meats' shop about two streets away, always being confused and justly irritating the family. Neither were the two Elphick families knowingly related. When Dad was going through a particularly bad 'alcoholic phase', he said that the only job he could imagine keeping him sober would be farming – early mornings and hard physical graft all day from first to last at night ... too tired for anything but a good meal and sleep at the end of the day.

As far as Herbert and Ray were concerned, there was no time to consider which trade to adopt before they went straight from school to the call-up. Herb had been a good student at school and something of a bookworm. He went to the same grammar school as the author, John Wyndham, and Dad remembers having all his books at home, *The Day of The Triffids* etc. But a scholarly outlook was of little consequence in the six years of wartime facing Herb. Like many of his local contemporaries he spent the duration in the Sussex Yeomanry and, like them, would never speak of those years. Suffice to say, the regiment saw action at Dunkirk, El Alamein and the storming of Monte Cassino, amongst other theatres of war.

Amid the gloom my Granny Joan had been one ray of light in Herb's life. At some social event in the Brighton area he had befriended a young saleswoman from a coat and gown shop there. Her name was Joan Haddow. She joined up too and went into the WAAF, the Women's Auxiliary Air Force, where she became a corporal, working in the quartermasters stores. Joan says that she was given her NCO stripes because her CO said that she had 'a commanding voice'! Joan originated from Ladbroke Grove in London, not far away from where I was born. Her father was a hairdresser and had worked in-house in a number of prestigious London hotels. The fact that his latest had been the Hotel Metropole in Brighton accounted for Joan choosing to work down there. Herb wrote to her every week for nearly six years.

Joan was one of four children and the only girl. Of her brothers, Claude was killed in the war with Japan, Les was a Down's Syndrome child and died young and only Peter was around in her later life. Dad was taken to see Uncle Les on a few occasions before he died and I always wonder if these visits prompted his later work for Down's Syndrome charities.

Joan and Herb demobbed at the same time in 1945 and got married. It was a Catholic wedding, as both Joan and her mother were of that faith, but neither were constant churchgoers. The young couple moved in with Herb's parents in a council house in the Wyke area of Chichester. Like many of his generation who were battle-weary, Herbert never fulfilled the academic promise that was evident before the war. He wanted a quiet but satisfying life and what he settled on provided both. He was employed by West Sussex County Council as an untrained librarian, driving a mobile library round all the local villages.

On 19 September 1946 Dad was born in a local nursing-home. 'He took four-and-a-half hours to arrive,' said Granny Joan. Three years later, Robin came along, 'and from then on my life was refereeing the lot of them!' But she enjoyed bringing up the boys and when they were old enough she returned to the hotel life she knew as a child and became a 'silver-service' waitress at The Dolphin and other Chichester hotels. Dad remembered those days in the 1950s with a soft nostalgia:

> I didn't read much, which I regret terribly now. My father was so keen that I should, so maybe I got pushed into it and rebelled. We didn't have a television at home, but I loved listening to the radio, especially at my grandfather's house, where there was a big 'wireless' on the floor and a large comfortable chair beside. *Journey Into Space* and *Quatermass and The Pit* were my favourite programmes; the second one made me so frightened I had to leave the room.

Like most of his generation, the first thing that he saw on television was the coronation: 'A neighbour had a set and everyone in the street watched it, standing on chairs and tables in the garden.' He also remembered in those days that his parents didn't have much money: 'I didn't get pocket-money, but my grandmother used to give me a pound now and then.' He also started his first paper round at 9 years old:

I got half-a-crown at the time ... [about 12p!] I spent it all every week – no saving – I didn't like saving. My Mum tried to teach me, but I didn't catch on. I spent money on model aeroplanes, pet food and going to the pictures. I loved *Batman* and *Flash Gordon* and I still remember seeing *Conquest of Everest* and realising that cinema was not just about adventure. I seldom bought sweets.

There were just three years between Dad and his brother Robin but that was enough, according to Robin, to make Dad refuse to have anything to do with his little brother. Robin remembers this more keenly than his sibling. There were a lot of children, boys and girls, to play with, and he would try in vain to attach himself to Michael and the older children, only to be rebuffed.

They shared a bedroom but Robin says there was a clear line between his and Dad's side. Both loved animals and Robin would gather his model farm animals into their own enclosures. Dad's side of the room was swathed in old sheets, the Big Top; Dad would be crouched within his tent, lit by a torch, making the roars, snarls and snapping teeth of lions and tigers, the crack of the ring-master's whip, the antics of the clowns, and the applause of the crowd. Robin knew that something infinitely more exciting was going on there, but it was not for him.

As the boys grew they became, like their father, ones for the great outdoors, whether they were playing in their garden or farther afield. Joan sent them off to scout camp in the New Forest. 'One night,' says Robin, 'there was a lot of shouting and carrying on, headlights, and what sounded like a bit of a skirmish.' In the morning he found out that the focus of all this excitement had been Dad. 'An adder had managed to get in under his groundsheet and bitten him, and he'd been taken to hospital. I remember the sickness of fear that he would die.' Robin remembers quite a lot of squabbling:

I had a bit of a temper and I always seemed to be in trouble, getting caught and being told off. I went for him with a knife once. We were playing leapfrog and he stepped out of the way; I got a knife and stabbed his arm. He'd broken my collar-bone! We were about eight at the time.

Dad used to talk about Granny Joan, who was then working as a waitress, leaving out their tea in two biscuit tins for when they got home from school, each tin containing a sandwich and a cake or an apple. Whoever got home first used to eat both, and more fights ensued!

The boys kept guinea pigs, up to sixteen at any given time, because they bred so fast. But Dad had one favourite out of all of them. One day Robin was mowing the lawn for his father when disaster struck. Dad's guinea pig became inextricably tied up in the mower's blades. Bits of guinea-pig were left on the grass, on the mower and on Robin. As Robin says, Dad could never, ever talk about it, 'even up to the time of his death'. A sort of payback came later, says Robin:

> Michael was made a prefect. He did his job very conscientiously. He was always the last to leave the house to go to school. I used to hang about for ages waiting for him. When we finally got to the school he used to report for prefect duties. They would ask him if he'd caught any latecomers. There was always the one and only one: 'Elphick. R'!

Years later, when Dad had money, he presented Robin with a Rolex – I can't remember what the occasion was. Robin stared at it for all of fifteen seconds, 'I'd never be seen dead wearing that,' he said, barely looking up.

'Sell it, then,' said Dad.

On a lighter note, it seem to me that it was a wonderful time and place to be young, with town, sea and country. Favourite haunt was a park at the back of Chichester cattle market called 'The Cinderpath', where they used to have imaginary speedway racing. Julian Sluggett, of Attic Theatre fame, remembers when he first met Dad:

> My father knew a couple called Nelson and Edie Fowler who were from Devon, like him. In fact, they used to run the Chichester branch of the West Country Society. Their hobby, or probably more of a business, was producing home-made wine; their parsnip was particularly lethal. Anyway, one day, my father and I were sitting

with them, on their back terrace, supping said brew (I would be about fifteen at the time), when we spotted this lad kicking a ball down the alley-way at the bottom of the garden. Nelson obviously knew him and called him over. So he sat with us and helped us sup our way through a few bottles that afternoon. Mike was nearly thirteen at the time.

The circumstances of this first meeting jogs Julian's memory about something else that happened with Dad:

It was some time later. My mother was getting very upset that I hadn't been confirmed and so made arrangements for my instruction. The day duly arrived for the Confirmation, and I don't know why it was that it was Mike who volunteered to accompany me to Chichester Cathedral; we didn't go to the same school, but we had obviously been hanging out together at that time and it must have seemed natural for him to pitch up to support me, in his best bib and tucker, on the day.

Julian can't quite remember the order of events, but at some point Dad was in the line with the others at the altar rail and took an inappropriate gulp of communion wine. The retribution was fast and furious, and both boys were summarily ejected from the cathedral, but what galls Julian till this day was the caustic comment by the Church dignitary that accompanied their departure: 'We don't want you brown boys coming in here again!' Julian says that their colouring suggested that they were the children of agricultural workers. Such was the caste system that operated in Chichester at the time.

There is a thread that runs through these stories that is echoed by Granny Joan in talking about those days: 'Herb was a real man's man and very handsome. He could drink fifteen pints and ten whiskeys and still stay really together.' Robin says that he can never remember his father appearing drunk. He used to take both boys to the pub with him, and they would sit outside with a packet of crisps and in Dad's case a surreptitious half. Herb would park his mobile library outside some of the loveliest pubs in Sussex.

He also used it to bring back farm produce to the house: duck eggs were his favourite.

The boys still used to accompany their father to the various pubs when they got a bit older. 'My father used to love a good old sing-song there,' says Robin:

> He particularly liked to sing 'The Muffin Song'. You balance a pint of beer on your head – he had a very flat head – and sing 'I am the muffin man etc.', without dropping a drop. If you did, you had to drink the pint straight off. Mike wasn't too good at it.

It seems, though, that he harboured a dream of emulating his dad one day because when he was playing 'Boon' he did a charity stunt that meant he had to walk a distance carrying a glass of vodka on his head. He cheated a bit and used a mortar-board! Bill Bray points out that there was a downside to Dad's early initiation to the pub: 'Michael got his first ulcer at fifteen. It was like a trophy and he always took medication for it. He knew that he shouldn't drink but he did.' When I started my teenage years (and recreational habits), Granny Joan told me proudly 'No matter how late your dad came home, or how drunk he was ... he would always make sure that he brushed his teeth!' Mmmm. Was that a lesson for life? Whenever I'm tossing up whether to just fall into bed after a heavy night without doing my teeth, or removing make-up, I think of those words and force myself to have a bit of discipline.

I never met Granddad Herb but I know that Dad admired him a lot. He once said:

> I don't know how I feel about religion. There's plainly a force that I respect. My dad wasn't religious and yet the last thing he said to me before he died, in his semi-coma, was, 'I wish I'd prayed more'. My dad died of lung cancer. I'd taken him a packet of fags the night before ... and I still smoke.

Granny Joan never spoke much of Herb after his death, although I do remember when I was little she would often look at me wistfully and say 'Your Granddad Herb would have loved you.' She was a rock to her sons and so proud of both of them. Of Dad she said, 'He was not demonstrative, but he was sentimental and would always introduce me to everyone. If I was in a bar with Michael and a fan came up and asked for an autograph, he'd say, "Do you mind, I'm talking to my mother!"'

4

Barefootin'

In the summer of 1966 Mum came down to London. The group of friends all applied to the Inner London Education Authority (ILEA) to teach in the most salubrious area of West London. They were given District 10, Wandsworth. She and Ros miraculously got jobs in the same junior school. In those days, after you qualified, you could immediately start work for the last six weeks of the summer term, which entitled you to holiday pay. This certainly had the edge on going back to the theatre to waitress through the summer, and besides, many of the reasons that they might be going back to Chichester had now decamped to London. They found a small, pretty, downstairs garden flat in Battersea Bridge Road, from which they could easily reach the school by day, but more importantly, within minutes in the other direction, lay Chelsea.

There was a slight setback, however: although the flat was fairly unprepossessing, its location, as described, was brilliant. This, sadly, was reflected in the weekly rent – so much so that it seemed likely to be beyond the purse of the two young teachers. That is where Sylvia stepped in, who was still going through teacher training in London, and was looking for accommodation. As Sylvia says today, they were an unlikely trio: she from an affluent Jewish community in Essex (her father ran a men's clothing factory), Mum from rural Hampshire and Ros from Chichester. They all got on really well from the outset, as young people can, although Sylvia today would say that initially she felt very much the outsider. She found Rosalind and Julia cool and sophisticated. She felt, next to them, raw and too fat. She was telling Ros this just the other day, as she was describing their first meeting, and Ros, of course was stunned – it was the first she'd heard of it, forty-seven years later. The three would become inseparable in the following three years and beyond. The year in Battersea Bridge Road would be followed by years in Edith Grove and Callow Street in that Valhalla of the 1960s, Chelsea. Even for impoverished probationary teachers at the time, to have the stigma of living the wrong side of the river was too embarrassing to contemplate!

As Sylvia was a student, her first year's tenure of the flat was given some financial support by her father. However, she will reflect now, as do others who lived in that part of London at the time, how cheap the trappings of 'swinging London' were. A new dress from Biba or a blouse from Ossie Clarke once a fortnight were well within the budget of these young teachers. The 'boys' they knew would have their flares hand-made by 'a little man off Ganton Street', by Carnaby Street, for £5. Hair cut *at* Vidal's, if not *by* him was *de rigueur*, and later Leonard did the honours for the cost of a meal. Meals were becoming cheaper by the minute in an increasing number of bistros. No one had a car (they were mostly owned by older men) so local travel was inevitably by bus and Tube. Travel further afield would always be by hitch-hiking.

Mum had hitched before going to college – down to central Bournemouth from Highcliffe. Then afterwards, from Bournemouth to Birmingham, or Birmingham to London, mostly with another girl, but sometimes alone. With a college mate she had been picked up by a racing-driver, Denny Hulme, who travelled at no more than 40mph down the M1. With Ros, once, returning to Birmingham from London, they were given a lift by David Kossoff, the actor, who was doing a one-man show at the Alexandra Theatre and offered them tickets for it. Mum and Ros had even hitched to Spain and back for a holiday with a couple of lads from college.

The lifestyles that determined the age had emanated from students. There were the art students from Chelsea College of Art, Dad's drama students, the demonstrating political students, Mum's teaching students, the students forming pop groups, like The Stones: all different but with a common affliction – lack of money. Nothing, therefore, would have to cost much, and nothing did, or so it seemed. Naturally, the heavy subsidy of grants did much to alleviate the pain, but cheap flat-rental was an added bonus.

Of course, this was also the time of unequalled employment opportunities, particularly for the young. Chelsea offered many job vacancies in the bars and restaurants for young resting actors and holidaying teachers – options that neither Mum nor Dad ever felt that they had to take up, unlike some. One of Mum's Wandsworth teaching colleagues found gainful holiday employment in Battersea Pleasure Gardens, where staff would be hired on a daily basis for whatever fairground attraction was in need of help. Mum's friend, Pat, was assigned to the Roll-a-Penny, where she found one of life's least inspired entrepreneurs in charge. Willy had failing eyesight, which made the task in hand almost impossible. With the mantra 'On the black, we pay you back. On the line, the money's mine' ringing in their ears, punters rolled their coins down little slides onto a chessboard matrix: those coins settling in a white square or only partly in a black square (the chances of which should be about 95 per cent) would lose their money; the others would win a coconut. When Pat first joined Willy he was completely out of coconuts an hour after the park opened.

Pat discovered Willy's problem was that, when his back was turned or he was attending to the needs of customers from different sides, the canny youths of Battersea and Wandsworth were placing the coins by hand in the required spot. She soon stopped that. Willy's coconut supply was now lasting a month, rather than an hour. He gratefully hiked her pay, made her 'permanent temporary' and suggested, without knowing her full-time occupation, that she might consider a future officially as his assistant. He never wondered why, at certain times, she would duck down below the counter and seem to wait while a particular group of children moved on past the booth – they would, of course, be children from her class. As the holidays were coming to an end, Pat found it impossible to tell Willy about her impending departure. Every time that she plucked up courage, he would sound off about the golden future that beckoned them both in an empire of Roll-a-Pennies. One day she just didn't turn up. Mum and Ros found her guilt-trip very amusing.

The three flat-sharers didn't find additional work because they never seemed to need extra money. There was hardly any travelling back to Highcliffe and Chichester. They didn't seem to spend much in London. As Sylvia says:

> In those days, it was simple. We got home from school or college, early evening, and had baked beans on toast, or an egg or something. Next, we went to bed with the alarm on for about 10 p.m. As soon as it rang we were up and dressed in our party clothes and off clubbing till about three. Then home and a little kip before getting up for school/college. Day in, day out! Where did we go? 'The Bag of Nails' sometimes. Sometimes 'The Speakeasy'. What did we drink? We usually found that one gin and tonic would last us all night, or what was left of it. We could be offered drinks by 'boys', but we seldom accepted. We just went there to dance, and dance we did.

And who were 'the boys'? Friends, and friends of friends, and friends of friends of friends – an assorted peacock army in satin shirts and leather bomber jackets. Mum seemed to favour at the time a European Bahamanian called Kai, profession unknown. Ros had discovered that Chichester had seemed to move its gilded youth en masse to Fulham and Chelsea, where even Dad moved later, so Mum met many of the people that she'd met at the Festival Theatre again. Sylvia met many that she would never forget. By this time, of course, Dad was well ensconced at Central, but as my parents had not yet settled down together, I am following their separate paths. For example, Pat from the fairground was getting married to the co-author of this book, Nigel, and invited them both to the reception, but only Mum and the girls arrived and Dad's place-setting remained embarrassingly vacant. It was 1968 and he was hung over. Ros did have a particular vested interest in attending, as she possessed some wonderful skills as a seamstress and had run up the bridal dress on the morning of the wedding, having returned from the 'Bag of Nails' at 3 a.m. before she started on it. She probably wanted to see if it held together.

Life in the flats followed the unstructured rhythms of the young: when it became impossible to move, they would start to tidy. In Callow Street, an unusual conversation piece in the kitchen was the bath – it wouldn't be allowed today but in those days it wouldn't be uncommon to find a bath in the kitchen. They'd be covered by a wooden board that served as a chopping surface or an extra food shelf. A typical tableau could be of one flatmate in it, shaving her legs, one washing up and one listening to Radio One, eating toast. Edith Grove and Callow Street were equally deficient in the bedroom department: they only had one. Divans were grouped around the edge of the main living area and the one bedroom was prioritised for those with *company*. *Company* meant that you would not be disturbed; you had full call on all resources, like cups and coffee; but you weren't to abuse the privilege and have more than three nights in a row. Eyes might have to be averted, as *company* was leaving. There could be last-minute arrangements. Sylvia recalls emerging from the bedroom, flustered and telling the other two that she had arranged to meet 'some fellah' for lunch whom she didn't want to let down: 'I pointed to the bedroom and said about the incumbent: "He's Number Two in the Hit Parade. Can you fix him some breakfast? I must rush!"'

The girls' parties were the stuff of legend: this, admittedly, at a time when legends were ten a penny. Sylvia remembers one when almost the complete cast of Zefirelli's *Romeo and Juliet* turned up. The young Olivia Hussey, who played Juliet, was sitting perched on the edge of the bath in the kitchen talking to John McEnery and Bruce Robinson, the actor-turned-writer, who was Dad's flat-sharer; and Dad, of course, was there. But at that time the paths of my parents were rarely crossing, or not so that the flatmates would notice. The girls may have been close but they weren't ones to pry into each other's separate lives, and changes of men were not matters for open discussion.

There was, in those days, an explosion of fame and celebrity. Up-and-coming actors, models, designers and photographers were making a name for themselves, but this was new. There was not the flooding of media obsession with 'slebs' that there is today, and from all accounts, the atmosphere was exciting and generous of spirit. Fame was seen as a temporary bit of luck – in fact every one in the girls' circles would regard jobs as something they could switch whenever they liked. The concept of settling down to a career was something that their parents had aspired to – for their children, opportunities were to be seized. People made quick and easy decisions to make life-changing choices. There was a feeling of insouciance and optimism. No one agonised over whether they were doing the 'right' thing.

Ros had made friends with an American seamstress working in a Kings Road boutique: Ros chucked in teaching at the end of her second year and went off to New York with the American to work in fashion for a couple of years. Fairground Pat went off to teach in Istanbul. Sylvia's father bought his daughter a lovely little Volkswagen, so she and Mum gave up teaching and decided to head off across Europe for a few months with their summer pay and the intention of giving English lessons or working in bars, as many of their friends had gone off to do. Sylvia recalled later the image of Mum, as they drove, the wind blowing in her hair, singing along to her favourite song, 'Hey Jude'. She spoke to me about it a few years ago, at a party at her house. 'My!' she said to me, as 'Hey Jude' blared out of another room, 'you do remind me of her. This was her favourite song.' It was strange to hear this for two reasons. Firstly, people seldom remark on me looking like mum. Secondly, coincidentally and unknown to Sylvia, I had just named my new son 'Jude'.

They spent a few days driving to Greece, got bored there and decided to take the ferry from Piraeus to Haifa in Israel. Sylvia had a distant relative living there, a cousin of her dad's, who in those days of limited communication would have had no notice of her impending visitors before they arrived. It wouldn't have been much of a problem because no sooner had the girls arrived and experienced the aunt's warm and rapturous welcome than they were off. Haifa in those days was a dull industrial port that was about as exciting as a wet Sunday in Grimsby. Tel Aviv, which was only a few hundred miles away, beckoned our two globe-trotters, so they went that very night, arriving in the early hours of the morning. They settled down to sleep in the car.

Israel was not offering the same sort of temporary work as London in those days. If young people went out there to work, it was in *kibbutzim* to pick fruit or some such manual activity, or to go and settle. Neither alternative appealed to the two adventurers. They found a bar in the main square and were having a beer when they heard English voices: a group of animated English girls were sitting a few tables away. They struck up a conversation and found out that the girls were dancers who had just finished a season of cabaret at the Tel Aviv Sheraton. They were off to England but they said that the hotel was looking for dancers for their newly opened discotheque. Needless to say, when they left, after a very brief discussion, Mum and Sylvia high-tailed it round to the Sheraton. They saw the manager, admitted that they were not exactly trained dancers, but explained that they were used to demonstrating all the new dances at a very impressive list of London nighteries. In the rather off-putting environment of the manager's office they demonstrated a few of these dances, accompanying themselves with a dirge-like hum. They were booked on the spot. They were given great rooms in the hotel, billed as The Go-Go Girls from Swinging London on posters through the city, had excellent working hours, great pay and stayed for nine months. Sylvia said Mum barely moved in her dance routine; the odd slope of the shoulder, a step forward and back, energy was being conserved on a nightly basis. And so we'll leave them here in Tel Aviv for the moment and go and find what Dad's up to!

In 1964 Dad was starting his three-year course at The Central School of Speech and Drama. As Bill Bray observed laconically at the time, the place was 'crawling with birds'. These were interesting times for young men from the provinces. If young Elphick had discovered the sweetshop of womanhood, while mixing with the theatricals of Chichester, at Central he must have felt that he had found a whole confectionery factory, and one of the most beautiful there was Domini Blythe whom he partnered, on and off, through most of his time in the college.

The 'swinging sixties' from the young man's point of view were measurably different from their predecessors' experience. The pill, recently available, had changed a lot of things and encouraged the young independently thinking girl to 'look at the world as if you were a man'. In those pre-women's-lib days, there was still a lot of pleasing a man, too! Marriage was seen, for the most part, as an unedifying institution to subscribe to; that was mostly the view of the career actress, or indeed any young, professional woman in this peer group. It was really unusual, by all accounts, for any relationship to last more than a few weeks.

Domini, sadly, died in 2010 from cancer, after a hugely successful acting career, most of which was played out in Canada, and much, interestingly, with the Stratford (Ontario) Shakespeare Festival company – for eleven seasons over thirty years. In 1970 she had starred in the ground-breaking new revue, *Oh! Calcutta!*. One of the cast was Canadian Richard Monette, and he persuaded her to join him on a trip home. She stayed with him until his death, becoming in the meantime, the leading classical actress of her generation in her adopted country. Dad, I am sure, would have cherished her success. In those early days their relationship was a matter of conjecture for the other flatmates, its only manifestation being the size of the room allocation.

Like Mum and her friends, Dad moved three times in as many years while at Central in Swiss Cottage. There was a looser arrangement in living together. You may be visiting a flat and stay over several days. You may have gone to sleep in a chair, or even a bath, and stayed overnight. You might have security of tenure of a small divan, but go away for two days and lose it. The permutations were endless. Michael Feast recalls their flat in Fitzroy Road NW1, where they lived for part of their first year and all of their second. There were about eight would-be tenants, including Viv MacKerrell and Bruce Robinson, the actor turned screenwriter. His sister, Ellie, who was an art student at St Martins, had a flat upstairs. Sometimes, if those staying over 'for a cushion for the night' reached saturation point, Bruce would high-tail it up to his sister's. Michael Feast says that they also had a shed in the garden, which 'acted as an overflow or drunk tank'. He says that Dad always claimed the best and private bedroom in the flats that they shared because he was the only attached member of the household. This was not a bone of contention, but he does remember a big row over whose turn it was to wash up, 'nasty names were used and we nearly came to blows – but we kissed and made up.' He also remembers Dad:

> [always] wanting to dance whenever we played records in the flat we all shared. 'Everybody on their feet!' was his catchphrase [a line from the song *Barefootin'*], 'We're doin' a dance that can't be beat!' We were both South Coast boys – me from funky Brighton and him from yachting-club Chi. We used to go down to Chichester some weekends and see shows at the Theatre; John Clements was running it by then.

Bill Bray says that Dad used to also reclaim his old job on the lights in the summer for some extra cash. Another interesting way of earning a spot of dosh, Dad used to say, *and* getting your face on the TV, was going down to the Rediffusion Television studios, where they shot *Ready, Steady, Go*, the big pop show of the time. 'You could sit in the audience, but some they picked out, like me, and invited you to dance on a rostrum, and you got paid a fiver for that. I'd practice the steps back at the flat, and so be well prepared.'

Of course, the reason Dad and his friends were at Central was not to have arguably the best social life that anyone might ever have experienced at drama school up to that time; they were there to develop their craft. Michael Feast again:

> Mike Elphick had tremendous energy and a strong sense of what he perceived as right and wrong. His theatrical acumen was precise beyond his years. Once when he and I played two tramps in *Sparrers Can't Sing* at Central, and we had an exit, one on either side of the stage, right next to the two proscenium arches, Elphick said that if we timed it right, by nodding to each other, giving a thumbs-up, and spinning round before we went off, we would get an exit round of applause – and we did.

Bruce Robinson reckons that Dad:

> [was] the best actor in our year at Central School – as a matter of fact, only he and Feast were *proper* actors. As a student, he could be aggressive by nature, and also by nature sweet; he swore at me once, and I told him not to, and he melted into apology. I was surprised by him in our first year in drama school, because he called the teachers, 'Sir'. I wondered why he would do that. I thought that he was a fabulous actor throughout his career, but I remember first seeing him in *The Crucible* at drama school and I sat there, actually shocked at how good he was.

A fellow student at Central, but a year below, was James Snell. He recounts the memory training exercises that Dad undertook, so he could learn lines: 'He'd sit on the Tube in one compartment and between two stops try to remember all the words of all the adverts in that compartment. Then he'd regurgitate them on the platform to us!'

Stephen Barnes, another more-or-less permanent feature of the Primrose Hill flat-sharers remembers there was a certain discipline beneath the anarchy there. He seems to remember that Dad's acquisition of the best bedroom for him and Domini didn't go without rancour; he was just bigger than the rest! Some rebellious little toad (forever nameless) put a kipper under their bed. It took a few days before it was discovered.

It was Steve's job, for which he had volunteered, to run the kitchen and complicated meals like Spag Bol and Chilli Con Carne and the occasional Shepherds Pie would materialise, as far as the rest were concerned, seemingly out of nowhere. He also remembers an ingenious means of rent avoidance; this entailed everyone leaving for a couple of days, without paying the outstanding rent. Then a new face, unknown to the absentee landlord, would apply to rent an empty flat in the same block, and they'd all move in and start again. Dad said that Catherine Deneuve lived just round the corner, but everyone thought that this was an apocryphal story.

During their last year at Central they moved to a second-floor flat in South Hill Park, Hampstead. It was pretty much the same group but they were joined by Bill Bray, who by this time was bringing his lighting skills to play on West End productions. Bill remembers the Central students' favourite watering-hole, The Winch. This was 'The Old Winchester Pub', no longer in existence, but now a youth outreach programme centre called – The Winch. Bill felt that even by this time Dad was beginning to exercise his thirst-quenching abilities a little too much. Stephen says that only he and Dad were the drinkers and that would be for a couple of pints a night, if the cash was there. In true student tradition it was Saturday night for the cheap plonk for all, and smoking a bit of grass, 'Nothing harder,' says Bill.

The final student move was to Albert Street, Camden Town, to a three-storey Georgian town house. The house had been bought by David Dundas, a fellow student at Central (in actual fact he was the real Marquis of Zetland). As Michael Feast says:

> we all moved in and it stayed as a place in town for us, on and off, for the rest of the Sixties and into the Seventies, thanks to David's generosity. Pretty much the same crew, but it constantly changed shape and you often just bedded down wherever you could or wherever you were last sitting. That house was the *Withnail* house really and the party never stopped until the Seventies. By Albert Street Domini and Mike had parted, and so he could no longer claim a special bedroom; he slept on a bed in the bathroom.

Bruce Robinson says, 'It was like a hill of fucking alcoholism – strange, Elphick, Viv Mackerrell, Mickey Feast and myself. Were we all alcoholics?'

Bill Bray also remembers sleeping in that bathroom, 'I had no rights in the house, as I was living there completely rent-free. I would sometimes sleep in the bath; it was a bedroom-sized bathroom. One morning I woke up to Viv MacKerrell singing and shaving.' Bruce Robinson flew off to Italy later to film *Romeo and Juliet*; by the time he returned, there was only the bathroom available to sleep in. According to Bill, home-cooking was now a thing of the past and 'we went to the Parkway Restaurant for all our food, from cornflakes to veal masala'.

As the house became more and more crowded, poor David Dundas felt he ought to move out, which he did, letting everyone else stay on. David abandoned the stage for a life with music, successfully becoming a pop star with his composition of 'Jeans On', writing jingles and scoring the music for successful films like *Withnail and I*.

As a postscript to the Albert Street years, most people, including Dad, moved away around the 1967 to 1968. Michael Feast and Bruce Robinson went for the holiday from hell to a very wet Lake District. Finally it was just Bruce and Viv MacKerrell left fending for themselves in Camden. Money was a very scarce commodity. David sold the ground floor, which became a separate flat for an architect, who must have got used to his milk going missing. These circumstances must have fed the creative mind of Bruce Robinson who started writing the yet to be published book *Withnail* that was the precursor of the film script. Dad would always see Viv as the archetypical Withnail, though Bruce has been quoted as saying there is also a lot of himself in the character and the experience of the Lake District holiday.

Both Stephen Barnes and Dad found Viv's erudition and general cultural awareness fascinating in one so young. The tragedy of his short life was that he never experienced the recognition that his early blooming forecast. He was truly a creature of his age and as the 1960s rolled into the 1970s, he was left stranded in the past. For Dad and Michael Feast the future beckoned full of promise, as both won the shared ATV best actor of the year award at Central. As Michael says: 'I think it was a hundred quid or so, each, and a job on an ATV show.'

5

Hey Jude

Dad's early confidence on the stage, in part, may well have been a consequence of the walk-on parts at Chichester he undertook at such a tender age. Experience is a great teacher. Michael Feast said that Dad and he took up their ATV offers. They were schools programmes. Michael played a pedlar, a sort of Autolycus figure in a feature about Shakespearian England. Dad's was something a little more obscure. However, these were not the acting experiences that three years at Central had prepared them for. The final productions at college had afforded theatrical agents the opportunity to attend and talent-spot. Stephen Barnes reckons that one of the big ones like Fraser and Dunlop installed Dad on their books, and very soon after graduating, offers of work came in. His first professional job was with a few lines in *The Cherry Orchard* at London's Queen's Theatre, but it was a short run and allowed him to take off for Yugoslavia (as it was then) for his first film role. The film was *Fraulein Doktor* starring Kenneth More and Suzy Kendall. Dad played a traditional heavy in this First World War drama; it was a European co-production, Italian and Yugoslavian, produced by the famous Dino de Laurentis. The score was by the equally famous Ennio Morricone. The fame of these two did little to help the film, which never went out on general release. Those who have seen it have reported that it is none too bad, with a strong spy film narrative and some bloody but believable battle scenes.

For Dad the whole experience was undiluted fun. To be a professional actor on location was recompense enough, but the Brits in the cast were a homogenous group, who knew how to work and play hard. Dad was particularly friendly with the young James Booth, who had a sizeable part. One evening, the group, which included at the time Kenneth More's wife, Angela, went out for a meal to a local hostelry in Novisad. The restaurant was made up of a number of little alcoves, which divided the cast up into intimate tables. All was peaceful, until a plate suddenly sailed across the room and landed in front of Mrs More. Dad swears that it had nothing to do with him. What you should know is that it was the custom, there, at the time, and still is, as far as I know, to smash any glass that you have finished using. Whole factories were set up to produce glasses that were very thin and therefore very cheap. Most taverns on a Sunday morning were ankle-deep in broken glass. How, on this particular occasion, the cheap glasses graduated to expensive plates, I can't imagine, but it seems that Mrs More had more than the devil in her when it came to reprisals. Soon the air was swirling with flying saucers, plates and even the occasional tureen. The band stopped playing and joined in. As far as I know the only recrimination was an extra service charge!

Back home, tensions in Camden were beginning to make themselves apparent, due mainly to the limited accommodation. Bill Bray, by this time, had found himself a regular job with productions at The Royal Court. Steve Barnes was off to act in rep. at Crewe. As long as people were away, of course, things were fine. It was when they all returned at the same time that the problems happened.

Dad, himself, was due to go away again. Throughout his career, it wasn't just a question of getting the parts – it was getting good parts, and these in some of the most memorable plays and films of a generation. And the fact that he measured up to those challenges so confidently makes me so proud to be his daughter.

His next adventure, then, was in Tony Richardson's *Hamlet*. This was first produced as a play at The Roundhouse; then it went to Broadway, with a further short tour in the States. It then returned to the Roundhouse to be turned into a film, again with Tony Richardson directing, who was equally at home with film as stage. Nicol Williamson was Hamlet in a star-studded production with Marianne Faithful as Ophelia, Judy Parfitt as Gertrude and Anthony Hopkins as Claudius. Dad played Marcellus and the Player King at The Roundhouse and on Broadway and the Captain in the film. I think that he was disappointed to have been cut down to size for the filming, but as one later critic pointed out, the extras included Angelica Huston and Roger Lloyd-Pack.

Nicol Williamson's Hamlet was described as a 'benchmark' Hamlet. It was different. He decided to use a Birmingham accent; he had been to drama school there. London audiences understood the nuances, but one New York critic described him as sounding 'like a museum guide crippled with a blocked sinus'. Nicol could give as much as he got. He was known for haranguing his audiences on occasions, and at The Roundhouse just walked out of one performance, saying he 'was too emotionally drained to continue', but he managed to replace his understudy for the second act. The prime minister of the time, Harold Wilson, raved about Nicol's performance to his opposite number President Nixon, so when *Hamlet* went to Broadway, Nixon went to see it. He was not unduly impressed but asked if Nicol could go to The White House and present a one-man show based on the production there. The actor agreed, and then went on to surprise his host by turning up in jeans and T-shirt to perform a series of country and western songs interspersed with poems. I somehow think it would have been typical of Dad to have put him up to it.

So the show did a brief detour to Boston before returning to London for filming in The Roundhouse. Dad was pleased to be home – but what was 'home'? This was the age of the 'squat' and that was what home had become. After going back to his parents in Chichester to tell them all about America, the Camden house was hardly welcoming. His old friend Bill was there, equally dissatisfied with his life, sleeping in a bathroom. These two young men had had differing backgrounds to the rest in the house. They had been apprentice electricians in Chichester. I'm sure that Dad considered himself an 'apprentice' actor rather than a 'student'. The whole 'student' thing was a bit of an anathema to both their working-class pedigrees. It was time to leave behind 'student' things, including, as Bill says, 'the fridge that was only used for storing things other than food and drink.' The big tidy up before the Saturday and the start of Trip Weekend was also a feature of life there. I know Dad was a bit sad to leave the place and its assembled company: they had all been together a while. I know that memory plays tricks but his later description of 127 Albert Street does create a real impression of Edwardian decline. There would be David Dundas's objets d'art and original paintings forming a background to the dissipated lives of the tenants. Dad felt that scenes in *Withnail* captured it perfectly.

Like a married couple, Bill and Dad started looking for a new *pied-à-terre*. Bill's money was guaranteed from The Royal Court and Dad was beginning to garner adequate funds from the work he'd done. He liked the idea of Chelsea and no wonder: when the two weren't hanging around The Spread Eagle or Gina's, the Italian round the corner, Chelsea is where they'd be. You got on the 31 bus and half an hour later you could be at 235, the popular restaurant near World's End, or San Lorenzo, in Brompton Road. The area was a Mecca for beautiful young women, looking for bric-a-brac in the Chelsea Antique Market, clothes in the Kensington market or Biba, and the Chelsea Kitchen packing them in, in the middle. The flat that they ended up with, at 68 Cheyne Walk, met all the criteria that any young budding actor could hope for. It was right in the apex of it, you might say. Today, such a property, in any form, would be well beyond the financial reach of a novice actor, or even a successful one, come to that. Most of the occupants these days are very rich emigrés. Then, Sean Kenny, the stage designer, lived two doors away in one direction, and Robert Robinson, the broadcaster, two doors down the other way. More importantly, Kings Road was a three-minute walk away. I'm also aware that Callow Street, which had become a rallying point for a number of exiles from Chichester, was very close but Dad was showing no signs of resigning his independence yet.

Like Mum, he found the local night-life fascinating. After work, Bill would join him to go clubbing. The Speakeasy in Margaret Street was the favourite. They'd hang around there and as Bill says, 'there was always a party after that; you didn't have to gatecrash. Sometimes you knew them, sometimes it was fame by association or you'd just slide along with the group and somehow be there.' Life, itself, was a party, and if nothing was happening, you could be sure that before long Dad would make something happen. Bill says that one night, after a session down the Kings Road, they were walking down The Embankment towards Chelsea Bridge when Dad spotted some Port of London Authority rowing boats. They reminded him of his ferryman duties back home in Itchenor so he decided to go for a ride. He was a powerful lad but the oars he was wielding were no match for the fast-flowing currents of the Thames that night, so when he slipped the line, he swiftly disappeared into the black, 'I thought I'd lost him,' says Bill, 'But there he was, twenty-five minutes later, cheerfully dragging the boat onto a little beach, about a hundred yards down river!'

Girls continued to be an ever-present fascination – this was the 'swinging sixties' don't forget! Dad started seeing an Italian starlet called Jolie Marinelli. She was gorgeous and as Bill says, 'It all seemed too good to be true.' It was. She was married but separated. Her jealous Italian husband, a rather ageing thespian, heard about Dad and in the manner of the day, decided to name him as co-respondent in the divorce courts. To which end he sent private investigators scurrying to the flat in Cheyne Walk, with photographers, who were joined by press photographers, who were always roaming round the area for a story. Bill arrived home to this carnival. Jolie stayed in the apartment until everyone cleared away and then left, never to be seen again – she left the country. Result: no court case; life returns to normal or as normal as it gets.

Dad's first big-production UK-based film was *Where's Jack?*. This was the story of Jack Shepherd, the highwayman, played by Tommy Steele. Tommy had had a run of popular musical films with *Half a Sixpence* and *Finian's Rainbow*, and this was intended to follow suit. The scriptwriters had just completed *Point Blank* for Lee Marvin and the producer, through Oakhurst Productions, was Stanley Baker, who had had the success of *Zulu* behind him. Stanley was also the co-star. Interestingly, the director was James Clavell, who subsequently became a very successful novelist, with titles like *Shogun*. Dad had a middle-ranking role as Hogarth the painter. The film was destined for box-office glory. Sadly it didn't happen.

Gwen Taylor, the actress who later became a good friend of my parents, remembers going to her local picture-house in Derby, before she even went to drama school. *Where's Jack* was showing briefly. She says:

> I can't remember much about the film, but I can remember Mike. This stunningly attractive gypsy-looking boy outshone those around him. It was the sort of appearance that means you have to stay behind and check the credits, to see who it was. Later, when I worked with Mike, I told him about this, our first unofficial meeting.

The film went largely un-celebrated but Stanley Baker had bigger fish to fry. The next film that he produced that year was *The Italian Job*.

Some of the location work had taken Dad to Hungary. It became the custom that any time he was abroad, on his return he would take out friends, family or both for a celebratory meal. This was no exception, and the rule was also applied to having just been paid as well. In fact, it's difficult to find an occasion when Dad didn't need to celebrate by lavishing all his funds on those around him! This time, he decided to take a large group to The Pheasantry in Chelsea, a prestigious eating-house that is there till this day. Among the friends was Pete Jacobs, one of Mum's friends from college, and Mum herself. It was Pete whom I have to thank for the recollection of that night. Everyone was having a lovely time but Dad was becoming infuriated by some braying 'chin', as Dad called them, a fellow diner with partner and an upper-class accent that cut straight through him.

What particularly rankled with Dad was the way this man was talking to the waiter. He evidently thought that belittling the waiter, whom Dad knew – they drank in the same pub – was behaviour that would impress his girlfriend. Finally, Dad could take no more of it. He was sitting at the head of a long table in the restaurant. In order to leave his seat swiftly, he jumped up on the table and walked the length of it, stepped down and advanced towards the table of this 'Flash Harry'. Uttering the immortal words 'I'm sorry about this' to the young lady, he removed the couple's wine bottle from the bucket, and then put bucket, water and ice over her partner's head. The restaurant responded with instant applause round every table. Dad returned by the same route to his seat, and said to Pete, 'Sorry about that. Now, where were we?' not a word was spoken by the doused diner before he left.

I was intrigued to hear that Mum was one of the assembled company at The Pheasantry that night. Bill says that both Mum and Dad were still 'playing the field', as it were, at this time. They had one long weekend together at some point during the time at Cheyne Walk. They also had one occasion when Mum called round to see Dad and he pretended not to be there. She rang the bell and Dad, who had arranged to meet someone else that night, asked Bill to say that he was out. Mum barged in but by this time Dad had managed to step out onto the ledge, outside the window, five floors up. Mum said that she was sure that Dad wouldn't mind her waiting, which she did for two hours. In true farcical style, it began to rain outside. As Mum left she gave Bill such a knowing look. 'He knows where to find me,' she said. But he didn't because the next week she left with Sylvia for Israel.

6

Cabaret

Looking at photographs of Dad in the late 1960s, as he was starting out on his career, I feel that I have to take issue with all those journalists, sometimes aided and abetted by Dad, who described him as being a 'career heavy'. He would agree with his friend Bob Hoskins, who described himself as 'resembling a beaten cabbage', and Dad as having 'a face like a brickworks', and Dad would probably add for good measure that 'crumpled prune' and 'deflated football' might also be mentioned as equally descriptive of his visage. He always reckoned that when it came to casting, Bob, he and Don Henderson were as far as most film casting-directors could see for this type of role. Although, apparently, Bob told him, 'if they want an *animal* they send for me. But if they want someone who looks like an *animal*, but isn't necessarily an *animal*, they send for you.' Dad would draw attention to his youthful acne and say

'I wouldn't like to have had a typical romantic hero face because those roles can be so dull.'

But when he started in minor film roles in the 1960s, these remarks could not be further from the truth. This was the age of male 'eye-candy' as much as female, and Dad fulfilled that expectation as well as any Terence Stamp or David Hemmings. These were early days, so he appears in credits as a 'speaking', if not necessarily as a named part. In *The Buttercup Chain*, he is merely 'Chauffeur', while in *Blind Terror*, he becomes 'Gypsy Lad'. This was the feature dubbed *See No Evil* in the States, where Dad's character gives shelter to Mia Farrow's blind girl when her family are murdered. In both films, he is good-looking with a sort of innate moustache-twirling menace, which he also brings to the part of 'Burke' in *Cry of The Banshee*, as he looks disapprovingly over the shoulder of his boss, witch-finder Vincent Price, at a denounced witchette; this story was 'loosely adapted' from an Edgar Allan Poe story. It featured lots of *deshabillé* young ladies – also a staple ingredient of current films at the time. The 1960s were a fertile period for a type of 'soft-focus/ soft-porn' feature film; suddenly shots were allowable that hadn't been before because the directors were merely reflecting 'the new morality'. How much was mirroring and how much the changes were manipulated by the media is difficult to judge. Dad didn't care. All he knew was that there was a lot of work there, and to be earning as well as honing your craft, surrounded by these lovely women, was not to be sneezed at. Dad's friend Andy McCulloch also appeared in *Cry of the Banshee*. As he says:

> The script was as bad as the title. We filmed at a large mock Gothic house near Stanmore. Vincent, the aging Hollywood film star, used to arrive every morning, holding the script, his eyes raised to heaven in despair. He would say to us in a camp American voice, 'Oh, my God, I can't possibly learn all these lines.'
>
> Mike grinned and said, 'Don't worry, Vince, if you don't want 'em, Andy and me'll take 'em.' Vincent laughed and went off to talk to the director. When it came to shoot the scene, the director took me and Mike aside. He said he was changing the script slightly and we were to say a lot of the dialogue which had been Vincent's. We looked at

the lines and quickly started to learn them. Vincent then came over to us and Mike thanked him for making our parts bigger.

Vincent smiled, 'Don't thank me, Michael. I should thank you two. The lines were awful and they'll shoot on me anyway – I'm the money!' Sure enough they did. In the final version, it was a close-up on Vincent Price, with us two speaking off camera.

Andy says:

Vincent really liked Mike. He got us to take him out on the town one night. For a joke, Mike took him to the Buckstone – a very down-market, after hours, basement club, mainly for theatre people, but not stars. It was certainly not very Hollywood. Vincent loved it and kept asking us to take him there again.

Talking of the Buckstone reminds Andy of another time when he and Dad were there:

One night in there, there was a large crowd of 'luvvy' type actors, not the sort that Mike normally took to. He sat at a table, listening to them braying away. He suddenly stood up and started to speak very forcefully: 'Quiet in the studio, please, we're going for a take!' He then went into a totally spontaneous monologue, made up of random theatrical terms: 'Darling, you were super ... curtain up ... Good Heavens, it's the half already ... your cozzy's absolutely marvellous, darling ... beginners, please, act two ... shush, please, god's sake, don't mention the Scottish play, whatever you do ... Larry absolutely loved the whole thing, darling. He was all over me afterwards ... It's going awfully well ... did you hear what Johnny said to Irene, in a taxi – it was priceless ... Last make-up and costume checks ... sorry, cut camera, sound, aeroplane noise ... and curtain etc.'

He went on for what seemed like at least five minutes. The entire club fell silent and listened. When he finished, he got a huge round of applause.

Dad saw himself now, quite rightly, as a jobbing actor. He had no pretensions about it. If his contribution ended up on the cutting-room floor he would be disappointed but not devastated. He auditioned and if he was given a part he accepted it no questions asked. Sometimes this could cause problems. The part of the chauffeur in *The Buttercup Chain* was a case in point. To his eternal credit, as a man who more than likely would have had a drink when he was socialising, Dad never drove a car. In fact, he never had a lesson nor took a test: 'There's enough danger on the road without me adding to it,' were his bywords. Thus, the part of 'chauffeur' was a bit of an anomaly. He had been told, however, that he would be driving a Rolls-Royce automatic, which a friend who had a garage had let him have a crack at, on the forecourt. It was only when he arrived at the location, a private airfield, wearing his uniform, that the further implications of his role became apparent. The director explained the situation: Dad was to drive the young couple at high speed in a brand-new Maserati, it had been decided, up to a waiting four-seater plane. He was to screech to a halt, as close to the plane's steps as he could, to let them out and then drive off, to where out of sight of the cameras, were waiting representatives of the owners of the car and plane and sundry accountants and insurance brokers. What could be simpler?

How he did it, I'll never know. He got a basic run-down from the guy who'd delivered the car, feigning no knowledge of 'this particular Maserati'. He says that his passengers pretty swiftly got the feeling that all was not well as he reached 60mph without much of a problem. He overshot the plane by just a few yards, which was great because for most of his journey towards it, not only he, but his passengers, and the director and the assembled 'money men', thought that he was going to hit it. He screeched to a swerving halt, let out the chastened occupants, and somehow started it up and moved slowly to the designated point. Getting out he said, 'Sorry about that. Shall I do it again, and stop nearer the steps?' The chorus of 'No!' from every quarter was nearly deafening.

Dad's acerbic view of cars was well-known amongst his friends and well documented. A great friend of his and Andy McCulloch's, Smudger Smith, was getting married. The wedding was in Bedford. As Andy remembers:

I had recently bought a second-hand Triumph Vitesse car. I thought it was the business. I offered Mike a lift to Bedford from London. He pretended for the entire trip that he thought we were going to Bradford. He practiced his Yorkshire accent for the occasion. I picked him up after he had had a fairly liquid lunch. He took a jaundiced look at my car and said, 'Most impressive, Andy, called a Vit-us is it?'

Playing the game, I explained that it was pronounced '*Vee-tess*', being the French for 'fast'. He nodded, completely unimpressed and started to doze off, 'Wake me up when we get to Bradford, please, driver!' When we got to our destination about an hour later, he woke up with a start, and looked at the clock on the dashboard. 'Bloody hell, Andy! No wonder they call this car a Vit-us. We've got all the way to Bradford in less than an hour. That's 200 miles, isn't it?'

I don't know whether Mum electing to work overseas influenced Dad's next adventure, but he volunteered to go on a British Council tour of the Far East. The project was a scaled-down version of John Barton's *The Hollow Crown* from *Henry IV Parts 1 and 2*, with Dad as Hal and his friend Anthony May as Poins. Anthony had been at RADA, but as contemporaries their paths had already crossed. The production, directed by Richard Eyre, much later to become Director of the National Theatre, had a pre-tour run at The Lyceum in Edinburgh; Zoe Wannamaker was also in the cast. The company visited Malaysia, Borneo, Singapore and the Philippines. As Richard Eyre says, 'I fell in love with the East, with travelling, even with falling in love itself ... It was, as they say, the time of my life, and for years acted as a kind of template against which all my other experiences were set.' Of Dad, he says, 'I loved working with him and being with him. On the tour, he was told that the Singapore Customs would be very tough and could forcibly cut your hair, as well as search you for drugs. He mischievously asked one of them if he knew where he could get hold of some marihuana.' Tony May remembers Dad and he having little difficulty in pursuing this aim. The pay wasn't great but the hotel accommodation was very comfortable and the afternoons spent smoking on the beaches before the evenings' performances were delightful. Carrying their competitiveness from their stage characters into real life meant a few crossed swords over the attentions of women on their journey, but Tony's abiding memory is also one of a totally joyful experience. There was also a soundtrack: this time Dad's favourite song was 'Molly 'Awkins', as in 'I met old Molly 'Awkins as 'er drawers were 'angin down ...' which Tony and he would regale anyone with at the drop of a hat. On the way back to England they both stopped in Penang, where they found themselves hiring trishaws for a bit of competitive racing in the style of Ben Hur. Tony remembers Dad's driver was rechristened 'Charlie'.

So back to Blighty and changes were being mooted on the domestic front for the 'star-crossed lovers'. The Go Go Girls' successful season at the Tel Aviv Sheraton had been sadly interrupted by the death of Sylvia's mother back in London. During their time at the hotel they had got to know the resident group well, and Sylvia came to know the lead guitarist, Mike, very well indeed. In fact, the following year she was going to become *Mrs* Mike Lahav, but this had to wait. And so, leaving lover, job, VW car and Mum behind, Sylvia flew home to London. It didn't take the one Go Go Girl long to realise that she wasn't really up to a solo career; the management probably agreed. Soon Mum was following Sylvia back to England, to see her family in Highcliffe and take a well-earned rest. Here she had time to reflect on the next stage of her life. She realised that she wanted to teach. She had missed the classroom and the children. She would return to London and whatever fate chucked in her direction, she would definitely be teaching again. Of course, there would be 'accommodation issues'. Ros had left Callow Street to go to New York. Sylvia and Mum had been in Israel and the lease had slipped into abeyance. Bill Bray, meanwhile, had left Cheyne Walk to return to Chichester; Dad didn't feel like keeping the place on himself and served notice accordingly. Would the two 'commitment phobes' end up together as a consequence? The answer was in the hands of the ubiquitous Pete Jacobs. He had for many years had a flat in Old Compton Street, in Soho, and for a long time had a string of 'visitors', friends staying sometimes for a weekend, or indeed, sometimes as long as a year. He had developed the personality of a 'hub', to whom the homeless could turn. So it was, in his new-found flat on the Finchley Road, Mum and Dad became his first tenants.

I'm aware that it wasn't just an accident of fate. Despite Dad's need to fly the flag for the single man, I know that he had a deep-seated, working-class need to follow the normal protocols of your average Joe to settle down and raise kids. Mum, also, who would rail against the tyranny of marriage, as any ardent feminist would, had a normal nesting expectation. For Dad there was the added appeal of the location: the Finchley Road. They say that those who move to a large metropolis like London usually settle nearest to the site of the railway/ bus station at which they first arrived; so ex-students will look for accommodation near their old college. According to James Snell and Smudger Smith, who followed Dad to Central as students, one of the first questions you might be asked as a fresher was 'Have you met Elphick yet?' Apparently, if he was not working, Dad could hold court down at The Winch, and be introduced to the new intake. He loved that Swiss Cottage area. As a student he had already done some work behind the bar at the pub, The Burgundian, in the Finchley Road, probably under the misapprehension that you might drink less while you were serving, than when sitting the other side.

So Mum applied to the Inner London Education Authority for a teaching post, and Dad found himself in another play, this time at The Royal Court. Throughout his acting career, he seemed to find himself in productions that were at the cutting edge of cultural development in this country. The play *The Changing Room* was written by David Storey, who had made his name as a novelist with *This Sporting Life* and other books that were to explore areas of Northern life with a new grittiness that had lately come into vogue. The play looks at a rugby league club and its players, their separate lives, but their strong sense of teamship. As the title would suggest, it is set in the club-house, and was one of the first plays in the new era to feature wholesale male nudity. It was directed brilliantly by Lindsay Anderson, himself a mould-breaking figure in the theatre. Not surprising, then, that the acid-tongued playwright of what had now become dated romantic comedies, Noël Coward, should remark, when leaving the theatre: 'Fifteen acorns are hardly worth the price of admission!'

The play was reviewed with superlatives: 'It is a masterly piece of writing and Lindsay Anderson's direction is beyond praise.' wrote B.A. Young in the *Financial Times*. In 1973, with an American cast, it won the New York Drama Critics' Circle Award for Best Play. The actors at The Royal Court really became a team and everyone commented on the effect on the acting that was achieved with the developing male-bonding. It was bitter-sweet to hear Alun Armstrong, one of Dad's fellow player/actors, talking at Dad's funeral of their times together in the play. David Daker, who was in *Boon*, was also in the cast. It was so successful that it transferred to The Globe, after its short run at The Royal Court. Dad, unfortunately, didn't travel with it. The actor/players had got together, independently from their director, to do a bit of keep-fit, as they felt the parts required. This entailed them forming seven-a-side football teams, which also included backstage crew, and playing in Regents Park on non-matinee days. Dad, who had been school football captain, was very enthusiastic and highly competitive on the pitch. On the final match before the play transferred, he broke his leg in a tackle. He somewhat ruefully reflected that 'acting an athlete doesn't mean you necessarily are one.'

When he recovered, he started getting quite a bit of television work in series like *Armchair Theatre*, *New Scotland Yard* and *Crown Court*. One, *Adam Smith*, seems a very unlikely port of call for him to appear in six times, described as a religious drama series in which a Scottish minister of the Church finds that his wife's death makes him confront the purpose of his local ministry, but finds spiritual comfort from the community. Even more unlikely was the part of a gay hairdresser he played in Alun Owen's *Norma*. All these parts would bring home the bacon, as it were, but the television company, 'Granada' were waiting with his first major supporting television role. They had commissioned a series of thirteen self-contained plays, based on the short stories of A.E. Coppard and H.E. Bates, under the generic title of *Country Matters*. The writing was of a very high standard and the viewing public were introduced to new young actors like Ian McKellen, Penelope Wilton, Peter Firth and Dad. *The Little Farm*, in which he appeared, starred Bryan Marshall in what one critic says 'is possibly Bryan's most brilliant and inspired performance of his entire career'. He plays an illiterate farmer who advertises for a housekeeper, who duly arrives, played by Barbara Ewing, a young woman trying to escape her past. Dad is the sly, wicked neighbour who spots their weaknesses and brings the play to a stomach-churning end. It does allow him to develop the characterisation of this interloper in a way that up to that time no previous television part had allowed, and was probably the precursor of roles in *Holding On* and *Schultz*.

While Dad was away filming, Mum particularly appreciated the atmosphere of the flat-share. It provided company and support, a very useful quality during his times overseas. But she was beginning to amass more belongings (through work and social commitments) than one room would allow. Besides, Dad was earning reasonable money and they needed to have room to entertain their friends. They found a little garden flat but a stone's throw away from Pete's, in Parsifal Road, with a sweet little garden. This was the year that Dad made the pilot for the series *The Nearly Man*, starring Tony Britton as a middle-class Labour MP It was written by Arthur Hopcroft, who won the Broadcasting Press Guild's award for the best single play of 1974. Dad played the part of a heavy-handed Bolton schoolmaster and Gwen Taylor played his wife. 'He was always such a considerate actor,' she says, 'both in role and out of it. He looked after you as if he'd been doing this sort of thing for years, and, frankly, we were both pretty new to it.'

That year had started with Dad joining the pantheon of stars that make up the historical assembly of *Coronation Street*. He played Douglas Wormold, the son of Ernest Wormold, who was reputed to originally own virtually all the property in the street. He didn't own The Kabin, however, and Dad's character spent most of his six appearances trying to dislodge Rita Fairclough from it, by fair means or foul. He always swore that one day he'd return, waving a set of deeds, and ask everyone to vacate their properties and find another street to live in. Dad loved the friends that he made in *The Street*, and would call in to see one or two, whenever the opportunity arose in the future. My dad was not the only actor to undertake roles in the two major 'soaps' in this country, but I am sure that his was the most upsetting transformation: from appearing first as that cocksure, young entrepreneur in 'Corrie', to the lumbering paedophile in his final appearance in *Eastenders*.

Television and films inevitably meant that opportunities for my parents spending time together was limited. Plays, on the other hand, allowed greater contact, even 'location jobs'. About this time, Dad appeared in the Ludlow Festival's production of *The Winter's Tale*. It was an outdoor production in the castle grounds; it got a bit chilly at night, even in June! However, it did offer Mum the chance to travel up there, with a few old friends from college days, to stay over and watch the proceedings, sometimes from the warmth of the nearby pub. Dad's friend Tony, from the Far-East tour, had also been persuaded to take a small part in the play. His memory of Dad and that pub is that somehow he spent many more hours there than he had in the bars overseas. It might have been just a climate thing. The *Ludlow & Bishop's Castle Advertiser* could hardly contain itself with its front-page critique:

> Audiences will be moved and carried with the intensity and ease with which the cast cope with the changing moods and passions demanded ... Michael Elphick, Oliver Ford-Davies and Matthew Guinness are professionals who not only know their Shakespeare, but also have the same 'feel' that he must have had for getting across to the audience.

Esta Charkham, who was to go on later and produce Dad in *Boon*, was an agent at the time, looking after another cast member. She remembers joining the cast in the Clarksons' coach home at the end of the run:

> The people of Ludlow had put on this fantastic party for the cast which finished very late. By the time the coach arrived in London, in the Finchley Road, it was six in the morning. We'd sung all the way home. Mike loved to sing. This was the first time that I'd met him, and somehow I'd been inveigled into giving a burst of 'Cabaret' – 'I used to have a girlfriend known as Elsie ... With whom I shared four sordid rooms in Chelsea ...' it went. This was not to be the end of it. The number of occasions over the years when he'd turn to me and

say, 'Give us the "Elsie song"!' were legion, and not always at the most appropriate of times.

Mum had a lovely time that weekend in Ludlow, but there was a sense of change in the air. Who knows when she broke the news that she was pregnant; all I know from both of them is how pleased he was with the news, and how excited they were as they prepared their little home in Parsifal Road for the new arrival.

7

Lemon Popsicle

The day I was born, so I've been told, it was snowing, which was unusual, as it was April. Saturday 5 April 1975, at around 10 a.m., I came screaming into the world. It was also the day of the Grand National. The horse that won the National that particular year was Escargot but, so my dad told me, running earlier in one of the other races was a horse called Fighting Kate. Of course Dad put a lot of money on her and she won. Mum told me how he came flying into her hospital room, throwing notes into the air and whooping for joy. My mum was 30 years old.

My parents' relationship, from what I can recall when I was little, was good. We lived in a small, two-bedroom basement flat, in Dennington Park Road, West Hampstead, that my parents had moved into just before my birth. On the right, as you faced the door, were wide stone steps to a grand doorway leading to the flats above; on the left was a steep, narrow set of stairs, down to our little, dark basement flat: Number 37. Through the front door, there was a tight corridor, at the end of which, if you turned right, you'd pass the box-sized kitchen, before reaching the living-room. I don't remember spending much time in either room, except occasionally to watch some television on the thick, cream carpet, or to feed the fish, who lived in the kitchen. 'Kipper' was one of a bag of fish that Dad had won at the Hampstead Fair one year. He was huge and outlived his bowl mates by years and years.

If, at the end of the hallway, you continued straight on, there was the bathroom on the left: a dark, little room, where, strangely, my parents had put up loads of funny paintings, prints, and photos, to alleviate any boredom, I suppose, while in the bath or on the loo. Dad even had his work schedule written on the back of the bathroom door. Ahead was my parents' room: a pretty room that backed on to the garden, as did mine, next to it. My room was the focal point of the house, being the largest one. My bedroom was the 'family room', used for entertaining any visitors during the daytime. At the garden end it had our dining-table, beside the French-doors that led you out. At the top end was my bed, wardrobe and a huge circular cane papasan chair that I was allowed to sleep in when we had guests to sleep over.

There was also a wonderful old horse-hair sofa, on which I would play boat games or 'King of the Castle'. Dad had painted a massive tree behind the sofa and one of our games was to add birds, animals and make-believe creatures to the branches of the tree. I remember finding birds very hard to draw. I also clearly recall that one of the hallway walls was covered almost entirely with different coloured writing and drawing. Beside it was a pot of pens. Each person who visited the house was supposed to leave something there. You would see cartoon pictures, drawings, poems, quotations and jokes scrawled in small, tall, straight and squiggly lettering styles in rainbow colours. We sadly painted over it before we left in 1982, when I was 7. I wish we'd thought to take a photo of it first. It was like a valuable work of art, with contributions from Dad's friends at the time, including Stephanie Beacham, Gwen Taylor, Dennis Waterman and Robbie Coltrane.

Dad was away quite a lot even then and I missed him when he wasn't there, but I do remember lots of smiles between him and

Mum when he was at home and they were together. They seemed to have a great social life with many friends and lots of parties. I would wake up in the middle of the night in my parents' big bed, hearing the sound of music and wander into my room to find it packed full of smiling and dancing people. I'd be allowed to stay up for a while and join in, before being put snugly back to bed. I loved it! I can recall so much from these childhood years; my long-term memory's pretty good. I can see those toys, enact the playground games, and remember conversations, thoughts and even dreams. They're all stored safely there, locked away ...

My earliest memories of my lovely mum are as all children's should be: that she made me feel loved, safe and special. She was my everything and I adored her. As I grew up I honestly thought that she knew everything; I believed that she was just about the cleverest person in the world. My mum, Julia Mary Alexander, was a person whom everyone seemed to like and respect. Her pupils loved her – and their parents seemed to as well. She was calm and serene, hardly ever getting cross; she was honest, hard-working and very, very bright. I should mention she was also elegant and beautiful, quite tall at 5ft 7in, with flowing, wavy auburn hair, pale skin and light green eyes. We were together all the time. I take after my dad: even more so when I was little, with long, dark hair and big, brown eyes. Once when Mum was out, pushing me along in the pram, a passer-by was heard to comment: 'Oh look! She's adopted one of those little Vietnamese babies!'

We would experience the usual chaos that most families enjoy every morning before school, trying to get out of the door in time. Mum would brush my hair, while I complained and she'd have to remind me ten times to go and brush my teeth. We would talk about everything during the daily drive to Hallfield, where Mum taught and I attended through Infants to Juniors. Occasionally we would listen to the radio or as I got older and more into music (and this will date me!) put on a tape. It was always the same one: Mum's 'Sixties Hits'. It's the one we mutually agreed on: her taste being mostly classical and my choice of Madonna, Wham or Aswad boring her. So, we'd sing along together to 'It's My Party' and 'My Boyfriend's Back'.

Fifties and sixties music always reminds me of my parents. Dad loved Rock 'n' Roll, especially Little Richard, but he had all the Beatles records, and John Lennon's 'Jealous Guy' and 'Imagine' will still be a trigger for me. Of course, The Platters were the favourites. I can still hear 'Only You' playing in the house or the one the words of which were framed in the bedroom, 'The Great Pretender', softly in the background on a Sunday morning, as Dad cooked us breakfast. He gave me an album called 'Lemon Popsicle' when I was quite little and I continued to play it to death until I was mid-teens. This music was like the soundtrack of my early life.

When my school day was over at 3.30 p.m., I would go to Mum's infant-school classroom and wait while she finished her work, usually marking, finishing off elaborate wall pieces for a project or meeting in the staffroom. Sometimes I would go outside and play in the playground alone: I had a wonderful imagination. Other times I would just sit with Mum reading, drawing or playing with the classroom toys. We would usually get home before six, so Mum would make a simple dinner before we settled down for the evening. She wasn't one for fancy meals or baking, and she often said that out of her and Dad, he had always been the better cook, and that he enjoyed cooking as much as she was indifferent to it. She was, however, an advocate of healthy eating: no sugar! I was very rarely allowed sweets and we never had a pudding: yoghurt and fresh fruit would suffice. I always remember how devastated she was when she discovered that the proprietary expensive brand of muesli that we'd had every morning for years was as full of sugar as all the other kids' cereals!

I shouldn't complain. I was weaned off chocolate for life and had my first filling when I was 26. Ironically, Mum was fit and health-conscious, yet repeatedly hit with cancer. Before his later ill-health, I am sure that Dad felt guilty that he had smoked and drunk and generally abused his body from an early age, yet had not suffered similar consequences. His cooking was not particularly aimed at the health-conscious either, but it was delicious. Mum was definitely right about that. When he was home at the weekend, he would be the one to cook a big roast, late in the afternoon, after a walk on the Heath, and we would always have a cooked breakfast when he was around. He made the best omelette – he tried to teach me how as an adult, but it was never the same – and I loved his bubble-and-squeak. His real speciality was the Christmas dinner and this was the day that he would never drink. Perhaps the presence of both my grandmothers would curb his enthusiasm! I can still see him now, receiving his annual gift from Mum's mum, Nanny Alexander, the home-made jar of spicy jam or mango chutney. She would say, "It's what you give to the man who has everything.' He said that it was the present that he looked forward to most every year.

During the school holidays we would go to stay with Nanny in the New Forest. The house in Highcliffe was truly wonderful to me. It seemed huge and was surrounded by garden and countryside. As you drove in from the road there were thick heather bushes lining the driveway, which in the summer would be full of fat, dark bumblebees lazily buzzing from one flower to the next. There was a small porch before the front door, next to the garage. This door never appeared to be used, as the back door led straight into the big kitchen, the heart of the house. It was the heart as Nanny was an amazing cook. She had one cupboard that I would make a beeline for on arrival. Inside would be biscuit tins crammed with freshly baked goodies: scones, brownies, biscuits, and my favourite flapjacks. I can taste them now. For dinner, my favourite was her Shepherd's Pie, followed by rhubarb crumble or tinned peaches with condensed milk – a pudding at last!

Nanny would often despatch Mum and me down the lane to pick blackberries and apples from her trees for future crumbles or pies. Granddad would be tinkering around in his shed with some tool or other, or fiddling with his bike; another time he'd be gardening, most often tending his beloved tomato plants in the greenhouse. Indoors he would pull coins out from behind my ears and we would play endless games of Monopoly. I loved it there. Mum and I would lie on the grass in the garden and look up at the sky, showing each other the changing pictures that we could see in the clouds, while making daisy-chains. It's such an idyllic memory. Often I'd play in the garden alone, galloping around and around on my imaginary horses. I'd leap over the pathways and heather bushes, winning umpteen imaginary ribbon rosettes. Sometimes I would go and investigate the interior of the musty caravan, carefully avoiding the spiders as I looked through piles of junk to find old treasure.

It was a neverland of discovery. I would walk to the end of Bracken Way, collecting what were the largest pine cones I had ever seen, and then walk into the woods. Usually I went with Mum but, occasionally, when I got a bit older, I'd brave it and go alone. There was a wide stream with high banks that you could jump over in places or find a shallow part to wade through if you were wearing your wellies. Coming from London this was for me truly an adventure. I also spent lots of time with Mum's sister, Aunty Sue. She always had horses and I would go with her most evenings to feed them at the nearby farm where they were kept. The London child could not imagine a more fun place to spend time: dogs, cats and horses and fields full of flowers. Then there were the sheep – one summer I named them all, and my favourite little lambs. There was a hay-barn to play in and there were tractors to ride and fresh eggs to bring home. I just could not get enough of the place.

Aunty Sue had two dogs, Ricky and Bengie, both black-and-white 'cross collies'. Mum and I would go with her to walk them most days. We would usually either go to the Common near where she lived, where the bracken was as high as me, or we would go on to the New Forest with its tall trees that changed colour like something from another planet. The walks that really appealed to me were the ones by the sea. We would go to Highcliffe beach and park at the car park at the top. As you got out of the car on a windy day you would feel that you were going to be blown straight over the cliff. The dogs would sprint off in pursuit of rabbits and we would walk for what seemed miles. The beach itself was pebbled and Mum showed me how to skim the flat stones across the water and make them bounce. Years later, we went there to scatter Mum's ashes. Well, Sue and Mum's best friend Elizabeth did, taking them down to the water's edge, to let them into the sea. I was 20 by that time. I sat up on the cliff, watching them, unable to move.

I've taken great comfort over the years from these early memories, almost in a therapeutic way. Unable to sleep, perhaps,

I've sifted through the comfort of the past and felt better for it. I could pick up the atmosphere, for example, of my Nan's old house in Highcliffe, remembering everything about it: the pictures, the ornaments round the fireplace, the swirls on the carpet and the junk kept in the caravan outside. You know, I can smell those tomatoes of Granddad's in the greenhouse and hear the sound of the wood-pigeons overhead. It does make me grateful for the security I experienced in those early years.

Because I had no siblings to grow up with (Mum having to have a termination because of her cancer treatments), she and I were incredibly close; the more so because my grandparents and extended family all lived far away in the country. Dad was always having to spend time away, usually because of work, but now I realise, probably also due to his drinking, one way or another. Funnily enough, because he was away such a lot, his being around became special. It was a break from the usual routine and therefore memorable. For instance my mum would have read me a million bedtime stories – she loved books and they were a massive part of my upbringing – but I don't have a clear image of her doing so. By contrast, the times my dad put me to bed are engraved on my mind. I would so look forward to it. He would make up amazing stories, usually based on characters under the sea, involving magic submarines, and a much repeated tale about a king and queen, who lived down a well with a giant octopus.

Sometimes he would get out a small, thick hardback book, a collection of Shakespeare's plays. I can smell its musty 'old bookishness' even now and see its thin gold-edged pages. Dad wouldn't read from it. He would just tell me the stories in a way that I could understand. I loved *Midsummer Night's Dream* and *Macbeth*. Dad's chosen play was always *Hamlet*. Later on, as I approached adulthood, Dad would drum into me the life's lesson that he said he so regretted ignoring himself, the quotation from *Hamlet*. 'Kate,' he'd say, 'Never a borrower nor a lender be.' That beautiful old book was illustrated with vivid drawings, most quite dark and gruesome. I found them fascinating and never scary, but then I had my dad with me. He was very loving and affectionate, unlike Mum who wasn't one for cuddles. My earliest memory of Dad would accord with my view of him just before he died: he could be quiet and kind, but also great fun and hugely interesting. I can remember that I'd know when he had returned to us after being away, by the *chug chug* of a black cab outside. Often I'd hear this having already gone to bed and I'd sleepily look forward to seeing him in the morning; this would be especially true if he'd been abroad as that would probably mean presents for me!

One such time he had been away in Helsinki, filming *Gorky Park*. He brought back these wonderful, strange presents: an extraordinary fur hat with ear-flaps and beautifully painted wooden puppets, together with the piles of forbidden sweets and exotic foodstuffs. Dad loved puppets. He had them hanging all over the place, with clowns for preference. I had a large coloured material bag stuffed full of hand puppets that we had collected over the years. We would do shows, either for Mum or for our own entertainment, and had characters ranging from one rather dodgy-looking fellow with a definite five-o-clock shadow, black trilby and a cigarette hanging from his mouth, dubbed 'The Frenchman' by Dad to a fluffy, blue bunny-rabbit and most of the cast of the Muppets. If friends came round, Dad would move into magician-mode. He would amaze them with the trick where you peel a banana and it's sliced inside or the other one where he could make cigarette ash appear and disappear on the side of his hand.

Because he was so good at doing this sort of thing, I can't imagine why for one of my birthdays he decided to hire a children's entertainer, but he did. It also went against all his socialist principles: hiring staff for a party was so middle-class. I think that he had just had a big payday and thought 'Why not?' To his eternal chagrin the entertainer, who arrived with his bendy balloons and limp wand was another, less successful graduate from Central. He met Dad in our kitchen and as Dad's star had not really begun to soar, the entertainer recognised him solely from his college days. 'Hello, Mike,' he greeted the ex-student, 'I didn't realise that they'd booked two of us. Do you want to go on first or second?' History has not recorded the reply.

Another feature of my childhood were the holidays Mum and I spent with Pat (fairground) and Nigel (co-author) her college friends, and their daughters Juliet and Charmian. It all began in 1978. Through contact at school Mum had met Gavrik Losey, the son of film director Joseph Losey, and a film producer in his own right (responsible for, amongst other films, The Beatles' *Magical Mystery Tour*). He had a cottage in the Devon countryside, near Honiton, and was happy for us to stay there in the summer holidays. This was very kind of him. The cottage was furnished, stocked and equipped for the worst a future Armageddon might throw at it, but all we had was the worst August in living memory. On the one occasion we went out, Juliet, Charmian and I found ourselves in the middle of a wet field being pursued by a herd of cows.

At the end of our week there, driving back to Camberley where Pat and Nigel lived, the adults decided to call in on Dad who was filming something called *The Blue Remembered Hills* in a village near Wincanton. This was a film where all the cast played the parts of children. We found Dad dressed in his boy's short trousers and pullover. He introduced the actress, Helen Mirren, who was playing the part of a 7-year-old girl. Hearing that Charmian was that age, she asked to 'borrow' her for a while for a bit of a chat and character research, which she duly did, taking her off and returning her after an hour. Helen said that she had been going to avoid the cliché of playing the child as a thumb-sucker until she spent the time with Charmian, who sucked away for most of her waking hours.

Because of the bad weather, the adults felt robbed of their holiday. The feeling grew and a plan was resolved to dump the kids for the weekend of the August Bank Holiday when the weather was forecast to improve, and go away. They drove down to Portsmouth with friends, boarded the ferry to Cherbourg as foot-passengers and then meandered down the coast in a local bus to Barneville-Carteret, a destination they had plucked out of their Philips School Atlas. They found a cheap hotel and an even cheaper restaurant. They spent two glorious days on the beach and fell in love with the place. Pat noticed there were a lot of single women lying on sunbeds while their children were supervised by play leaders in a 'Mickey' club on the beach. They looked so relaxed, languidly smiling, sipping a coffee, smoking and flicking through magazines. She got chatting to a couple of them; it seemed that it was their practice to spend the summer by the coast, while their menfolk continued to work back in Paris. 'What a good idea,' the women thought, and it was resolved that the following year a house would be rented for the summer and such a plan would be put into operation. Thus began our annual French holidays.

The next year the adults found a large house in the centre of Carteret and rented it for the whole of the month of August, through the local 'Syndicat d'Initiative'. Mum and I only stayed for the first fortnight, as we were going on to Highcliffe. This was when it was just four women and seven children, the 'other halves' coming for the second two weeks. We had a wonderful time, four little girls and three boys, with miles of empty beaches and the daily 'Mickey Club'. The only mortifying event began in the ferry car park in Portsmouth, when Pat's elderly Renault 4 (with the pronounced gear-stick) could not be restarted and burly ferry-hands were persuaded to push it on. Similarly it was given a running kick-start the other end. Welcome to France! The original of the 'roll-on, roll-off' concept.

What Mum found about these annual forays into France was how cheap they were. Apart from the ferries, and we only had the one car for all of us, everything else was relatively cheap: food, certainly, and rented accommodation seemed half of what you'd pay back home. The following year we stayed in a truly beautiful fortified farmhouse in the Vendée, plucked from the local Gite Guide to the area. It was just we three girls, but we had numerous adventures round the ramparts, or paddling in the little stream. We'd also drive to the sea and I do have a memory of my brilliantly unfazed mum lying on this French beach, topless, two years after her mastectomy.

The following year we went to southern Brittany. The adults found a large holiday home a few kilometres from the beach. Again it was very reasonably priced. I'm sure this had a lot to do with the fact they only booked it about ten days before going (a precursor again, this time of 'lastminute dot com'). Some of the friends, who had been in Carteret with us, had booked a tent for the same period in a nearby campsite months before and apparently were paying much more than us. For no obvious reason, except that life seems to go in cycles, this was to be our penultimate visit to France with Charmian and Juliet. The venue for next year's jaunt was to be a beach-side villa in La Baule, and it was made signally different from the previous holidays because Dad decided to join us.

We had been in the house for a couple of days when he suddenly pitched up one evening. I know that Pat and Nigel weren't expecting him; I'm not sure about Mum. He had been filming in Paris and said that, on the spur of the moment, he'd decided to come down and visit us. He'd hailed a cab just off the Champs-Élysées and the driver had agreed to take him the 500+ kilometres to our holiday home. He had a suitcase with his clothes in and another hold-all that he was particularly protective of: there was a little bag inside, which he said had 'something special' in, and also what appeared to be lots of rolls of money. Anyway, we all had a lovely time. We girls collaborated on a play, and gave him the role of the waiter, which he took very seriously, and the next day we got up early, for all of us to do a bit of sight-seeing.

Sadly, the sightseeing was mostly of Dad. He'd been recently on television a lot and was beginning to be recognised in the street, particularly by the British holiday-makers there, and also some French ones who'd seen him in a film he'd made with Alain Delon: 'Gangsteer!' they shouted. As Dad was autographing for one Brit, Nigel was asked, 'Are you anyone, too?' Dad really hated all this attention in those early days. Leaving the women and the girls to continue on their way, he dragged a willing Nigel into the dark depths of a welcoming bar and stayed there until dusk. When they emerged they were really not fit for purpose. However, they had already agreed to take us kids to a nearby circus and they wouldn't let us down. Sitting in the audience, no one would possibly notice that our two adult companions were not quite themselves.

That was the theory. As the performance finished, Dad set off at high speed, 'backstage' with Nigel and us children in tow. Asking his mate to translate into the French, he asked to see the owner, to explain that he would like to join the circus, preferably as a clown, but that he would consider working with animals. Although dubiously translated, the assembled company got the drift and, thanking Dad for his understandable enthusiasm, they declined his offer. So with heavy heart, he trudged home with us in train. What happened during the rest of that night still remains a mystery. We children went to bed, as did Mum and Pat; the men retired to a large bottle of Armagnac. Later the whole house heard raised voices and a splintering sound. Nigel remembers only going to the downstairs lavatory cheerfully and then waking up next morning unscathed but as if from an anaesthetic. In the morning, we children tiptoed downstairs to find an axe sticking out of the loo door, the Armagnac bottle empty and Dad gone. The adults continued the rest of the holiday breezily without comment.

Despite this episode we moved from Dennington Park Road just before my eighth birthday, and I can honestly say that during all the time we lived there, I don't remember my dad's drinking being a problem. I know that I was little, but kids do have a sixth sense. Anyway, I guess what I'm saying is, if he did have a problem, he didn't bring it home. Mum never smoked and rarely drank alcohol, but we'd often go down to the pub or had friends round to drink. Dad was always very entertaining. Every May the whole family would go down to Pat and Nigel's in Camberley for a big party. On one such occasion, he and all the children went missing for a couple of hours; he'd warned the adults beforehand. We were carol-singing – round Camberley – in May. We collected quite a bit for one of his charities. At the appointed hour, a large chauffeur-driven limousine arrived to cart Dad off to whatever rehearsal he was required for that day.

Our favourite local point of call was a huge pub on the Finchley Road called The Burgundian. Dad was very friendly with the landlord and his wife at the time, and sometimes used to help out behind the bar when they were short-staffed. It had a massive yard at the back, where I would sit with my lemonade and crisps and Dad, with his Guinness. With my friend 'Buster' Casey we'd play on the fruit machine, with pennies from Dad. We'd randomly push the colourful buttons as the images spun round, hoping to win more pennies. I particularly remember the walk to and from the pub. This was the best bit. It must have been a good half an hour each way, especially with my little legs. We would talk and talk and talk.

There were two ways to go there. One was down what Dad called 'Billy Fury Way' (I never knew its real name), which was an alleyway alongside the railway tracks from West Hampstead; I thought that it was miles and miles long. The other way meant walking from the Finchley Road, down Lymington Road to West Hampstead. Sometimes I'd draw arrows on the pavement, on the way there, to find on the way home. We'd walk past a house where Dad said a friend of his lived. Every time we passed, he would get me to go down the stairs and ring the bell. No one ever answered and I thought it a little odd, particularly as Dad would have his mischievous grin on. It was every time we passed. Maybe the house was empty or maybe he was playing proxy 'knock down ginger'. No one ever came and I will never know.

I have a lovely memory, also, of being with Dad and his brother, Uncle Robin, in a boatyard on the Thames at Hammersmith. Dad had been doing a play down there and had heard that a 'cabin cruiser' was for sale. It was a 'heap' as far as my Uncle Robin was concerned but this did not deter Dad from feeling he was returning to his seafaring days, so he bought *Quaker Girl* and had it moored in Little Venice. I remember having the odd picnic on her but she was never moved. I was so pleased to have been there when she was bought, and as the school-run took us past her everyday, I had a welling of pride, as I had my daily view of 'our boat'. Those journalists who referred to Dad's 'millionaire lifestyle', with his luxury cruiser, however, had obviously never seen it. And not long afterwards, neither did I. One day as we drove home from school in the rain, we saw a crane, lifting her out of the water. Vandals had broken in and torn at her covering; the rainwater had poured in and *Quaker Girl* had sunk. Dad had the carcass removed and despatched to a boatyard near Uncle Robin's for dismantling: the end of our luxury lifestyle.

You will gather that the memories I associate with my first home in Dennington Park Road are happy ones. I would never be aware that my own blissful experience was protected by my mother's refusal to let the diagnosis of breast cancer impinge on our lives. She was 32 when she had her mastectomy. Friends remember that she accepted it with remarkable stoicism; there was no fuss or outward sign of grief for her lost breast, and she had elected not to have reconstruction. When I was 5, Mum's cancer returned for the first time. I remember a friend of hers, Caroline, who taught at the same school, coming to pick me up in the mornings and take me in. I knew that it was something serious, even though nothing was ever discussed in front of me.

8

Pennies from Heaven

In talking to Dad's fellow actors while collecting the material for this book, it's been interesting how many of them dwell on his innate skill in embracing every aspect of the character he'd been asked to represent. Yes, the funny stories are there, many of them, and the downsides too, but producers, directors and actors have been unanimous in their need to emphasise that here was a very fine actor indeed, and that this should be documented. If anyone believes that he was a 'one-trick pony' or that he was typecast, compare these two descriptions from reviews, early on in his career, from productions already referred to:

as the alarm clock shattered sleep and the candle was lit in the dawn, we too were pulling on our clothes to share the day's hope and despair, powerless ourselves but yet powerfully involved as Barbara Ewing's handsome Edna and the stolidly gentle Tom of Bryan Marshall came together but did so only to be parted by the grubby ferret that Michael Elphick made of Jack.

(The television play *The Little Farm* from the series 'Country Matters', reviewed in *The Times*)

And then:

Michael Elphick's Polixenes is magnificently imaginative, bohemian in the widest and most pertinent sense. With his shaggy, tanned, buck-skinned, buccaneering swagger and electric sexuality he brings a necessary animal magic into the neurasthenic world of Leontes' court.

(Review in *The Stage*)

Less than two years after my birth Dad was to find himself starring in two major dramas on television at the same time. The TV magazines said that this had never happened before. Paul Knight, the producer of one, *Holding On*, says that Dad was a stand-out candidate for the lead role. The actor had to age fifty years in the part and Dad was deemed to be one of the few young actors who could carry it off. The series appeared on London Weekend Television on Sundays, while Dad also had the major role in Granada's *This Year, Next Year*, on Tuesdays. Whether it was fortuitous or not to have such full exposure at this point in his career, I don't know, but I'm guessing it was. Then it was more luck than judgement. Paul says that the filming actually took place in 1975, the year of my birth, but for 'political' reasons its broadcast was delayed nearly two years. Whatever the subtext it proved to be the major launch-pad for Dad's career. However, actors, particularly those in 'soaps', are often out of kilter with what they're doing at the same time as the characters that they portray. Dad was a 'new dad' when filming *Holding On*, but I was 3 years old when it finally appeared.

Before then he was to have a near-death experience that might have affected all of our lives. After the success of the Far-East British

Council tour, another was mooted to go to Iraq and Japan; it was a six-man group, under the director, Nick Kent, from The Tricycle Theatre Company. The featured play was *Macbeth* with William Gaunt in the lead. Tony May once again joined the company and said that he and Dad sometimes found themselves playing witches, but mostly Dad would be the tour 'Macduff'. Tony says that Iraq was awful but Japan was a different matter:

> We stayed in this beautiful hotel, especially designated for visiting artists. We visited an English bar, where bowing geishas were on hand to light our cigarettes and we even managed to get a lot of sight-seeing in, unlike our last trip to the East; we were especially bowled over by the golden temple at Kyoto. Mike was certainly tucking away the booze, but somehow he could take it without any evident side effects. His secret, he told me, was to take two valium before the evening's excursion and all would be well.

Famous last words, particularly when you're appearing in a play with the reputation of 'Macbeth'!
Tony continues:

> We were no more than a week into the tour ... It was a matinee, and the audience were mostly young girl students. Mike was Macduff and I had entered as Ross, bearing the news of the family's annihilation. He was just intoning: 'All? What, all my pretty chickens and their dam, At one fell swoop ...' when an arc of red liquid seemed to sweep the stage and disappear into the stalls. It was blood and it was cascading from Mike's mouth as he fell to the ground. There was silence, then a bank of adolescent screams broke from the audience. A stage-hand grabbed the curtain across, as I and fellow actors half carried him to an adjacent lavatory, where he collapsed into a cubicle, blocking the door.
>
> I shouted out, 'Are you OK?' to which there was no reply, so I climbed over the top and heaved him out. Thankfully our touring bus was parked close by and a hospital was quite near, so, although we called an ambulance, we actually got to the hospital before it left. I cradled Mike's head in my lap on the way there. He was in

a terrible state, with very shallow breathing; I was convinced that he was going to die. Apparently, we learned after the event that he had lost four pints of blood in twenty minutes. Luckily for him, a surgeon, an expert in duodenal ulcers, just happened to be visiting the hospital at the time and did a brilliant patching-up job, prior to him being sent to a specialist hospital in Tokyo. Naturally, the play was cancelled, but for only two nights, by which time a replacement had arrived from England.

Dad was advised to convalesce for at least six weeks in the hospital but after a fortnight he was getting bored: 'The only English-language books I could find were four or five volumes by Hans Eysenck, the psychologist, which, although interesting, were slightly repetitive.' So, he decided to go and convalesce in a place he'd got to know well on his last trip east, Penang:

I arrived there with only about £100 and checked into a little Chinese hotel at Batu Ferringhi, which latterly has become a big tourist spot. My agent was supposed to send £1,000 to a local bank, but it took ages to come. I ended up having to borrow from the poor tri-shaw driver, Charlie, who I'd used as my 'charioteer' the last time I was over. When I no longer had the funds to pay the hotel, this driver took me into his own home; it was literally a landing in an apartment block, where his children slept on mats on the floor. His real name was Sate, or, at least that was what I called him, as his own name was virtually unpronounceable. We became firm friends, with him feeding me and cycling me to the bank every day to see if the money had arrived. The answer was always in the negative.

The beautiful islands are not quite as idyllic as they look: they have killer bees, sea snakes and poisonous crabs. I learned this as I used to go fishing with Sate's friends, using a net from a small boat. When we got back, we used to sit and flog our haul in the market. One night, Sate woke me and said: 'Come and see the turtles.' It was incredible; we saw hundreds of them walking up the sand, dropping their eggs and then letting out this haunting cry. If anyone ever asks me where is my ideal place to be, it's there, chilling out under a palm tree, in Penang with a glass and a book. The place had an enormous impact on me. When my money eventually arrived, I offered Sate half, but to him it was a king's ransom and he wanted none of it. I had to secretly buy clothes for his kids through a relative, and cooking stuff; I also managed to get a deposit put down on a real apartment for him, which was next to nothing. His one request was that I should cycle/drive him to a nearby brothel, pay for his services there, wait outside, then pedal him back home, so he could imagine what it was like to be a rich tourist. I duly obliged and you can probably understand how the locals viewed this particular exercise: they couldn't stop laughing. I never went back to Penang, and as Sate could neither read nor write, that was the end of our relationship, sadly.

Dad managed to catch up with the *Macbeth* crew, at the very end of their tour, although not to perform. Tony May says that he got a note in his dressing-room, with the message, 'I'm O.K. now, but I've been told I must never drink again.' And, then, ominously, 'See you in the bar after the curtain.' So there was Dad sitting, as Tony arrived, with a large glass of milk in his hand and the whisky chaser on the bar. 'Apparently it'll be alright,' he said, 'if I keep taking the milk.' However, he did appear more restrained; so much more sober was he, that later in a bar, he intervened when two drunken British sailors were abusing a waitress. 'Don't you dare talk to her like that,' he said, 'Apologise now!' and they duly did. As Tony observed, 'There was no danger of a bar-room brawl. He had such authority that they submitted without protest.'

So Dad returned to Mum, healthier and wiser than when he left, and Dad's and Tony's paths were soon to cross again in a bizarre fashion. They had both got to know the playwright David Halliwell. Tony had been involved in a street theatre project with him at the time of the protest against the development of Covent Garden. David Halliwell had come across a single line advertisement in the *New Statesman*, saying 'Lifer needs help.' The advertiser turned out to be George Thatcher, a prisoner serving a life sentence in Albany Prison on the Isle of Wight. He had actually received a death sentence, but this had been commuted by the Home Secretary just half an hour before he was due to be hanged. He indicated by a somewhat coded letter to David, who had got in touch with him, that he needed to talk. And so it was that Dad, Tony and David found themselves on the Isle of Wight ferry en route for Albany, and whatever George had to say.

As it turned out, it was not a lot. There were a number of strictures in force on a Category A prisoner, and he was very limited in what he could say. After interminable pleasantries, Thatcher asked his warder if he might give his guests the present he'd prepared for them. Another warder was despatched to get the gift, which turned out to be a rather nondescript painting. George presented this to David, with the traditional smile, nod and wink, and then the three visitors were on their way. Back on the ferry again, returning to the mainland, David started tearing at the underside of the painting and pulled out a large exercise-book. This might have been the end of the story because the three were sitting outside on the deck and at the point of disclosure, a large gust of wind almost wrested the book out of David's grasp overboard. Luckily he caught it in time, as it contained the play Mr Thatcher had been writing, about a prisoner in circumstances similar to his. This was the play that David Halliwell added the flourishing touches to, and later directed at The Theatre at New End in Hampstead, starring Dad. The play was called *The Only Way Out*. Jack Tinker in the *Daily Mail* wrote:

> This play comes to us by way of Her Majesty's prison. Its author is serving a life sentence for a capital crime – for which he has always protested his innocence. Its central character is a man convicted of a murder he steadfastly denies. The setting is the death cell during the three lead-booted weeks of his appeal. The time is pre-abolition. But although the prisoner constantly argues the injustice of his conviction, the author is altogether too fine an artist to write this play merely as a platform for personal grievances ... The prisoner Redmond neither excites nor asks for any obvious sympathy. Michael Elphick gives him a truculent, goading gallows humour, guaranteed to turn the prison screws the wrong way.

Smudger Smith played one of the two 'screws'. *The Stage* reported:

> The prisoner, in a deeply committed study by Michael Elphick, showing the frustrated despair of a man absolutely convinced he was framed by the police, endures the psychological claustrophobic effect of being crowded by two prison officers, watching his every action, yet preserves his sanity through an awareness of the grim humour behind it all. As a view from the inside, the play seems authentic to the last clang of steel bars.

Dad loved working in the theatre but it was on television he was to make his name. Before my birth he had been acting in the pilot play, *The Nearly Man*, which was then recommissioned as a series. This story about the skulduggery surrounding a Labour politician had been well-received by critics and public alike. Once again, Gwen Taylor played Dad's wife. She is such a natural, 'down-to-earth' sort of person, and a beautiful actress. As she says, she was a late entrant to the profession, having risen through the ranks of her local amateur dramatic society in Derby, to which she is incredibly loyal, and still makes a point of visiting whenever she can. She was 'nearly thirty' when she left the E15 drama school, but hasn't she caught up? 'Barbara' in *Duty Free*, *Coronation Street* and *A Bit of a Do*, and that's only some of her television work! She loved working with Dad, and as I've said, found him incredibly protective. She's under no illusions, though, about some of the stories that emanated around him:

> Of course, handsome men like him were bound to have a reputation. I once spotted him eying a pretty girl in the hotel, where we were staying.
> 'So, what do you think?' I asked.
> 'No,' he said, 'I don't think so. That would be the type that I might fall in love with, and I don't want to do that.'
> He was such an easy actor to work with as well. There was talk of all manner of evening carousing, probably embellished through word of mouth, but nothing affected the acting the next day. I, for my part, because I was still probably centred on my life in Derbyshire, kept well clear of the evening jollifications – thankfully. So what I

know, is only ever by report! It's a lifestyle choice that has certainly helped me out over the years.

Gwen discovered during filming that she and Dad were near neighbours in London, living as they both did in the Fortune Green area, West Hampstead:

> It was the beginning of a lovely neighbourhood relationship with both Mike and Julia. I was such a great pal of Mike's: it was great to get to know Julia as well. You'd go round there and Mike would open a bottle of wine and put on the soundtrack of 'Pennies from Heaven' or he'd cook for the three of us or they'd be having one of their parties. It was always a great atmosphere. Sometimes, I'd find him with the rather strange tipple of milk and brandy, which he explained was 'medicinal', but the problems that I heard about in later years were never apparent then. And as for Julia, from the time that I first met her, I was always struck by the strength that she displayed. I was around when she was first diagnosed with breast cancer and her fortitude was incredible. She was always calm and resolute, and seemed to provide Mike with the sort of support that empowered him.

After *The Nearly Man*, Dad was soon to appear on the small screen in *Holding On*. As Paul Knight, the producer said, they needed an actor who could age fifty years which was no mean challenge. Dad played the part of Charlie Wheelwright, the stevedore, who humps sacks of seeds on his back. He reckoned that there was one job more exacting.

> That's putting a changing face on acting the part, having to age gradually from a teenager to a 70-year-old. Sometimes they would film young Charlie in the mornings and the old Charlie in the afternoons. I was putting on and taking off wigs and moustaches so fast that I was exhausted by the time I reached the set. Once I went out in front of the cameras as an old man when the scene being shot was for the younger Charlie.

101

A six-parter was not the ideal length to encompass the whole story, abridged from Mervyn Jones's novel, but as Paul says there were 'budgetary restrictions'. Belhaven Street in Bethnal Green was used as the central point for filming; it became Steadman Street for the series and it took Paul and his team a week to restore it to its appearance at the turn of the century. Telephone poles and television aerials were removed and modern house doors were taken away and old ones fitted, 'The residents were very helpful,' said Paul, 'and gave us a lot of technical advice.'

It was Paul's casting director, Sheila McIntosh, who had suggested that Dad had the range for this demanding role, 'What a great decision that was,' says Paul. 'He was a very attractive man and a terrific actor.' He mourns for the days when a compelling drama series could be launched on the back of good writing, acting and production values alone, without the need that television companies now have to link it to a 'celebrity star'. *Holding On* gave their first 'leg up' to not only Dad, but also Kenneth Cranham, John Duttine and John Nettles among others. Ken Cranham still thinks it hilarious that John Duttine and he both played Dad's sons although Ken is actually older than Dad. He does feel that the relationship developed in those roles did actually bring about a sort of 'family' closeness between the two that endured over the years, both professionally and socially. One thing Dad had heard was that it might be difficult to be accepted by the dockers who resented other television programmes that had presented them as being flash and greedy. He said at the time, 'Of course, they're built like horses to do the hard work they do, but they are genuinely kind and understanding. They have a tremendous pride in their work and life.'

And so to *This Year, Next Year*, which began its thirteen-week run at the same time as *Holding On*. As the *Sun* said grandly at the time of Dad's double exposure, 'It is believed to be the first time in television history that a double like this has happened.' Philip Purser's television review in the *Telegraph* nimbly combines a critique of both:

> That Michael Elphick should bulk large in concurrent voluminous serials is a sign of the times. Barrel-chested, capaciously bellied and judging by his morning splosh in the water tank in the opening of

John Finch's *This Year, Next Year*, well hung, he's one of the few younger actors of heroic mettle who doesn't conform to the lean, mean, narrow-loined ideal of recent years. Not so stockily aggressive as Colin Blakely, less homely than Ernest Borgnine – to name two predecessors in this mould – he still has the bullet head, wide smile and general cheerfulness to provide the perfect contrast while remaining physically not too dissimilar, to his jaded towny brother in the story, played by Ronald Hines.

As the grown-up Charles Wheelwright, in *Holding On*, adapted by Brian Phelan from Mervyn Jones's life-span novel of a London stevedore, the Elphick character is harder, more cunning and a good deal shorter on truth. In the First World War battlefield scene last time he treated a vapid subaltern to a real lip-curling sneer; home again on demob, he sent his sister's gentle fancy-man packing. Yet both times he personifies better than anyone else what each of the serials is about. *This Year, Next Year* is responding very directly, almost literally, to the prevalent feeling of the last two or three years that the whole rickety structure of civilisation is about to collapse, the cities are where it's going to happen first, and the only hope is to get back to roots in the soil. Harry Shaw (Hines) is going to attempt that very thing, but brother Jack has got it already. *Holding On* is yet another rear-view saga, the appeal of which is more complex and more interesting than one merely of cosy nostalgia but does rely heavily on the same yearnings to retreat to where life is or was simpler, straighter, and if perhaps, harder, certainly fuller of zest.

These two roles inevitably acted as a massive springboard for Dad's future career in television.

9

Schultz

Dad had a chequered career, according to the distinguished television critic, Philip Purser.

For he it was who wrote the *Telegraph* review that closed the last chapter and he was also the author of Dad's obituary in *The Guardian*, where he recanted on his somewhat peevish earlier comments in Halliwell's Guide: 'I can only claim, in mitigation, that it (said review) was written when Elphick was newly occupying his most popular – and populist – role as Boon.' He had been patronisingly disdainful, calling *Boon* 'a worthy format' and that it made 'rather obvious use of Elphick's stocky physique and ready scowl'.

But Philip Purser was the author of Dad's next project, a television film of the life of a famous striptease artist, *The One and Only Phyllis Dixey*. It was a fairly straightforward docu-drama of the mostly wartime exploits of the lady performing, as bombs dropped. Lesley-Ann Down starred as Phyllis, aided and abetted by Patricia Hodge and Elaine Page. Dad played the impresario, Wallace Parnell, brother of Val. The whole was slightly censored in a made-for-television way. There was a sense of it being 'all in the family' as Lesley-Ann Down was with Bruce Robinson at the time and therefore a visitor to the Fortune Green houses.

This was another substantial role for Dad but unlike the guaranteed limelight that he was going to find in a role like 'Boon', he continued at this time still to have a mix of billings in the film and TV roles that he undertook. Obviously, his agent, Peter Crouch, would have a strong say in what was right for him, and whether he was available at the time. Dad, of course, would say 'yes' to everything if he could. But, rather like the time-lag with *Holding On*, delays and postponements by the television companies gave an uneven progress to Dad's earlier career. There would be simultaneous appearances in minor and major roles on different channels. This was definitely the time when his 'tough-guy' image was identified, be it in *The Sweeney* in an episode called 'One of your Own', where he played a crook named Jimmy Fleet, who helped Regan and Carter capture a gang-leader in return for a lenient sentence for his crimes; or in *The Professionals*, in an episode called 'Backtrack', where he played a policeman, Sergeant Garbett. In *Hazell*, he was a gang-leader, this time with a French accent, and he even managed to appear in a Children's Film Foundation production as a thug – an escaped prisoner who is found by two children on a remote island on a school trip. There were also good 'bread and butter' jobs like *Crown Court*. He appeared on this in a three-parter as Neville Griffiths QC, prosecuting the daughter of a Selsey family for harming her abusive father. It was commented at the time that he was the only actor to pronounce 'Selsey' as 'Zell-Zey' in the manner of the West Sussex village near Chichester.

There was a very jolly little BBC2 Playhouse called *Pocketful of Dreams*, where Dad played a villain who used a film unit to disguise his robbing of a bank, predating *Argo* by a good many years. In the series *Cribb* he appeared in an episode with Kenneth Cranham. Ken was appearing as a participant in a Victorian walking marathon, the type where you walked till you dropped. Dad played the entrepreneur masterminding the event. After a hard day's shooting they both retired to the welcoming warmth of a local pub. There was a lot of catching up to do and one thing led to another, and Ken remembers getting Dad back to the hotel and into bed. He was a little dismayed, then, the next day, when Dad failed to appear for the shoot. The director, Gordon Fleming's caustic comment – 'I like a drink like Elphick, but I happen to be upright and speaking' – didn't help. As Ken says:

Suddenly there was this flurry. As all the extras were busily applying their false sideburns and handle-bar moustaches, through their ranks swept Mike, with make-up girls busily adjusting his mutton-chops, while costume were trying to manhandle him into his waistcoat. He seemed to enjoy the whole element of risk attached to it.

Once, when Dad was playing one of these tough-guy characters for TV, his friend Andy McCulloch was there. He says that it was a summer's day, and they were filming on location in North London, all playing characters looking a little the worse for wear.

Mike and a couple of other younger actors, between scenes, all in costume as seedy-looking guys, were having a drink, sitting at a table, outside a rough, local pub. They all looked up as an attractive young woman, in a stylish summer dress walked past them and into the pub. Several younger heads turned. Mike just continued with the story he was telling. Almost immediately, the young woman came back out of the pub and walked off down the street. Several of the young actors watched her go. One shook his head – 'That's a shame. She didn't hang around long!'

Mike looked at the pub and the assembled company of derelicts sitting outside, and said, 'Don't blame her. If I looked like that I wouldn't hang round a dump like this either.'

This was a time when Dad was working with two very good stage directors. There was Peter Gill at the newly opened Riverside and Stuart Burge at The Royal Court. There was an electrifying atmosphere about their productions, before any actor stepped on the stage, because their reputations went before them. Peter Gill had just become the first Artistic Director of the Riverside Studios in their new incarnation as a theatre. He, himself, had made his name in a number of milestone productions, some at The Royal Court, and later at The National Theatre. Stuart Burge was the new Artistic Director at The Royal Court, which by that time had been going through acute financial problems and was in danger of losing its Arts Council grant. It badly needed the fillip of some good productions to steady its course. Gill's *The Cherry Orchard* in 1978, with a cast including Dad, Judy Parfitt, Eleanor Bron and Julie Covington was the 'hot ticket' that January with brilliant reviews. Then Gill's *Measure for Measure* opened at the Riverside the following year: again, with plaudits from the press: 'Peter Gill's treatment of this treasure is controlled, spare and dynamic. Using minimum of set, but effective, emotive lighting on a vast stage area, the action complements the grandeur of verse, yet concisely controls the parameters of truthful playing.' According to George Baker, who played the Duke, the very vast stage seemed even vaster to the waiting audience for about fifteen minutes of the proceedings one evening. The audience, still respectful, and only just beginning to cough, sat with growing apprehension waiting for the appearance of either Pompey (Dad) or Isabella (Helen Mirren) or both (George doesn't say). Apparently Dad was somehow unable to get out of Helen Mirren's dressing room, where he'd popped for an interval cup of coffee. The door had stuck completely and stage-hands had to break it down. Between Gill's productions, Dad also managed to fit in Burge's *The London Cuckolds* at the Court, with Stephanie Beacham and Kenneth Cranham, another hugely celebrated revival. Ken says that Stuart Burge let him and Dad, as the two Restoration men-about-town, develop their own business in the many scenes that they shared together. It gave them great ownership of their parts and the moves were instantly memorable; it was also tremendous fun.

Television continued to hand out the cameo roles of the hard man that the public recognised, but one beautifully written character part stands out from these: this was Gordon Weller in *The Knowledge* by Jack Rosenthal. The play examines the lives of those 'doing the knowledge', learning the roads of London like 'the back of your hand' in order to qualify as a black-cab driver when you are tested on it. Dad's character used the opportunity of leaving the house daily to escape his wife and womanise his way round London. Ken Cranham relates a story about Dad at this time. Apparently, he had studied a lot of cab 'lore' for his part, and one night, with Ken, in Soho, hailed a cab to go to his favourite haunt, The Burgundian on the Finchley Road. The driver refused, saying it was too far out of his way. Dad, sober, with a newfound authority on the subject, reminded him of his statutory duties and the penalties he faced if reported. Dad got his ride and, as Ken remembers, probably the only tip-free one of his life. Dad's wife in *The Knowledge* was played by Maureen Lipman, who was the real-life wife of the playwright, Jack, who sadly is no more.

Another great television playwright who is no longer with us is Dennis Potter. Like a few others – gamekeeper turned poacher – he was a TV critic who started writing for the screen, and how successful he was: *The Singing Detective*, *Pennies from Heaven* and the elegiac *Blue Remembered Hills* that Dad appeared in. This play was very unusual in that the cast of seven-year-olds were played by adults. It was the summer of 1943 in the Forest of Dean, when the Second World War was raging elsewhere and the children were kicking their heels, playing 'war games' and generally, in their bullying and in-fighting, reflecting the morality of their 'elders and betters'. Dad later reported: 'There was none of the usual stuntmen, or even choreographers. They just let us go out and have a bash. It was great fun. We got terrible grazed knees and bruises, just like kids do.' He adored Dennis Potter's writing. Dad was the big lad, Peter, with a great cast that included Colin Welland and Helen Mirren, one of only two girls, and Colin Jeavons as the bullied boy Donald, who finally dies in a fire. Dad told me that the director kept this actor purposely lodging in another pub in another village than the rest of them to encourage his sense of isolation when it came to doing improvisational exercises for their roles.

For those who couldn't get enough of Dad at this time at the theatre or on the television, there was always the cinema. In 1979 alone he appeared in three, what would now be called, I'm sure, 'cult movies': *The First Great Train Robbery*, *Quadrophenia* and *The Elephant Man*. The first starred Sean Connery and Donald Sutherland; Dad played the part of a Victorian guard on the South

Eastern Railway train. Dad tells a story from the time of filming, about Sean Connery; he could never sing his praises enough. 'That man,' he'd say, if ever he saw Sean on television or in the papers, 'That man saved my arse. I'll never forget him ... and if I can do for any young actor what he did for me ...' I could tell him now that I've had enough feedback from people who worked with Dad to indicate that he repaid the debt in spades. So what was the story? Well, Dad had, needless to say, gone out 'pubbing' the night before a big shoot, but unlike his usual self, had woken up with the mother-and-father of a hangover. He staggered into costume and make-up and appeared on set not really convincing as a Victorian guard. He muffed a couple of takes and then, to his surprise, realised that Sean Connery, who was the only other actor in the scene, was having an even tougher time – forgetting lines, losing cues and seeming not to remember the moves they'd worked on the day before. The director announced that it was a wrap and they'd start again in the afternoon. Dad was tremendously relieved; he knew he'd be able to get his act together by then. Sean Connery came over to him: 'Never do that again, son,' he said, 'you're replaceable. If they get rid of you in these circumstances, no one's going to hire you again. I had the advantage here, but I've done it so that you'll never forget.' He had deliberately screwed up to save Dad, who couldn't believe it: 'He took a bullet for me. What a man!'

According to the celebrated actress, Kate Williams, who worked with Dad on *Quadrophenia*, he could show huge generosity to fellow actors, himself. Her casting for the role of Jimmy's mother had been somewhat last minute. She'd been asked to attend a meeting with the director, Franc Roddam, and she remembers that it was at the end of a long day's shooting at the studio in Wembley. Mike, who was still in the building, was introduced to her, and both of them were directed to improvise a row between the parents of an errant son who'd been hiding drugs underneath his mattress, 'Franc's direction to us was that he wanted one of those relationship arguments where all the character flaws in the son are laid at the door of the other partner, and all the good qualities are claimed as one's own contribution.' Kate notes that, while she 'doesn't mind' improvisation – (she's brilliant at it – she had come from Stratford East, where it was seen as an essential character development tool) she had no idea whether Mike would relish it. 'I dived in, and, so wonderful, Mike just upped and slammed into me like we had been together for years.' She says he was 'fabulous to work with'. The two of them yelled and abused each other soundly for about five minutes and 'then, catching a look, we stopped, and Mike said to Franc, "Is that enough?" He agreed that it was. Mike gave him an almost imperceptible nod, winked at me and ambled out. God bless him, he got me that job!'

I wonder what experience he was drawing on to get inside that kind of row. Certainly, I never heard my parents engage in it – my mother used the silent, icily polite weapon. I think my dad, though, would have quite liked to get his teeth into something more energetic and emotional. When we're in the throes of a meaty, substantial row (I own up) at least there's a sense of acknowledgement: 'I see you – I might loathe you at this precise second, but I do see you.' Somehow, being ignored must be the most discomfiting, isolating feeling.

Back to *Quadrophenia*. This was when my Dad's 'accentuated maturity' was given a bit of a kick-start. I mean, he was 33 years old at the time, playing Phil Daniels's dad. Talking about his own youth, he said:

> I was a rocker. I had all the leather gear and we used to ride down to the seafront from Chichester to Brighton with all the mods and rockers. [He must have been on the back of somebody else's bike.] The funny thing was that when the film *Quadrophenia* was being mooted, the director was telling me about it and he said, 'We're going to make a film about a young mod who goes to Brighton for a weekend ...' And I was thinking, 'Terrific, I can get all the rocker's gear out again!' And he said, 'We want you to play his dad.' That was the first time it hit me that I was actually getting on.

To be playing the older generation in a youth-oriented rock-opera must have been a weird experience at the time. Esta Charkham, who later produced Dad in *Boon*, was brought in as casting director when Patsy Pollock, who was appointed, went on holiday. She remembers the casting of Kate Williams. Franc Roddam later went on to produce Dad in the 'Harry' series.

If Dad were ever asked if there were any jobs that he didn't enjoy, then filming *The Elephant Man* would be one of them, although, as he said, 'It was certainly an amazing experience.' He appeared as the sadistic hospital porter in this award-winning film, which starred Anthony Hopkins and John Hurt. 'It was very traumatic. Every time I saw John with all the make-up on, I was so aware that there had been a real man who actually looked just exactly like that. It was all a bit daunting. And I played such a horrible person.' Dad's dislike of this particular part has its roots in a very frightening event that happened in the aftermath of filming. After the film's release, Dad had gone down to visit Granny Joan in Chichester. He was just coming out of Victoria Station when this large figure approached. With a shout of, 'You, you evil bastard! Think you're hard, do you!' Dad was thrown to the ground, in front of astonished but frozen commuters, and kicked and beaten until he lost consciousness. The police and ambulance were called but the perpetrator was never found. As he used to say: 'There's a downside to playing heavies that casting directors should never forget.'

Leaving filming for a while, Dad returned to a play and a theatre that he really loved, and to work again for a director for whom he had the most massive respect. As Richard Eyre has written:

> I'd been asked to direct a play for The Royal Court' in 1980; I was producing a 'Play for Today' at the BBC, and hadn't worked in the theatre for two years. I think Max Stafford-Clark hoped that I might suggest a new play, or revival of a contemporary classic – in short a 'play for today'. I thought I had, and so, I imagine, did he, for he accepted the notion of *Hamlet* with Jonathan Pryce with no visible ideological struggle. If the production belonged in any way to a 'Royal Court tradition', it was in its casting (Jill Bennett as Gertrude, Michael Elphick as Claudius, Harriet Walter as Ophelia), and what I thought of as a strain of rational humanism.

There was a fair bit of anxiety amongst the cast as they rehearsed at Awful House, the rehearsal rooms in Kennington; Thatcher was cutting back on the Arts; the Court had a reputation for the outlandish, and was the world ready for this Jacobean version of a classic? The opening reviews were not totally appreciative, but by the time the weekend critiques rolled in, there was a very palpable hit. *The Stage* wrote:

> Pryce is an actor of great range and mercurial illustration of thought and emotion. His performance is excellent. Michael Elphick is a suspiciously hearty Claudius, a villain yet touching in his origins when conscience strikes him. Jill Bennett is a splendid Gertrude, a woman of large character and flowing desire, but also of keen mind and sensibility.

In retrospect, Richard Eyre writes of Dad:

> When we were doing *Hamlet*, he had a crate of beer under his dressing-room table, always empty by the end of the evening. How did he do it? Why? He was always good company. After the show we'd often go to a club on the Kings Road. I never knew him to be maudlin. Or really drunk.

There was a development from Dad's playing Claudius, this time, that Neil Morrissey told me about recently. About a couple of years after the performance, Dad got a panic call from the director of the play at the Royal Exchange Theatre in Manchester. His 'Claudius' had fallen ill and the understudy would not be available; could Dad possibly step into the breach the next evening? He could travel down the day of the call, and next morning could go through the blocking, ready for the evening performance. Ever the man who likes to say 'yes', Dad agreed. He'd got a space before going abroad for another film, so he quickly bundled a case together and headed towards Euston. About half an hour into the journey, he came to the sickening realisation that he could not remember one line from the play. He raced up the train and found the guard, who luckily had his wits about him. As far as he could remember, the station with the largest WHSmith's bookstore adjacent to the platform, on which their train arrived, was Stafford. Dad shot off like a greyhound there to buy *A Complete Works* or some anthology including *Hamlet*. He swears that the guard waited to see him safely on, before blowing his whistle. He started relearning straight away. After the performance, the other actors gathered round offering their congratulations. The director duly appeared smiling broadly, 'Well done, Michael,' he said, 'So good, and so inaccurate!'

Dad, himself, believed that his next role was his game-changer. He says of his friend, Bob Hoskins: 'We were both up for *Pennies from Heaven* and then *Private Schultz* came along and the director wanted either Bob or me. It worked out very well. Bob and I agree that they got the best casting for each part.' This six-part series was described by BBC Enterprises when they released it on video as:

The last in a line of distinguished dramatisations by the late Jack Pulman. *Private Schultz* has been hailed by critics as a television classic with the hallmark of genius. Poignant, exciting and extremely funny, this macabre tale follows the extraordinary exploits of a quite remarkable SS clerk – the inventor of an outrageous plan to disrupt the British and Allied wartime economies by money forgery.

Dad said later:

Schultz was considerably important. I suppose because it wasn't too far from me. There's a lot in me that understands how he behaved. I didn't have a clue when we started. Imagine being told that it had concentration camps, jack boots and Nazis – and it was a comedy! Schultz is one of life's survivors. He is not a Nazi; he is not even a war patriot or a 'mercenary' soldier, so it is easy for the audience to sympathise with him without discomfort. He is a victim of circumstance who puts in for a sleepy niche in Postal Censorship, well away from the military action, and finds himself, instead, appointed to the post of confidential clerk to SS officer Major Neuheim in Counter Espionage.

Dad's single reservation regarding *Private Schultz* was whether a Nazi comedy might not prove too unedifying a prospect for Jewish viewers. He raised the question with the actor Cyril Shaps, who was Jewish and played Solly, an ex-jailbird friend of Schultz, who becomes his leading counterfeiter. 'Shaps,' Dad said, 'felt that, though we should never lose sight of the appalling reality of that time, there was also, perhaps a place for poking fun at this particular Nazi episode which has such preposterous overtones.' Dad had a great admiration for Ian Richardson, who played Schultz's chief, Major Neuheim: 'Ian Richardson has a powerful personality, and clear-cut ideas about what he intends to do. I decided to wait, and build my performance around his.' Also, in one of those self-belittling interviews, where his looks once again came under scrutiny, he said, 'People who write scripts don't conceive of me in a sort of romantic lead way, but I did end up with Billie Whitelaw in *Private Schultz*, which can't be bad.'

Before this happens, *The Stage*, in a glowing review, highlights

> what lifts the series above the sit com level is the comedy and, most of all, Pulman's dialogue which abounds in subtlety and satire. Regard these examples. At the beginning of episode one, the bedrooms in the city's brothel have been bugged and a monitoring point set up in the basement by the SS. Schultz's first job is to listen in. 'It's like being permanently tickled with a feather and never being allowed to laugh,' he tells Berta upstairs; and she refuses to go to bed with him because, 'I have a psychological block about sleeping with anyone below the rank of major. Besides,' she adds, 'I'm tired – I haven't been on my feet all day.'

Dad's greatest regret was that Jack Pulman never saw his finished oeuvre, having died before it was completed. The story was loosely based on an actual SS clerk, called Johann Rasch, and the 'Operation Bernhard' that he mounted. Pulman's widow said that after he had heard the story, 'It became one of Jack's main objectives in life to show how very nearly our world was brought to a standstill by what he called B-feature film gangsters.' Esta Charkham remembers when Dad was filming *Boon*, in one episode, a young actress called Corey Pulman was appearing. When Dad discovered that she was Jack's daughter he just grabbed her and gave her a great big hug, tears in his eyes, 'Your Dad changed my life forever,' he said. *Private Schultz* was an international triumph, winning award after award, but the sensibilities of the Jewish lobby in the States restricted its network coverage. However, it was on Public Broadcast, and as a consequence,

Dad, as the lead actor of *Schultz*, made it on to the Johnny Carson Show. Johnny Carson said, 'Nice to meet you – you speak very good English for a German!'

10

Going Global

We've all been to the cinema or watched TV dramas where some well-known actor has put in an appearance. We recognise the face – can't place the name. Older readers will be familiar with a cohort of British character actors of my father's generation – I'm thinking of people like Julian Glover, Clive Wood, Jeremy Child and the late, great Peter Postlethwaite, and many more. These actors tend to make whatever they're in that much better. By 1979, my father had joined them.

He seemed to be everywhere: cameos, series, full-length plays, you name it, comedy, drama, television and film. In *The Quiz Kid* television play he was reunited with Helen Mirren, where she is the brassy barmaid to his over-protective boyfriend. The story, which follows his jealousy of the intellectual interloper whose ascent through the ranks of the pub quiz team to the barmaid's heart, was always bound to end in tears. Bill Hays, who directed the play, had been responsible just before for the highly original series *Rock Follies*. As the writer, Alan Plater, summed up in his obituary in *The Guardian*:

> He achieved some of the most spectacular visual effects ever produced in a television studio: 'Basically, we just twiddled all the knobs to see what would happen. God knows whether they'll ever work again.' Gregarious, charming and irritatingly handsome, Bill had an attitude to work characteristic of the period; rehearsals started early but were carefully planned to harmonise with licensing hours. This was not, however, an approach that sat easily with the management strategies which invaded the television industry of the 1990s.

Soon after *The Quiz Kid*, Dad appeared in a comedy series, this time linking up again with Jonathan Pryce, in a very different role than *Hamlet*. Pryce is the anti-hero of *Roger Doesn't Live Here Anymore*, a musician going through a divorce who finds solace with Rose, played by his real-life wife, Kate Fahy. The script, by John Fortune, explores Rose's need for the titillation that adultery affords her, and so, when Roger's divorce comes through, with the possibility of her romance fading, she swiftly gets married herself to an all-in wrestler. Dad played the part of the wrestler, Stanley. Each episode was treated as a separate play and there was, unusually, no studio audience. It was while Dad was working on this series that something happened, Mum told me later, that gave her such an insight, in a funny sort of way, of the sort of pressure he was under at this time. He was almost like a one-man repertory company, having read-throughs on one production, takes on another and performing on a third, all at the same time. One night, Dad had come home late when Mum was already in bed. He looked briefly at the script by the bed and then fell into a fitful sleep. Very early in the morning Mum was woken by Dad staggering round the bedroom, evidently asleep, but trying to get into the wardrobe. 'What on earth are you doing, Mike?' she asked, 'Lookin' for the jokes in this bleedin' script.' was his immediate, somnambulant reply.

The next script-writers were two of Dad's trusted actor friends, Andy McCulloch and John Flanagan, who had already written a lot for television. This time, though, they were writing for the stage, a comedy set in a funeral parlour called *Stiff Options*. The play was premiered at The Theatre Royal, Stratford East, and starred Dad, as a gangster, and the great Brian Pringle, as the undertaker. As ever, when Dad was involved in anything, life always seemed to upstage art. First of all, two of the coffins were stolen from the theatre, before rehearsals started. New ones were acquired and installed. But as Dad recalled:

> In my role, I had to move the coffins around and then jump in one. It was as black as ink and then I couldn't move the lid. I was wedged. I could hear them standing around and talking. I shouted but no one heard. There were no air holes and I couldn't breathe. I'm a bit claustrophobic anyway. I felt giddy and blacked out. Luckily, they found me soon after, when they took the lid off. But I was a temporary hospital job.

A fellow actor provided the helpful observation that coffins don't necessarily come 'with air-holes included'. A lighter, chipboard coffin was used thereafter.

This was an era when the great mini-series were beginning to appear from the States. British actors could pick up well-paid cameos, whilst staying often in luxurious surroundings. Usually it meant playing some sort of 'baddie': a criminal mastermind, or a German officer or a Roman soldier. It was as the latter that Dad found himself cast in *Masada*, also known as *The Antagonists*. He was Vettius, a Roman, as were all the many British actors recruited for the series that depicted the events surrounding a Jewish rebellion against the Roman occupation. No prizes for guessing what parts the American actors played. Richard Eyre recalls the time that Dad was out in Israel for the filming: 'I love the story of him making that film in Israel, sitting up all night on a balcony, looking over the beach. Some of his fellow actors (American, of course) ran past in jogging gear at sunrise. "Hi, Mike," they said, "Training?", "Sure ..." said Mike, raising his nth glass of beer.'

It was undoubtedly thirsty work on location, particularly when they were working in a more desert-like environment. Dad said it was his good luck to get to know Peter O'Toole, who undoubtedly was 'the money' on the film. O'Toole had a large and comfortable air-conditioned tent structure, where he could afford to house other British thespians away from the heat of the day. On one particular day it was fairly evident to all but the most insensitive of assistant directors that the likelihood of Peter O'Toole and his air-conditioned tent parting company for a bit of outdoor filming in this most broiling of temperatures was a bit of a no-no. 'But Mr O'Toole,' pleaded the young director, in desperation now, after half an hour of cajoling, 'We have a camel waiting very close by for you to mount.'

'I know,' said the actor, shovelling more ice into his glass, 'Go and get me a photograph of it, a Polaroid, so I can see what it looks like!' The hapless wunderkind leaves and returns at length with a picture. O'Toole stares at it in disbelief. 'Good God! What's this? I'm not working with this. I want a *pretty* camel.' he said and guaranteed that neither he nor Dad would have to face the rigours of the burning sand for some considerable time. Another of his fellow 'togaed' Brits was that great actor, Denis Quilley, who was playing the part of a general. Dad was to meet him in his next project, again in uniform, but in a role that could not be more different than this. He would be playing the flamboyant, queenly Captain Terri Dennis to Dad's Sergeant-Major Reg Drummond in the film of *Privates on Parade*.

Peter Nichols's play of the same name, with a film-script by the author, transferred well to the large screen. Indeed, most of the cast had travelled with it from the theatre, including Denis Quilley in the starring role. The two exceptions were John Cleese, as a mad major, and Dad. Handmade Films, which were mostly funded by George Harrison, and seemed to be one of the few organisations supporting British films at the time, felt that Cleese, who was starring in Monty Python, was very bankable. Dad's part on the stage was played by David Daker, who was going to be his co-star in the future, in *Boon*. Peter Nichols based his play on his own experiences in a Forces concert party in the Far East. Although the characters, for the most part, would be amalgams of several personalities, some had more than a passing likeness to specific individuals he'd met. Sergeant-Major Drummond is as tragic a figure as you are likely to find in any play: he is homophobic, corrupt and sadistic and his early death is not mourned. Of his characters' progenitors, Nichols writes:

> a couple have taken their own lives. The first suicide was our company sergeant-major, who is roughly Reg Drummond in the play. Critics found him far-fetched and perhaps his life *was* too bizarre for fiction. He took cyanide in the presence of several other men and died babbling about the Special Investigation Branch, as Reg does in the play.

The film was greeted with polite, but unenthusiastic reviews.

If only the same could have been said about *The Curse of the Pink Panther*, which totally justified its title. This was to be the last in the original series, although more than a decade later, an earlier one was reconstituted. The franchise didn't just run out of steam, it lost its star, Peter Sellers. When he died, the director made another film with out-takes of Sellers and a rather garbled storyline to accommodate them. *The Curse* followed this, with an even more strained narrative, involving a clone of Sellers's bumbling detective, purportedly in a hunt for the original, missing one. All ended in grief, with the director suing the distributors for a lack of contractually obliged promotion. Dad was interviewed at the time, saying:

> My work schedule has been extraordinary. I went to Spain and France to film my role as Chief of Police of Valencia. In fact, I met Blake Edwards, the director quite casually and he suddenly said, 'Hey, you look a little Spanish. You wanna come to Spain with us?' So there I was, flying down to Spain in this pink jet called Panther 1 with his wife, Julie Andrews. Me and Mary Poppins. I thought, 'This isn't real.'

I daren't think what the cost of each spoken line worked out as. While involved in *The Curse*, Dad met David Niven who was making his very last film. 'David had been destroyed by motor neurone disease. It was terrible to witness this fine actor brought low by such a cruel affliction. I was determined to do as much as I could for the charity that was seeking a cure.'

About this time there occurred a rather difficult interlude. Anyone monitoring Dad's career, using the standard reference works, will notice that among his performances is listed a detective chief inspector in John le Carré's televised *Smiley's People*. However, among the credits for the film there is no mention of him. John le Carre was interviewed about this at the National Film Theatre:

> I think the parts in *Smiley's People* weren't as good as in *Tinker, Tailor* – they weren't written as well in some ways. They weren't as contributory to the main theme as they should have been.
>
> Michael Elphick is also sadly dead. On the night shoot in *Smiley's People* where the General is lying dead on Hampstead Heath, Michael Elphick plays the copper. He was so nervous about acting opposite Alec Guinness that he over-refreshed himself. That was his problem. So the scene had to be abandoned, which was a very expensive thing to do on a night shoot. Because it was near our house in Hampstead, we brought everyone in for a drink. Alec was seething. My wife took him downstairs and gave him a large scotch. He said, 'It is exactly the same as far as I'm concerned, as a soldier going to sleep on sentry duty.'
>
> He had his drink and then straightened himself up, went upstairs and was sweet to everybody. He gave Elphick a little pat and went home.

Dad's next venture had all the signs of having its run extended, or at least Yorkshire Television thought so. It was to be written by Roy (*Last of the Summer Wine*) Clark as three one-hour plays. The publicity machine had Dad in a flurry of interviews, I'm sure, under duress, to promote it:

> I'm playing a guy who must be the world's most unusual private eye. He's a Leeds-based sleuth who's got a serious heart condition. He's a seedy character, useless at his job, and his Pakistani assistant, who wants to become a Catholic priest, has only one leg. It's very funny.

Roy Clark has a beautiful touch. It's such an offbeat idea that I'm sure it's going to click.

It didn't. It was called *Bloomfield* and it wasn't re-commissioned. Dad was always very unhappy about the part, as this review in the *Mirror* will illuminate:

Bloomfield's Big Bloomer. Have you caught that odd little series about the cardiac case and the crippled coon? Don't immediately rush screeching to report me to the Race Relations Board, because I am quoting from the dialogue in this week's episode of *Bloomfield*. Frankly this odd three-parter – one more to go – from Yorkshire on Tuesdays has got me baffled. I turned to it eagerly because it stars the extraordinary Michael Elphick who happens to be a hero of mine. Apart from the fact that, unlike *Minder*, the odd mixture of humour and violence doesn't really work, it began to annoy me with all its racist jibes.

I started to write the lines down, then I found I was writing out the whole script: not an opportunity is missed to call Bloomfield, himself (rather unconvincingly played by Mark Zuber) coffee-coloured, a Paki, or that he ought to 'frig off and see if the curry's ready'. Nobody ever says 'You', it's 'You Dago bastard' or 'You cripple'. People may or may not speak like that in real life. I don't really want to hear it on television, thank you. Could it be because it's written by Roy Clark – whose dazzling success with *Last of the Summer Wine* may have blinded Yorkshire to its glaring faults. I wonder ...

The gap between the publicity machine and reality couldn't be illustrated better than in the press release that accompanied the one for *Bloomfield*: 'Michael Elphick's next big project is a big-screen, medieval times film called *Krull*, playing in Italy, a bad guy, opposite Francesca Annis.'

Krull was actually a science-fiction fantasy film, one of the most expensive to be filmed up to that time and directed by Peter (*Bullit*) Yates. It was filmed at Pinewood and in Italy and the Canary Islands. For the American market, one of the stars, Lysette Anthony, had to be dubbed by Lindsay Crouse. Inexplicably, Dad's involvement was in dubbing Robbie Coltrane, in the role of Rell, for which he was not credited. One can only suppose that, in this case at least, first-class air tickets to Italy were not going to be necessary.

Tickets would be required, however, to take Dad to Helsinki, where he would be acting a part that would lead to a BAFTA nomination for Best Supporting Actor. That part was 'Pasha' in *Gorky Park*, the film from the successful novel of the same name; the script was by Dennis Potter, whom Dad admired so much, and the director was Michael Apted, whom Dad had first come across in the late 1960s, when working on *Parkin's Patch*, a long-running series about a rural policeman set in the Yorkshire Moors. The environment of *Gorky Park* couldn't have been more different. This was at the height of the Cold War and, although the action, a police drama, was set in Moscow, the Finnish capital, Helsinki, had to double up; this it did very effectively with temperatures in the high minuses. I wouldn't describe it as Dad's favourite excursion. Later, the whole crew moved to Berlin. The two stars of the film were Lee Marvin and William Hurt. The latter was just not Dad's cup of tea for a number of reasons. One night, Dad and he were in their hotel bar with others, relaxing in the way you do. Hurt was going on about the difference between American actors and British ones: he was being particularly dismissive about Dad and his fellow-countrymen. As spectators recalled, it all happened so quickly. Dad was out of his chair and knocked Hurt clean out, and then left the bar. Hurt was brought round and helped up to his room. There was no mention by either thereafter, but Lee Marvin, who was the real 'money man' of the film, arrived on the set for the first time the next day and said to Dad:

'Are you the guy who hit William Hurt?' Dad nodded.

'Congratulations!' said Marvin. 'You saved me doing the job!'

Naturally, the two bonded immediately. Marvin was hugely jet-lagged and later was freaking out that the restaurant couldn't provide him with eggs Benedict for breakfast. Dad calmed him down by telling him that it was actually 6 o'clock in the evening. Though nominated for a BAFTA, Dad wasn't to win, but like most actors, he didn't really relish awards ceremonies. He was awarded a special gift, however, by a jeweller whom he got to know in Helsinki: a watch that ran backwards. It used to delight him, that without drawing attention to it, people would gradually notice that something was wrong with it.

You'll sometimes find the 'back' story of a film, how it was conceived, financed, delayed, or indeed, never appeared, almost as fascinating as the storyline of the film itself. *Memed My Hawk* was a case in point. An international best-selling novel written by the Turkish author, Yasar Kemal, in the 1950s, the film rights were quickly gobbled up by Daryl Zannuck and Twentieth Century Fox in the early 1960s. Terence Stamp and Peter Ustinov were to star. However, the right-wing government of Turkey, at the time, asked the US State Department to intervene and have the film idea scrapped, as they saw the story as being part of a communist conspiracy. This duly happened. Later, a Turkish opera stage director, Fuad Kavur, who had been working as an assistant to Ustinov, gained the rights from Fox, and persuaded his boss to get it refinanced, to play his old role and get a new cast. A left-wing government was now in power in Turkey in 1982, so filming was also possible in the country, with a state subsidy.

The project continued apace: Dad and old acquaintance Denis Quilley were among the actors recruited. As a simple matter of procedure, the script was submitted to the Turkish Film Censorship Committee. Sadly, this organisation was still under the control of the military and they rejected the script. The Prime Minister sacked the Committee. The Opposition insisted on a vote of no confidence and won. The right-wing was back in harness again, and no filming could take place in Turkey. For the producers, this was a disaster: contracts had to be honoured but costs had risen dramatically, as all filming had to take place in nearby Yugoslavia. *Memed My Hawk* was eventually completed and had its Royal Gala Premiere in London in May 1984, in aid of UNICEF. The event was attended by HRH Prince and Princess Michael of Kent, and about thirty foreign ambassadors in London, except the Turkish ambassador. Dad went with Mum to the post-premiere party. He was an excellent dancer and danced a lot with Princess Michael that night with whom he was photographed. He told the story that he was sitting at the same table as the Prince and Princess. He looked about him at what appeared to be a preponderance of single men, sitting in their vicinity, and asked of the Princess, 'Are there any Royal Protection Officers here?'

'Ask me to dance, and you'll find out,' she said. He did and immediately half-a-dozen be-suited carers also got to their feet, but gradually sat down and relaxed as the dance progressed.In the long-term, sadly, there were going to be quite a few rumblings among the cast about the inadequate settlement of fees for the film.

In more ways than one, it was time for a change from the international filming schedules. Dad kept a sort of rough diary on the back of the loo door with dates and places chalked up: Israel, Spain, France, Finland, Germany, Yugoslavia ... Sheffield. For the next port of call was Yorkshire for the BBC film *Bird Fancier*.

I find the obsession with which the pigeon-racers pursue their sport absolutely incredible. Their whole lives revolve round it. If they're not at work, they're in the pigeon coops up on the Dales. They're rarely at home, and therefore their wives are very bored, and this is an essential comment in the play. The character I play, Joe Desmond, is a bird fancier in the classic double sense of the words. I first came across what the women have to put up with some years ago. I was playing in *The Winter's Tale* in Ludlow Castle and was staying in a local pub. There, one evening, I fell in with some pigeon-fanciers and their wives, one of whom complained how, when one of the birds was ill, her husband had kept it company all night. I'd never come across pigeon-fanciers before, never given them a moment's thought, but this picture of a man hunched up in a coop, sleeping with his ailing bird, always stayed in my mind.

The author of the play, Mal Middleton, was a former long-distance lorry driver, who at the age of 50 found himself redundant.

I realised that if I was to have a job again, I'd have to create one for myself, so I decided to, as a writer. It wasn't a decision taken completely out of the blue. I had been writing as a hobby for years, and even completed a novel. I'd never dreamed of doing it professionally, however, until I was unemployed.

Mal had kept pigeons, until the long-distance driving prevented it happening, so he had that in common with the hero of his play, but he protested his innocence as to the womanising proclivities of his creation. Dad became a real convert to his author's hobby:

> Do you realise pigeon racing is one of the nation's most popular sports, yet many people know nothing about it? When we were filming, I hardly saw anything of Sheffield. I spent most of the time up on the Dales with the guys who fly ... just talking to them about their sport gave me immense satisfaction. They keep their birds – one man can have as many as thirty – in coops on their allotments, so when they're not flying them they're digging the potato crop or exchanging tips on the ins and outs of leek-growing.
>
> Handling the birds is not too difficult. I mean they don't have talons piercing you or anything! It's amazing how light they are – like a ping-pong ball. To think of them flying those incredibly long distances – 400 miles, or as far as from Nantes – is incredible. The main drawback was that they kept shitting all over me. I think it was out of fear. They're used to just being picked up, put in a basket and sent off, but I was having to hold the birds all day long, and it terrified them. I've never heard and felt such a loud, thumping heartbeat coming from something so small.

According to Dad, the blue pied hen, Joe's champion flyer in the play, in reality belonged to a young lad, Dennis. As usual, before too long, Dad had developed a real affinity with Dennis, and noticed that he was constantly having the mickey taken out of him because his bird never won any races, 'On the day of the race we were filming, he said to me "I had a dream last night that my bird will win today."' Dad said that the two of them stood together, scanning the skyline to spot the blue pied hen ... 'There was something almost primeval about it – deeply emotional.' Dennis's bird came second – 'not quite as good as Kes,' said Dad, 'but almost.'

The next project was a return to Shakespeare. Stuart Burge, who had directed Dad at The Royal Court had been asked by the BBC to direct *Much Ado About Nothing*. Dad had been offered the lovely cameo role of 'Dogberry' and Clive Dunn, of *Dad's Army* fame, was to be 'Verges'. Dad said that he felt 'very relaxed' with Stuart directing: perhaps, some would say, too relaxed. This was not to be Dad's finest hour in keeping off 'the sauce'. Inevitably, the scenes involving Dogberry and Verges were filmed later in the day, resulting in more 'takes' than most of the rest of the play's scenes put together. Stuart would take one look at Dad and say: 'You've done it to me again, haven't you?' However, the viewer would never know ... For Clive Dunn, it was to be his last acting role, before retiring to the Algarve to paint, quite understandable in the circumstances. However, he thought that Dad, too, needed a break and invited him out there to stay at his villa, and a new chapter opened in all our lives.

11

Portugal

It was 1984 when Dad first came to Portugal. He stayed with his friend Clive Dunn of *Dad's Army* fame, who had a house in the central Algarve. Whether it was the memory of the boatyard in Itchenor, where he had worked as a boy, or the more recent disaster of *Quaker Girl* (that you might have thought he would want to forget) that drew him to *Rosaminha*, we shall never know. But when he saw that battered motor-cruiser, tied up alongside the fishing boats in Faro harbour, she had to be his. He said at the time that, if he couldn't join the circus, he had always thought of running away to sea as a boy and that many of his classmates had joined the Navy. Down at Itchenor he had once helped rescue a couple who had capsized in a storm: 'They were trapped under their boat; it was pretty hairy, standing on the hull of an overturned boat, trying to pull it upright in a stormy sea!' But not 'hairy' enough to put him off boats forever.

Dad as a boy.

Dad in *Murder in the Cathedral*.
Chichester Remembered

Dad sweeping snow outside Chichester Theatre.

Dad in *St Joan* at Chichester Theatre. *Plays and Players*

A young Mum and Ros on their travels.

Dad and Domini Blythe.

A poster advertising Mum and Sylvia dancing in Israel.

Far East tour: Zoe Wannamaker, Dad and Tony May on the beach.

My parents, looking very young and smart for a night out.

With Mia Farrow, Dad as 'gipsy lad' in
See No Evil, 1971.

Dad on *Quaker Girl*, his first boat.

Dad, Donald Sutherland and Mum.

The 'girls' on one of our holidays in France. Charmian sits at the front, with me and Juliet behind, Pat sitting on the right and Mum standing. Nigel must have taken this photograph. Happy days!

Dad and a little me reading a script.

Dad in Faro harbour, Portugal, on the *Rosamina*.

Angela Thorne and Dad, *Three Up, Two Down*.

The *Boon* gang, early years.

Dad doing 'the shortest sponsored walk in history'.

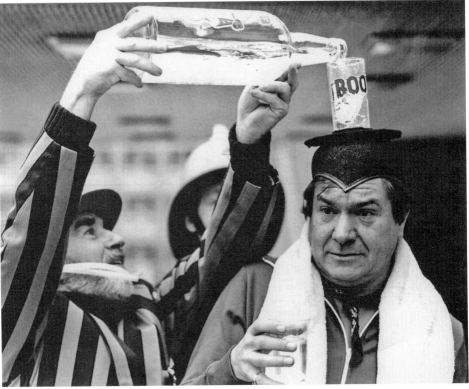

Dad at the White Swan, Henley-in-Arden.

Dad and 'Rocky' Neil Morrissey. For a laugh, Dad had written under this photograph 'Give us a kiss!'

Dad and Clive Dunn in Portugal.
Photograph from Cilla Dunn

Dad making prawn finger
puppets at the beach restaurant,
Olhos d'Agua.

'Cheers!' Clive Dunn and Joan, Christmas 1990.

'Poppy', as she called him, Jasmine and Liz.

Dad and me before the British Soap Awards ceremony.

Dad in the 'Cabin', *Coronation Street*.

Dad and his bike, 'White Lightning', *Boon* days.

Dad outside the White Swan.

Visitors who had read reports of Dad's 'yacht', anchored in a 'marina', would be taken completely by surprise. The harbour then was a quiet, unprepossessing sort of place that suited his needs exactly. *Rosaminha*, who had apparently been built for a Portuguese count some thirty years before, had been impounded (the story goes) four times for smuggling dubious substances. She was about 10 metres long with a cabin at the back the size of a double mattress, and an open middle section with benches and a small fridge. On the other side, down three little steps were a table and two benches, which when pushed together made another small double bed. In here there was also a tiny kitchen with a cooker, sink and a shower/toilet, which my dad must have struggled to fit in! At the very front of the boat was my 'room' – an arrowhead-shaped cabin with two child-sized beds that came together to a point with drawers underneath for the clothes. I loved the way we were rocked gently to sleep when we stayed there.

The occasional journalist who made it out to Faro, when Dad first took up residence there, would be courteously received; he was almost at the height of his fame at the time. One pronounced that the boat resembled a gypsy caravan with its 'plastic flowers and cheap gew-gaws'. He appears lucky to have survived 'the precarious gangplank'! Dad, on the other hand, regularly missed his footing and fell in. Whether the waiter from the Hotel Eva felt it his responsibility to maintain round-the-clock watch, we don't know, but inevitably he'd be the one to drag him out.

It is interesting, though, how that Romany-theme seems to be taken up. Julian Slugget remembered them both being called 'brown boys' and indeed, Joan told me that somewhere in her past was a Spanish gypsy. I can't help thinking that it explains Dad's colouring and need to roam – and my own? There was a large gang of gypsy children who inhabited the dockside area, 'I made friends with one of them,' he said at the time:

He was only about ten. I gave him money and food, and asked him to keep an eye on my boat when I was away. A friend said: 'You're not going to trust that kid, are you?' I said, 'Yes, I am and we'll see what happens.' Nothing happened. There was money on board, a camera, food. He didn't nick anything; he even cleaned the boat up while I was away! My friends had been doubtful because a few weeks before I'd let two educated 'beach bums' stay on the boat for a week or two. They ripped off all my clothes, my radio, everything. But it didn't put me off. It's better to be the sort of person that gets ripped off than the sort of person that rips off, and that gypsy boy was one of the bonuses of life.

In those early days there was nothing Dad liked better than spending a morning in Ollie's bar with its dartboard, television and stacked up beer crates, chatting to the locals, smoking Portuguese cigarettes and supping the odd pint; then, back to the boat. As he said at the time,

> My idea of real enjoyment is to lie in a little boat in the sunshine with nobody around. No telephone. Absolutely nothing to disturb me. I can fish and I can swim. If I've got a few days off from filming, which could be every three months, I'd come out and do just that.

For the most part, Mum teaching and me still at school in term time didn't coincide with these breaks, and Dad wasn't always by himself in Portugal. There was certainly one occasion where his mood of tranquillity was broken, when he admitted to being a bit high and thereby courageous beyond his natural expectation. He somehow foiled a carjacking, by grabbing the rifle from one of his would-be assailants and firing it wildly in the air. They all ran off!

Dad was an habitué of The Coach and Horses in Soho, known as The French because of the nationality of its landlord. Another habitué, or perhaps more aptly called, 'fixture', was the writer Jeffrey Bernard. He was known for his weekly pieces in *The Spectator*, under the heading 'Low Life'. His friend, the writer Keith Waterhouse, wrote a play about him, entitled *Jeffrey Bernard is Unwell*, the entry that the editor was bound to put in every so often when Jeffrey failed to come up with his script for obvious reasons. Peter O'Toole took the award-laden role of Jeffrey in the play, which mirrors what would have occurred if Jeffrey had found himself locked in The French overnight. Anyway, somehow or other, Dad persuaded Jeffrey to join him out in Portugal for a few days! There are quite a few locals who remember this happening. They also remember what happened to Jeffrey. Dad, at least, managed to get onto the boat after a protracted stay in the bar. Jeffrey was not so lucky: falling asleep in the midday sun in his swimming costume on the beach was not the best idea, as probably 'sun' and 'swimming costume' were novel concepts to him. He had lain on his side, so one half of him was white, and the other deep scarlet!

So I had had the occasional holiday on the boat with my parents, but never together. When Dad was really drinking, Mum didn't want to go. In fact, she suggested that he went there by himself rather than come home. So you can imagine I was quite taken aback when, in Easter 1988, she asked me if I'd like to go out to Portugal with Dad on holiday. He'd seemed to be off the booze for a while and the fact that he'd always spent a lot of time working away had meant that I'd never really spent any time with him by myself. So slightly apprehensive, I asked if I could take my best friend, Cathy, with me to Portugal. She came. We were just thirteen, and we had a really wonderful holiday.

Dad amazed me. He would get up each morning, before we woke up and would have the table in the cabin set, and covered in goodies for breakfast. It brings a tear to my eye just thinking about it ... there would be yoghurts, juices, prosciutto and breads. Dad would then spend the morning looking like a local, in his black hat, at the café at the other end of the harbour. He would relax in the sunshine, quietly enjoying a bit of anonymity, sometimes 'people-watching', sometimes reading the paper or a script, and drinking strong, Portuguese coffee and water. Cathy and I would sunbathe on the top of our little pointed cabin at the front of the boat, watching the jumping fish, looking out for boys and generally laughing and chatting, as you do at that age. I remember listening to Terence Trent Darby or the Beach Boys, and covering our faces with towels when the water levels got really low and the harbour began to stink!

One day we were at our usual place at the front of the boat when we could see Dad walking back to us, earlier than usual. When he got back, I could see that something was wrong. He was not his usual smiley self; he looked upset. I finally got him to tell me what had happened. First of all, he swore to me that he hadn't had a drink and I had come to know when he had and he hadn't ... I could see that he had not. It helps to bear in mind that at this time, although Dad was *on* television a lot, he very rarely had any time to watch any.

He had never heard of the 1980s American show *Knight Rider*, in which David Hasselhoff played Michael Knight, the hero fighting crime in his artificially intelligent car KITT. Outside the café, where Dad was sitting, there was a kiddie ride, one of those that are coin-slot operated; the child sits inside and is rocked backwards and forwards. This particular one was the KITT car, shiny and black, with the flashing red light moving across the front. It was quiet at the café and Dad was sitting outside alone, enjoying the peace and the morning sunshine. Suddenly his calm was shattered by a voice saying 'Hey Michael!' He looked around for the source, but couldn't see anyone. 'Hey Michael!' the voice said again. He studiously avoided it this time but, as you will guess, he was being 'addressed' by the kiddie ride or rather 'Michael Knight' was! As the disembodied voice continued to call out to him, Dad beat a hasty retreat; he quite literally thought he was losing his mind, and headed for the boat to lie down. Cathy and I still laugh about it now.

We stopped our sunbathing on the roof of our cabin about halfway into the holiday. We had gone inside after being up on deck all morning as usual, to shower and dress before going to lunch. The tide was low and the gangplank, which we used to get on and off the boat, was almost vertical against the wall. We came out of the cabin, to climb up it, when we saw the man, standing at the top at the other end. Not being used to seeing naked men, it took us a little while to understand what was going on. Our flasher was fat and his body flab was jiggling up and down. Shrieking, we turned and ran back inside. Thinking about it now, it makes me feel ill, especially when I think how young we were. However, at the time, I remember being shocked at first and then finding the whole episode hilariously funny – a natural response I suppose. So, when Dad returned, we had stayed inside and not moved. We tried to be quite casual when we told him what had happened. He listened very calmly, asking us quietly what the man looked like and a few other questions. It was while we were talking that Cathy and I both noticed that, while he was sitting listening, he was slowly and coolly unscrewing the handle off a large broom. He left the boat carrying it and saying: 'I'm just going for a little walk ...' Luckily for that pervert, and ultimately, probably for Dad, he didn't find him.

During that magical week, Dad took us to the beach, to watch traditional dancing, and out to eat every night. We would love to ask him philosophical questions about life and the universe. He would amaze us with his answers and theories. He definitely inspired me from that time forward to be more questioning and self-reflective. He was a natural psychologist who seemed to have an understanding of people and the world around us that was deeper and totally different than any other that I had come across. Those conversations on that holiday made it easier for me to talk to him in the years ahead and shaped the way I think and see the world today. Perhaps they also influenced my view of the country I now call home.

I said that Dad's first trip to Portugal was to visit his friend and fellow actor Clive Dunn. Clive suggested a holiday to Dad, and that is how it all began. Whenever Dad went out to Portugal, he'd make a point of seeing Clive and his wife Cilla and their daughters. During one such visit, Clive told Dad about a little ruin for sale, with a beautiful view, which was just along the hillside from his own place. It was in a fantastic location in a quiet, traditional village, with panoramic views of the sea. Cilla told me, when I was grown-up, that there was little discussion about it. Dad was taken over to it, loved it and bought it outright. There was another reason. From being left alone by the press originally, he was now being stalked at the boat. His friend Liz remembers him telling of there being only three trees on the dockside near the boat, at one point each bearing a portly photographer in its lower branches. What is so remarkable is that the house next to the Dunns' is now *my* family home, where I live with my partner and two children. Obviously the 'ruin' had to have a fair bit of attention to make it habitable, and Dad wanted this to be achieved as soon as possible. For once the clout and growing income could be used to our advantage, and within weeks it was ready.

In 1990 it was decided we would all spend a family Christmas in Portugal: me, Mum, Dad and Granny Joan. I was fifteen and bored; my friends were all in London and I was stuck in a little village on a hill, where there seemed to be no one my age. I was smoking sporadically at this time with my mates in London, so, being bored one day, I nicked one of my dad's cigarettes and crawled down the hill to smoke it. My legs were scratched to bits, as I tried to find a nice, flat rock to sit on, one that was suitably hidden by a low hanging *alfarrober* tree, from the house. I lit up. These particular cigarettes were Portuguese and called SGs. They came in different coloured packets, depending on their strength. The one I had stolen came from a dark-blue packet; they were very strong, containing black tobacco, I think. As soon as I'd smoked it, I felt incredibly ill. Faint and sick, and looking, I'm sure, a brilliant shade of green, I sat up there, on that hillside, for most of the rest of that day. It's funny how we remember our Christmases!

We had no Christmas tree, so Dad cut down a sort of twiggy, dried branch, which we stood up and decorated. Dad had been off the drink for a time, and had started to buy 'Aqua Libra', described as 'the adult soft drink of the Eighties'. It came in a sophisticated, tall glass bottle, like wine, and was the sort of thing you could take to a dinner party. Anyway, as we poked round the little local shop, in our picturesque, remote Portuguese village, looking for Christmas goodies, Dad was delighted to find that they sold bottles of his new favourite, non-alcoholic tipple. We carried our bags up the narrow cobbled streets alight with Christmas decorations, back to the house. However, that evening, as Dad took the bottle from the fridge and poured us both a glass, we realised that we had, in fact, bought something quite different ... I watched as Dad spat his first mouthful all over the walls of the kitchen. He had bought a bottle of *Aguardente*, meaning literally 'Fiery' or 'Burning' water, a drink of distilled spirits, made from up to 60 per cent alcohol by volume. I think Dad suggested that we use it to light the fire.

We joined the Dunn family for a lovely Christmas meal that year. They had a restaurant that they had leased for their daughter,

Polly, who was a chef, and where their other daughter, Jessica, and her partner helped out running and managing it. Polly described how my Dad, a regular customer there, would sit on the sofa, just outside the kitchen and talk to her while she worked. Her younger sister, Jess, now a successful artist, had decorated the place with a Parisian cabaret theme, like the Follies Bergère. It was a fantastic fun place to be and we had a lovely night, made more delightful when Granny Joan found out that she was born in the same year as Clive.

As I got older, my parents would allow me to stay at 'The Ponderosa', as our house was now called, through the summer holidays without them. Mum would usually come out for a week or two, but my Nan was needing more and more care, so Mum would spend every other weekend in New Milton with her, while my Aunty Sue was working. I loved it. Friends would fly out to see me, sometimes overlapping their stays – I counted seventeen bodies on one hung-over morning, of whom only half I actually recognised – and sometimes there would be a few days when I would be staying alone, without any guests.

It was during one such period when, one evening, while I was watching TV in the living room, a sudden storm arose outside. One moment I was curled up, barefoot, comfortably on the sofa; then suddenly it was dark, pitch dark, so that, with the shutters closed as well as the electricity off, I actually couldn't see my hand in front of my face. I didn't know what to do. After waiting a few minutes to see if the power returned, I decided to try and make my way across the hillside to Clive and Cilla's to see if I could borrow a torch. I crawled on my hands and knees to the front door, trying to avoid the furniture and stepped out, still barefoot into the torrential rain. Once outside the visibility was better but the wind was wild and the rain really lashing down. Dramatic booms of thunder accompanied my progress, as I ran on tiptoe down the pathway to my neighbours, horribly, but guiltily, crushing snails between my toes as I went.

I arrived looking like the proverbial drowned rat. I entered to see a candle-lit table crowded with people. The power surge from the storm had taken out the electricity for the whole area, but the Dunns with their customary style had gone ahead with their planned entertaining; there were a lot of jolly faces round the table whom Cilla later dubbed her 'lovely old queens'. Being the wonderful person that she is, she insisted that I stay and eat with them. She dried me off and lent me some clothes, before she sat me down. So I enjoyed a wonderfully impromptu dinner, with lots of laughs, great food – and no electricity. Sadly, during the writing of this book, Clive died, and with his passing went a lovely man and a great friend. I will so miss him.

I spent time at The Ponderosa at least once a year and it really became my home from home. Dad started to spend his time more equally between England and Portugal after my mum died in 1996. Although I worried terribly about his drinking while he was away from our London home, I also knew that the sun, the countryside tranquillity and particularly the walk up the hill from the bar to our house would do him good. He also had lots of friends among the locals of Boliqueime, who would look after him, often driving him home or chasing off reporters. Unfortunately, there were always a few hangers-on eager to spend Dad's money and take advantage of his generous nature, but that would happen anywhere.

I now live in Portugal, still at The Ponderosa. When I moved here in 2006, my first job was in one of the local bars where both Dad and I had spent so much time over the years. It was weird to pass, on my way to work, the spot where Dad would always sit, choosing to be facing the street, where he could watch the world go by. It felt lovely to have the locals treat me like they'd known me for years after hearing that I was 'Mike's daughter', even if they hadn't met me before. It made me feel as if I had a history there and so integration was instant. What better way to hear about your father's exploits than by standing at a bar, serving bottles of Cristal beer, or Sagres, while the locals expanded on the subject.

One friend told how Dad had decided to hold a big barbecue party at the house. It had all gone well and continued until the early hours of the morning when the final stragglers had either left or crashed out somewhere. This friend had woken up and seeing the state of the place, decided to help Dad by attempting to start clearing up. He felt sorry in a way for Dad, who had forked out a lot for the party and now had to get up to deal with such an appalling mess. He started trekking round what is quite an extensive garden, collecting up plates, rubbish and empty bottles. After a while my dad surfaced and, probably still the worse for wear, suggested that it might be easier to wash up the plates if they put them all in the Jacuzzi. They did and it never worked the same again. It would spout out a piece of chicken bone or old coleslaw for months afterwards ...

I also heard one afternoon, while working at the bar, that Dad had at one time bought a donkey. I'd seen the traditional leather head-collar that had hung by the door for years, but had always assumed it was merely decorative, there to create a rural look to our Portuguese 'Casita'. The donkey didn't appear to have the same staying-power as its tackle. As there was no perimeter fencing for the property, just a low dry-stone wall, it had either simply wandered off across the hillside one day or been stolen. These days, because of my equine enthusiasm, the four-legged members of our family are treated differently. The Ponderosa has a beautiful post and rail fenced paddock, built by my partner Luke, and a lovely big stable. Our rescue ponies, Rango (a palomino falabella) and Rupee (a 4-year old chestnut gelding) are very happy.

Dad was always an animal lover. He abhorred any animal cruelty and I remember him telling me that when he was taken to a bull-fight in Portugal, he would cheer every time a bull laid into a bull-fighter. Usually in his cups he would talk about building a huge aviary on our land to house all the birds kept in little cages in Portuguese houses, very popular pets in Portugal. Or buying up caged iguanas and lizards and letting them free on our land. Bless him! The garden here has always had wildlife of its own proliferating: bugs, butterflies and huge wolf spiders; many types of birds, including noisy tawny owls, and toads the size of saucers, who would entertain Dad, when they would come bravely up into the house, when the door was left open and hide behind the floor-length curtains in the hallway. Walk round the garden and you can see geckos, camilions, lizards and hedgehogs. The pond is home to coloured frogs, carp and even a snake.

However, after the donkey it seemed Dad needed another personal pet. Could he be searching for a replacement for his childhood guinea pig? Anyway, his next unusual choice was to be a duck – Daphne. At the local market, where it seems you can buy anything under the sun, from rosemary-flavoured honey to sparkly stillettos, you can also find for sale kittens, puppies, chicks and, on the day Dad happened by, ducklings. So on a whim Dad bought Daphne and brought her home. I'm told that Dad and Daphne were great companions. He would get up in the morning and sit outside the front of the house, where the sun first hit, with his breakfast and then give her a call. She would waddle up from the pond, climb the steps onto the terrace, and greet him, hoping no doubt for a share of his cornflakes or toast!

After a while, Dad received news of a job and so had to make plans to return to London. But what to do with Daphne? Friends convinced Dad that the best place to take her would be Alte, a picturesque typical Algarvian village high up in the hills, with stunning views. Famous for its springs or 'fontes', this village was decided to be the perfect new home for Dad's beloved Daphne, because the area around 'Fonte Pequena' was a well-known picnic area, where people would go to feed the numerous ducks. About six months after her move, Dad returned to Portugal and decided to go to Alte to see if he could see Daphne. Well, so the story goes, when Dad got to the water at 'Fonte Pequena' and called out her name, his little feathered friend came waddling up the grassy bank to meet him. I'm not sure whether the locals were to be believed, but whenever I take my children there now, we always call out her name – just in case.

In the years before Dad died he spent much more time back in England. Back home in London, one of his favourite ways to spend an afternoon, after returning from the bar, would be to watch the birds on the bird-table in the garden, often with my little daughter Jasmine. She would join him to feed the squirrels as well. Liz and I drew the line and teased him when he insisted on leaving out fish-

and-chips on the lawn for the foxes. It was with all these thoughts in mind that, when Dad died, I had the idea to engrave a stone bird-bath, instead of a gravestone. It's at the beautiful garden of remembrance at Chichester Crematorium, with a bench nearby under a willow, where one can sit and watch the birds as Dad used to do.

12

Three Up, Two Down

Back in 1985 Fortune had a mixed bag of assignments for Dad: a film he starred in was nominated for the prestigious Palme d'Or at the Cannes Film Festival and he had a guest appearance as Roly Roofless in *Super Gran* on children's television. The film, the first feature by the now celebrated Lars von Trier, took Dad, once again, way out of his comfort zone. Sometimes it was as if he were deliberately challenging himself. *The Element of Crime* was filmed in the director's home country of Denmark (he has a well-documented fear of flying), but the film is set in Cairo. Dad plays a detective pursuing a serial killer. The film is really strange on a number of levels: the dialogue is stilted and full of contradictory statements; it is lit almost entirely with sodium lights and takes on a sepia look; there is a general mêlée of everyday objects lying around to create a surrealistic impression; and it never stops raining. At the time, it was the sort of film that, when you left the cinema, you'd be saying, 'What was going on there, then?' Certainly that must have been what Dirk Bogarde felt because he was President of the International Jurors of the Festival, and insisted that von Trier's contribution should receive no honours at all. Dad went to Cannes and was pleased not to have been nominated for an acting award in the circumstances. Anyway, some of the jurors were evidently impressed by the new *auteur* and a compromise was reached and von Trier was awarded Technical Grand Prize. Wim Wender's *Paris, Texas* won the Palme d'Or, and Helen Mirren won Best Actress for *Cal.*

A more traditional detective's role was waiting for Dad back in England, and you can't get more traditional than Agatha Christie. The film was of the book *Ordeal by Innocence* and Dad played Inspector Huish. He was once again acting with an old friend, Donald Sutherland, who was joined by Faye Dunaway and Christopher Plummer. This is an unusual story by the doyenne of detective fiction, as there is no Miss Marple or Hercule Poirot. The mystery is explored instead by a visiting palaeontologist, Dr Arthur Calgary (Sutherland) assisted by Dad's Inspector. Future film versions of the story were to interpose a Miss Marple but sadly these were not being true to Agatha.

There's a picture of Mum at the premiere of this film, smiling convincingly, with Dad and Donald Sutherland. It does remind me of what Mum used to say about these events. They weren't exactly her cup of tea, but to see Dad enjoying himself so much really did please her; however, there was a drawback. Inevitably, when it was time to go, no amount of cajoling would move Dad from the social scene. And Mum was not a cajoler. She simply went home by herself. This was typical, now, of the pattern of any social occasion involving the two of them outside the house. Dad was always in his element – ready to party. My mum, a teacher, needed a clear head in the morning and was ready for her bed. It was nobody's fault, but the two differing lifestyles were having an effect. Tony May, who was with them on one occasion, says that he, personally, never had the stamina to match Dad, anyway. Driving Mum home, she poured her heart out: 'Should she have stayed?', 'Should she not have gone in the first place?' Tony says that she reminded him of a beautiful rabbit caught in the headlights. 'There were a lot of us half in love with Julia in those days.'

Dad's final piece of film-making this year couldn't be more parochial, and it had a very interesting pedigree. It was called *Arthur's Hallowed Ground* and was directed by Freddie Young. Young was an Oscar-winning photographer, who had made his name particularly working with David Lean on films such as *Lawrence of Arabia, Dr Zhivago* and *Ryan's Daughter.* He had finally decided that he would like to direct too, and chose to do it with this film at the ripe old age of 82. The film was produced by David Puttnam. It was a sweet story about the love of Arthur, an old groundsman (Jimmy Jewel) for his cricket pitch, and how the revolutionary forces of the board of directors of the cricket club, led by their chairman, Len Draycock (Dad), wanted him to change or retire. For a man who had featured in the credits of classics, as Freddie Young had done, this was a slight film that did not make distribution and went to television, and he never directed again. The one line that sticks out, that Dad always recalled with some relish, was when Arthur, who is always refusing to pick up a ringing phone, says: 'It'll only be somebody wantin' me to do something.'

It was mostly television work now that was keeping Dad's nose to the grindstone. I think that he would have really liked a sustained series, but that was not to be at the time. The jobbing actor, in Dad's case particularly, would not turn down any substantial role, but a long run was the ideal, and at this time none seemed forthcoming. Little did he know what the future held for him. So he alternately played a Bad German in *Hitler's SS: Portrait of Evil* and a Good German in *Jenny's War* – two mini-series. He joined others who were enjoying extended runs in *Auf Wiedersehen Pet* as Magowan, the Irishman whom nobody liked so they conspired to get rid of him; thus Dad only made three appearances. However, he did have the opportunity of getting to meet a man who in the future would become his near-neighbour and metaphorical sparring partner, Jimmy Nail. There swiftly followed two pilot projects for sitcoms: *Pull the Other One* and *Late Starter*. The first ran for six episodes with Dad playing against type as Sidney, a henpecked husband; the whole thing was really a very long 'mother-in-law' joke. Lila Kaye played the lady in question, the character described by the publicity as 'very devious indeed – hardly your mouth almighty Peggy Mount type, much more subtle about getting her own way.' Dad chimed in with 'I reckon I've robbed about fifteen banks in my acting career, but they were a pushover compared to Sidney's mother-in-law.' The series was not re-commissioned. *Late Starter*, starring Peter Barkworth as a homeless academic, with Dad as his friend, proved a quick finisher after two episodes.

This was the time of the Citizen Band radio craze and Paula Milne, described by the BFI as Britain's leading female scriptwriter, wrote a one-off playlet for Channel Four called *CQ*. As the *Sunday Times* said:

> Norman is in his radio shack under the staircase of his little home 'waiting for an important TX from a maritime mobile'. The man next door works for the council and Norman's signals are interfering with his television. Nasty questions are being floated about 'planning permission'. Norman's unemployed son, Terry, is a cynical punk. In bleak, unsympathetic suburbia, Norman's search for his maritime mobile, a redundant polytechnic lecturer, circumnavigating the world to draw attention to the dole queues, takes on a desperate urgency. *CQ* tells what happens when he locates, loses his job because he won't abandon his shack and becomes famous on television as the man who keeps in touch with the drifting mariner. Like its title (it means a general call to 'Seek you') *CQ* is a gentle play about urban loneliness played to perfection by Michael Elphick as Norman.

Frederick Raphael, the celebrated novelist and screenwriter was commissioned to write a mini-series for the BBC called *Oxbridge Blues*. This would be familiar varsity territory for him. Of the seven 75-minute teleplays, Dad would be in the first, which gave its name to the series. It was about two competitive academics, one whose life was transformed by writing an erotic novel. Dad played the

American 'money man' who bought the title for 'big bucks'. The play was nominated for a BAFTA television award for the Best Single Drama. Of course, what is amazing about Dad's acting roles at this time is the huge range of accents, attitudes, ages and sometimes physical shapes that he was having to encompass to fulfil them. Soon, though, he would find out that writers were beginning to write with him in mind, or at least, with roles that he had shone in, in mind.

There was one show that he was in at this time that had a really fascinating back-story. It was called *Walking the Plank*. If anyone was asked to list the best UK sitcoms ever, *Dad's Army* would be bound to be on the list. What wouldn't feature, though, would be its little-known sequel – a radio play called *It Sticks Out Half a Mile*. Harold Snoad and Michael Knowles were responsible for the original radio adaptations of *Dad's Army* and, when it finished in 1977, with the agreement of its originators, Jimmy Perry and David Croft, they started on *ISOHM*. In it, Captain Mainwaring has returned home after an unsuccessful spell as a cuckoo-clock maker in Switzerland. He finds out that Frambourne Council want to demolish the old pier, and he is determined to save it. When he applies to the bank for a loan, who should deal with his request but Wilson – now Bank Manager of Swallows Bank. A pilot was made, with Arthur Lowe and John Le Mesurier reprising their original characters. Lowe wanted the pilot to have been made for TV, but the BBC weren't interested, and it was made for radio. He was then struggling with the effects of a lifelong relationship with alcohol and can clearly be heard in the broadcast slurring his lines; he subsequently collapsed with a stroke a few months later and the series was never made. But his widow, Joan, encouraged Snoad and Knowles not to give up with the idea, and they made a second pilot, this time with Hodges and Pike, joining Wilson in the central roles. This led to a successful twelve-part radio series, but unfortunately Le Mesurier died two days after the first part was broadcast. Undaunted, the two writers persuaded the BBC to produce and run a pilot on television, with Dad playing the Hodges role (now renamed Archer). For TV the show was rechristened *Walking the Plank*. It attracted 11 million viewers. For some strange reason it was not re-commissioned. It appeared later as a series on Yorkshire television with Bernard Cribbins and Richard Wilson, this time called *High and Dry*, and that was pretty much the end of it. *Walking the Plank* became one of the many recordings that the BBC have 'lost'.

When Dad's extended series came it was a gentle comedy called *Three Up, Two Down*. There was nothing to suggest that this programme, while garnering no awards, would settle at a viewership of about 12½ million weekly, and would run for four series with a total of twenty-five episodes over five years, with an American adaptation. Perhaps writer Richard Ommanney did but Dad was very doubtful originally, considering it quite a lightweight undertaking. However, he trusted Richard, as they'd both been together at Central. The public and the press took little convincing:

There's nothing special about *Three Up, Two Down*, BBC1's new sitcom, except how it made me laugh. No, not laugh, roar. And somehow I don't think I was the only one. The 'sit' has been used a dozen times before: working-class oik marries posh girl but *her* Cheltenham mummy can't stand *his* common-as-muck dad. The 'com' is what happens when they clash, and a fat lot of good it is trying to stop them clashing. What partly makes this work is marvellous Michael Elphick as beaming out-of-work Sam 'over the bleeding moon' at becoming a granddad. And it's also Angela Thorne, formerly Penelope Keith's twittering stooge in *To the Manor Born*, now an acid-tongued supersnob in her own right as the 'terribly thrilled' new Grandma Daphne. Both are lonely and both want to move into the basement flat of their children's home to become nanny to the grandchild, so trendy mum Angie can go to work. So for the next five weeks (first series), the basement will become a battle-ground.'
(One of the excellent reviews whose authorship Granny Joan excised. Possibly from the *Daily Mail*.)

Dad loved working with the cast on this first series and they with him by all accounts. Angela Thorne said:

Michael watches people. He's a serious actor, with a great sense of comedy, too, as he showed in *Schultz*. He can play a wide range of parts instinctively. He's as warm and friendly with the camera crew as with people who come and ask for his autograph when we're filming. That's unusual. I enjoy working with him. I never know how the scene will finally turn out.

Angela is reminded of filming one particular scene for the second series; horse-riding was involved and the pair went to stay for the weekend with a wealthy pop-star with impressive stables:

> I got on the horse in full riding gear, but when Michael got on behind me in cap and mackintosh, the horse wasn't having any. It shied, throwing Michael who fell on his back. Then the horse bolted off, making for a wood, with me still on. I thought, with all this wind and all those trees, I shall be decapitated! And so I leapt off, too! Michael and I were both quite bruised. Next day, they wanted to take it all again, to get a better shot. But again the horse started to play up. It was soon obvious that there was going to be an encore, but Michael and I still needed to get back on the horse for a close-up. It was finally decided that it would be less risky to film us without the horse, from the waist up! So Michael and I stood on the ground with our legs apart and bent as if we were still on the horse. It must have looked so funny. He had his arms round my waist, murmuring sweet nothings. I was in full riding gear, and both of us were acting our socks off. The crew, filming us from the waist up, was in hysterics.

Ray Burdis, who played the part of Dad's son, remembers that most of the filming for the outdoor shots was in the Bournemouth area. Interiors were filmed in front of a BBC studio audience on Sundays and Mum and I went on quite a few occasions. As the first series came to an end, the reviews became even more ecstatic, the *Daily Mail*:

> Two up ... and going places. Battling Michael and Angela in a Class of their Own. In the too-often trite and tired world of television sit-coms, chemistry between characters is everything. So when a new blend bubbles merrily over the bunsen-burner, its success is all the more satisfying to its creators. For the twelve-and-a-half million fans

who tuned into the BBC's *Three Up, Two Down*, it was the magical double act of Michael Elphick as the downtrodden Sam and Angela Thorne as the abrasively elegant Daphne that had them coming back weekly for more. And though its final episode was shown last night, Daphne and Sam are the kind of durable duo set to return again and again. The combination worked so well because, unlike most male comedy roles on television, Sam was neither ludicrous nor a wimp. He held his corner against Daphne's waspish wit.

Both leading players are surprised by the series' success. Elphick, big, burly and with the sort of crumpled, lived-in features that look in need of ironing, believes it worked so well because the ingredients of romance and human tragedy are traditionally successful. But the best humour has a trace of sadness in it. One thing is glaringly obvious. Michael and Angela look set to become a comedy couple sharing a rapport which produces the sort of marvellous entertaining television that many feel has been absent from our screens too long.

This was a time when any show at all successful in the UK was immediately seized upon so that it could be parlayed up into a significantly higher-earning bracket US version. As Ray Burdis says, this was quite difficult, since the whole premise of the plot was based on the British class system. The American answer? Make it race not class. So you have the black male protagonist saying to the white mother-in-law, something of the order of, 'That's some nice butt you got there lady!' The pilot, called *5 Up, 2 Down* (the younger couple having given birth to triplets) aired in 1991, but didn't develop to a full series.

The British episodes were shot in front of a live studio audience on Sunday evenings at the 'beeb' and Mum would take me (aged 10) each week to watch. Sometimes Joan would travel up to London by train and join us, or I was allowed to bring a friend. It felt amazing driving past the queues of people outside waiting to go in, and being waved through the gates like real VIPs. This was all before *Boon* took Dad really into the limelight and was the first taste I had of feeling what it was going to be like having a successful actor for a father. Once inside, I loved to walk around exploring; nobody seemed to mind as I wandered, looking at the pictures of all the famous faces on the walls lining the corridors. Dad's dressing room felt equally exciting, and I remember Mum looking smiley and animated.

I found the whole experience extraordinary. I would gaze around at the lighting rigs, huge microphones on booms over the actors' heads and cameras swinging around them as they moved. The sets were so obviously fake here, yet so realistic on TV.

There would be a 'warm up' guy getting everybody in the mood and filling the gaps when the technicians were taking their time doing their thing. I found it amusing when they had to reshoot a funny bit and we would have to laugh at the same joke three or four times in a row. I'd always try and laugh louder each time to make up for anyone in the audience who might have got fed up by then and not bothered.

I remember one night when the very beautiful Lysette Anthony was, for whatever reason, just having a bad night and kept crying. The whole thing seemed to be taking forever and the atmosphere seemed to me to be getting dampened by the constant stopping. At one point, mid-scene, Dad had to make a reference to bin liners. It came out as 'lin biners' for some reason, and the audience found this incredibly funny – everything came to a halt, and Lysette couldn't stop laughing, which, I know, was the intention. His efforts to disrupt proceedings seemed to lift her mood, and he was evidently enjoying the interaction with the studio audience, and could 'play' and have fun with the lines.

After the show we would go outside to the BBC bar. I remember thinking that Ray Burdis was very 'cool' and his younger brother, who played Stewpot in *Grange Hill*, even more so. I loved sitting at that bar, feeling very important to be there. I'd sit watching my dad getting drinks and looking after everyone as he played host, in his element. My mum talking away, usually to Angela, relaxed, smiling and proud.

I remember coming back from one of those *Three Up, Two Down* performances to this day. We'd just got in and Mum went to answer the phone. It was 'Crouchie', Dad's agent, Peter Crouch. Dad went off to speak to him and returned, looking pretty pleased with himself. 'You know that writer, Jim Hill, who worked with me on *Pocket Full Of Dreams*. He promised me he'd write a series for me. Well, he has, and Central have bought it, with me starring. It's going to be called *Boon*.'

13

'Go Number One'

Jim Hill had been true to his word. He and *Boon* co-creator Bill Stair came up with the series, originally called *Anything Legal Considered*. It was the time, however, for single-name titles, and not wishing to be difficult, they followed suit. The story goes that both authors loved to watch the 1950s American TV series *Have Gun, Will Travel*, about a lone cowboy who rights wrongs along the trail. His name was Paladin and he was played by actor Richard Boone. By way of tribute the two scribes named their hero similarly. On the subject of tributes, the title song of *Boon*, 'Hi Ho Silver' was written by Jim Diamond, originally as a tribute to his father who had recently died and who had been a fireman, like Ken Boon and Harry Crawford. Dad named our house in Portugal after the name of his caravan 'office' on the allotment in Chaddesley Corbett – 'The Ponderosa'.

And so like the proverbial London bus, it wasn't one big series, but two that came along for Dad. He should be so grateful! Even Peter

Crouch, Dad's agent, was beginning to say 'yes' to everything. Central Television entrusted the *Boon* production to the secure hands of Kenny McBain, who was promised the chance of turning Colin Dexter's *Morse* novels into television drama, as a reward, when the task was completed successfully. Production was to be fairly straightforward. Readings, rehearsals and interior shots would be done in London, at Shepherd's Bush, and exterior filming would be up in the Midlands. This was life lived according to the Central Line for Dad: Shepherd's Bush for Ken (of *Boon*), Wild West enthusiast, and then, White City for Sam (of *Three Up, Two Down*), another Wild West enthusiast. The first *Boon* series took 9 months to produce. The very first day of the very first read-through was a strange experience for all concerned. Dad said:

> We had all our rehearsals in a community centre. I'd just stopped for
> a fag break and there was a scream of brakes downstairs in the street.
> I went down to inspect and it was a police-car that had just arrived.
> An ambulance had gone before. A 13-year-old girl had jumped from
> the seventeenth floor of a block of flats nearby in a terrible act of
> desperation. What an awful reminder of any day in your life!

It was a day that couldn't be cheered, but by coincidence another team of actors in the building were just *completing* their series on that very afternoon, with a 'wrap' party in the evening, to which the cast of the new series *Boon* were invited. What better way was there for a new cast to get together and meet each other? What Mum probably never realised was that her old acting partner from college, Roger Hume, also appeared in 'Box 13', the very first episode of *Boon*.

The first series, although eminently re-commissionable, was very pedestrian technically by the standards of the series that followed. Sets were simple and only the outdoor filmed shots had any real vibrancy. That said, the very first filmed scene could also have been the last. Like any other series, the order of filming bears little relationship to the chronology of stories within it, so it would not be unusual, say, to film Episode Three first of all. Some of those behind the cameras suggested, unkindly, that if the lead character, for whatever reason, were to be unable to continue the series after this filming, then there would not be too much of a problem replacing him: so it would be best to get the dangerous filming over with at this point. The episode called 'Answers to the Name of Watson' featured a storyline about a lion that had been released from a circus by some animal rights activists. The outcome would be that the lion was discovered in a suburban house, and it was from there, Ken Boon, our intrepid hero, would rescue it.

Liz Summer was the stage manager on *Boon*, and this was the first time she had met Dad:

> I checked with the 'lion people' in the morning as to what sort of meat we should provide for the lion, but they said that the lion was very picky, and only ate heart, and they would bring it along with them. First they came with a huge cage that completely encircled the house. When the lion, which actually *was* called 'Watson', eventually, arrived, it was a poor moth-eaten looking specimen. The trainer told us that there was no such thing as a tame lion – only a trained lion – and that Watson would only allow us three tries at a manoeuvre before becoming unpredictable, and basically unsafe to work with. So, everyone got outside the cage, apart from the trainer, who had a gun, a tranquilliser gun, and Michael. Michael had this leash with a hooped end, to put round the lion's neck. He was then supposed to lead it to the back of his van and put it in. The first time he tried, the lion gave him a huge yawn, enveloping him in a great gust of meat breath. Don't forget this was all being filmed. The second attempt he got it round the neck but it moved in totally the wrong direction. He knew that this was to be the final take. The noose was round the neck and the lion seemed to be obediently heading for the back of the van. It planted its foot on the top step, turned its head and with a look that definitely said 'Make me!' moved no further. Without further ado, Michael gave him a huge shove into the back of the van and closed the door. No one could believe it. We stood transfixed. Michael went round the back and reappeared visibly shaking. 'Can we get you a cup of tea?' someone said. It was the first time I'd ever spoken to him, 'Can I get you something a bit stronger?' I asked, 'Oh, yes, please,' he said.

Dad survived and so did the series.

Two or three years on, in the part, and he'd talk about being insured for 'a million pounds', but not when he started out. To launch Series One, the *TV Times* features a typical day's filming in 'leafy Edgbaston'. This episode, which concerns the attempt by some heavy to kidnap a child outside his school as part of a custody battle, has Dad going through his paces with a fight co-ordinator from *Minder*, Peter Brayham: 'You go in after him, try to get him on the floor and – if you want to – in with the knee.' In the next take, Brayham, who thankfully is a brilliant driver, has to race down a street, brake and skid as a removal van looms into his path, reverse round and drive at full pelt, ending up inches from Dad's knees, allowing Dad to 'feel the warmth from the radiator'. It must have occurred to him that this was a strange time, now that he was over 40, to be starting a career as an action hero. It was also ironic that his chosen form of transport was a motorbike; motorcycling, like driving, was a total anathema to him. As his future co-star, Neil Morrissey, was to say: 'He could start it, move off with it; he just couldn't stop it.' By all accounts, the atmosphere on set was joyful from the beginning. Dad loved the cast and crew and they seemed to reciprocate. Every episode they bought him a little gift to remind him of the storyline. My children still have the toy lion named 'Watson'.

The series, following the lives of two retired firemen, one a hotel/club entrepreneur (David Daker as 'Harry'), the other, a 'Have Bike Will Do Anything' character (Dad as Ken Boon) garnered a reasonable-to-good following on its first few weekly outings. Mary Kenny, in the *Daily Mail*, celebrated the end of Season One on a very promising note:

> You can always trust a man who likes the Western. For the Western is all about honour, decency and the guy in the white hat turning up trumps in the end. There is something romantic and honourable about firemen too. They are naturally heroic figures. You always picture them dashing from a flaming building, carrying a prostrate child, having put their own lives at frightful risk for the sake of others. Michael Elphick as *Boon* in the series of the same name fits perfectly into all these categories. As an actor, he radiates a vulnerable humour, a brave sense of humanity and humility. As Boon, he is the fireman who does indeed save a family from a burning building – damaging his lungs irreparably in the process.

But as a man who loves Westerns, you can tell that he considers the sacrifice worthwhile. That was what he liked about being a 'smokey', as the fire fighters call themselves. 'It was a real job. It was saving people's lives.' It was, in short, specially made for the guys who wear the white hats ... This is a lovely, lovely series – I was enraptured by it. It has such attractive characters who immediately win your interest and sympathy.'

As the series came to a close, everything was in place for a second one to follow. Kenny McBain was duly released to start work on *Morse* and Esta Charkham was brought in from being Associate Producer on *Robin of Sherwood* to take his place. She says that it was a really big promotion for her, as *Boon* was heading towards being one of ITV's most watched programmes. 'I was new to this challenge and I felt that I wanted to give chances to other new talents,' she says. 'I had a great Associate Producer in Laurie Greenwood, and a fantastic script editor who was as keen as I was to develop new writers; the number of "names" who made it first on *Boon* became legion.' Esta has always run a dual career as a successful drama teacher.

One of her drama school discoveries had been told that she couldn't find a role for him in *Robin of Sherwood*. 'She said that she had something else in mind for me,' says Neil Morrissey.

'I also managed to entice Amanda Burton over from *Brookside*,' Esta tells me. It was decided to upgrade the production values on the programme, and so all parts were due to be filmed, meaning no more rehearsals in London and Dad moving full-time into the Holiday Inn in Birmingham for the duration.

Before that happened, however, there would be another season of *Three Up, Two Down* to rehearse, perform and get in the can. Poor Dad! The downside of fronting two of the most popular shows on the two leading television channels at the same time was beginning to become apparent. It wasn't the acting that wore him down; he lapped that up; it was the interminable promotion of the programmes. He felt less than enamoured of most journalists, and yet here he was giving his precious spare time to interviews. He began to blur his professional and his social life, with his post-prandial refreshments being shared with all and sundry. Wherever he went, there seemed to be a party. Down in London, Ray Burdis remembers that as soon as rehearsals were over in White City, Dad and he would get a cab over to Soho – 'usually Gerrys Club' to meet other 'mostly resting' thespians – 'I would leave early evening, feeling a little unsteady, to go home,' he says, 'but Mike would carry on showing no obvious side effects.' The benefit of the private club, of course, was not to be underrated when it came to media intrusion. It was more difficult at the Holiday Inn in Birmingham, when *Boon* Series Two began. The hotel staff endeavoured to make 'the Central Television floor' as impregnable as possible but they would be no match for the new breed of rubber-heeled journalist.

Dad loved to hold court at the big bar on the 'Central floor' in the hotel. They were always jolly times there. Liz Summer remembers one evening there, when Dad was conducting all the McGann brothers in a pitch-perfect rendition of 'Bohemian Rhapsody'. The emphatic hand-clap that greeted the end of the performance turned out to come from Tom Jones, who emerged from the shadows; he was also a guest at the hotel whilst he was performing in a concert in the city. He was then treated to a medley of his own numbers by the choir. This was, thankfully, a press-free occasion; but Esta Charkham remembers another time, when Hywel Bennett, who had been making a guest appearance in *Boon*, met her in the hotel corridor and complained that he was suffering from insomnia, 'Has anyone got anything like Benylin?' he'd enquired. He had no sooner left for his room than a journalist materialised from the gloom, asking whether he was 'on drugs'. In the same corridor, at a later date, Liz came across a very diminutive reporter, 'little over five foot, I would guess'. He asked her if she was staying in the same room as Dad. 'Well, you're standing in front of my door,' said Liz, 'and I think you'll find, although it's absolutely nothing to do with you, that Mike's room is at the end of this corridor.'

'"Boon" has Giant Girlfriend' screamed the headline the next day. Liz says Dad was furious on so many levels, for family, friends and colleagues. What he did next hardly made it better. He found the name of the journalist and his phone number and rang every half-hour for the whole of the next day with 'further exclusives', ending up with the news that he, 'Rocky' and Ronald Reagan had been enjoying 'three in a bed sex'. He shouldn't have been surprised that 'Boon's Gay Romp' was duly reported in the paper the following day, although Ronald Reagan was not mentioned.

Esta Charkham says that Central Television used the Holiday Inn for a big launch party for Series Two. At the end, Dad took one look at all the food that was left over and insisted that he and Midge, his driver, should take it to a homeless centre in Birmingham. Esta says that this became a matter of routine, after a day's shooting, that whatever was left over in the catering wagon was delivered to the same place. This was also a significant time for Dad and charities in many other ways. Because of his national fame, he was asked daily to contribute money and time to a growing list of very deserving causes. He found it impossible to say 'No'. He was always particularly keen to help charities for fire-fighters and their families but there were many others too numerous to mention. Among the events that he attended was one described as the shortest sponsored walk in history: from Central Television headquarters to the Holiday Inn, not more than 100 yards. However, in an echo of Granddad Herb, from all those years ago, Dad completed the task, not bearing a pint of beer on his head but a bottle of vodka, carefully balanced on a mortar-board. This was all part of Central Television's Telefon that year.

If Dad sometimes felt hounded in the Holiday Inn, he felt at his most relaxed in his motor-home that doubled as transport and dressing-room. He also enjoyed the company of friends there. Neil Morrissey, who always called Dad, 'Elph', looks back on those days with great affection: 'He only ever called me "Rocky". I think he used my real name twice, and that was probably at some awards ceremony.' *Boon* had a series of guest stars, of whom quite a few were old friends from the past. If you were an old friend, according to those who were, you had a very different experience of *Boon* from those who weren't. Dad's motor-home hospitality knew no bounds. Kenneth Cranham, one of the cognoscenti, says that Dad also got a video in for them, of *Holding On*, to watch in the Holiday Inn in the evening, as a treat for his on-screen 'son'. Despite the lure of the stacks of refrigerated Stollies, which were waiting mostly for day's end refreshment in the van, Dad would inculcate in Neil the need to be ready, as soon as the call came, to appear on set. It was dad's custom to always emerge down the steps of the van like someone on a parachute jump, and to encourage anyone with him to do the same. 'Go Number One!' he'd shout, pushing the other party out first, and then 'go Number Two!' as he followed on; he literally sprang into action. The van was also used to drive Dad to different locations and back to the hotel at night. Sometimes it would take him further afield, to the pub in Henley or even back to London. However, as he explained to his protégée, 'Rocky', an actor must be punctual and always on the mark at the appointed hour.

There was, however, one time that this piece of advice failed to register with its author. Dad, inexplicably, appears to be one of the first people to have had a mobile phone in the UK, one of those large brick-like objects that were about as mobile as a wheel-clamp. He had not been seen since mid-afternoon on the previous day; it was now ten o'clock and filming was due to begin, and he was not in the hotel and his driver had no idea where he was. The number of the mobile was called and eventually Dad's voice could be heard mumbling a few profanities and seeming to become acclimatised to his surroundings. 'Hello, Mike,' said the director, 'How are things?'

'Fine,' said Dad.

'So where are you?'

'It looks like a hotel bedroom,' and he added reassuringly, 'and I'm by myself.'

The director, still trying to appear reasonable, asked, 'Have you any idea where this bedroom might be?'

'No.'

'Well, would you like to look out of the window and tell me what you see?' There was a pause and the sound of lots of shuffling. Dad returned to the phone. 'Well?' asked the director.

'The Eiffel Tower,' said Dad.

This lapse was sadly accompanied by others as Series Three got under way. It seems that the culture of easy drinking was ubiquitous – almost standard regulations. Ken Cranham points out that the big TV companies outside London, in encouraging the 'names' to leave their metropolitan lairs, became very free with their advance expenses then. Working it out on the basis of how much they would have to pay the unionised electricians and allied craftsmen to move on a per diem rate up and down the country, their calculations for the actors were more than generous: 'We got these lovely little envelopes, with windows down the side, so you could see the crisp fivers waiting to be used.' said Ken. Dad, of course, had a constant stream of well-wishers to guarantee that his glass was never empty. Neil Morrissey says that Dad remembered a tip that he had picked up from Peter O'Toole, to disguise drinking on set; for Peter, it had been a subterfuge that he had used in Arab countries. This was to inject oranges with reasonable levels of vodka beforehand, so that when squeezed, they provided a delicious refreshment. Dad's driver became a dab hand with the syringe. How Dad found time for partying is the great mystery, because, apart from the two long-running series, he also thought it might be opportune, then, for him to make a couple of films. The first was to be an American-financed, television film of *Little Dorrit* with him playing Mr Merdle and Eleanour Bron as Mrs Merdle.

He spoke of his fears to Neil in the van: 'You see, Rocky, I'm moving out of my comfort zone. I haven't done this sort of thing for years. And the worst thing is ... it's Alec Guinness. He's William Dorrit. It's him I've got the scene with. And after the last time ...' As often in these situations, our worst fears ... Dad wasn't called to perform until nearly five in the evening. By then it was far too late, and obvious to all including Sir Alec, who said: 'Well, I, for one, would prefer to start again tomorrow. I've had a very busy day and now I'd like to rest,' and turning to Dad, said, 'and I look forward to working with you, young man, tomorrow as well.' Dad was down and ready to go at nine the next day.

This was not quite the experience of those who worked with him on *Withnail and I*, in which he played the poacher. Bruce Robinson, who wrote and directed, has said that the part of the poacher is completely redundant except to rev up the paranoia a bit:

> But he was bloody good. He played the part because we were old buddies from Central. He arrived to shoot as arseholed as it gets at seven in the morning and quickly discovered where the booze was

(in the wardrobe trailer) and burgled that and got on set so ruined. I didn't call takes but let the camera run – he was busted but brilliant, annoyed with me for being annoyed with him – I can't think of Elphick (as he was known to all of us) without thinking of UTTER inebriation – Elphick was always pissed – he was a much greater actor than he allowed himself and I don't know where that continual basement of pain came from – but he was in agony about something or another, and vodka was his mate.

After the films, it was back to *Three Up, Two Down* and another series. Ray Burdis said that the changes in Dad were now ominous:

> When I first got the role, the idea of playing Mike Elphick's son was the most thrilling opportunity I could think of, but as the different series progressed, the outcome was becoming more and more depressing. His whole personality had changed. Instead of being that charming and encouraging figure who had given me so much guidance when we first met, he had become petulant and short-tempered. It was seriously as if he had exchanged one father-figure for another, a supportive friend into a critical scold. If he muffed his lines, he blamed my cues; worse, as we both disappeared off together to 'the drinking dens of Soho', I began to be blamed by the producer for leading him astray! The cause of his change of personality was fairly evident: instead of shifting one bottle of vodka at a sitting, it had now become two. And that would probably just be the start of the evening. It was becoming increasingly difficult to find a window in which to rehearse and live performances were a nightmare for the director, with endless takes and re-takes.

John B. Hobbs, the producer, was according to Ray, 'one of those old-style BBC producers, very diplomatic and gentlemanly, who had never come across the like before, and basically didn't know how to deal with it. The cast and crew were all enormously fond of Mike, and somehow we all battled through.'

Things were little better back in Birmingham. Tony May, who hadn't seen Dad from the days of the trip to the Isle of Wight, was guest-starring on *Boon*, with an episode that he'd part scripted himself about an ex-fire-fighting chum of Ken, who ends up kidnapping him.

He says that he was 'staggered' to see Dad again, 'where once he was the life and soul of the party, here he was hunched up by the bar, surrounded by his acolytes, mumbling away and buying everyone anything they wanted.' Tony continued:

> I'm afraid it came as no surprise, in one respect, to me. In recent years I'd worked with both Richard Harris and Oliver Reed. They, sadly, both had retinues of sycophants who had learned to accept the largesse of the drunk, seemingly free of conscience. For me, the closeness that we had evidently shared in our younger years was no longer there and this was very upsetting; but his eyes didn't just seem dead to me, it was as if he'd just shut out the whole world. I visited him in his motor-home after the shoot. He was drunk obviously, enuretic, and pushing a fork around unenthusiastically in a plate of tepid food. 'Just a bit of fuel,' he croaked. I left him, and after that day's filming I never saw him again.

Esta Charkham says that day-to-day filming on *Boon* had to be dovetailed into Dad's available hours: the hours that he could perform at all:

> On more than one occasion, I'd had to contact Peter Crouch in London, and say that Michael couldn't hack it. Crouch had come up and talked to Mike, and the next day it was all sweetness and light, and it would never happen again, and usually, and ironically it was sealed by Crouch and I having a drink in the bar. And so we soldiered on. We had been paying a man six days a week to ride the bike; we now had to pay two men to actually lift Mike on to the static version, before filming. His triumph throughout had been his ability to remember lines, but he was losing that. I was mentoring a young actor at the time, Daniel Craig, who came on set with me. He took one look at Mike, flailing and failing to follow cues, and virtually signed the pledge on the spot, certainly when it came to a professional environment. Amanda Burton was pregnant, but was keeping the news secret (she had let me know purely for insurance purposes). She started surfacing fears about rehearsing with Mike, who was a big man, because she felt there was a chance that he might fall into her. He appeared on set, soiled and reeking of booze as well.

I think that Dad was not just losing it to alcoholism. I think that he was having a nervous breakdown at the same time. He'd say to Esta: 'Don't hurry me. Stop chivvying me. It's "Hurry here" and "Hurry there". It's "Hurry, Mike" all the time.' And Esta would say, patiently, 'The reason I'm saying it, Mike, is that we're behind on our film schedule, because you don't appear when you should.' Then, almost in a state of distress, Dad would say: 'You see, I've got to make money. I've got to do the work. There's people depending on me. I can't afford to let up. I've got to keep going.' He was like a walking cry for help. Esta says now that she recognises all the signs of an alcoholic and how, then, it needed to be handled:

> We were all accessories [she says], the drinking friends who were with him in this wonderful culture of co-dependency; his professional colleagues who made allowances; and people like me, who by whittling down the working hours to accommodate his 'illness' were enabling him to continue to get worse. I said to Laurie, 'Why are we doing this? We're just enabling him. We're all enabling him!' It had to stop.

The day it happened, Esta says that she had been getting more and more stressed herself. They were behind schedule and they still had four more of the series to film. That day Dad had not put in an appearance although he was in the van. Esta thumped on the door and a muffled 'Don't hurry me!' was heard from within:

> I was holding a mug of hot tea at the time and when he eventually came to the door, I threw it all over him. 'You're fired!' I told him. I went away and came back in a few minutes brandishing the Equity Rule Book. 'An actor,' I said, reading from the relevant text, 'must present himself fit for work. You haven't, so you are in breach of contract. And I am ringing your agent, Peter Crouch, because he is in breach of contract.' Then I marched off to my car, got in, slammed the door and sobbed. Here I was, a greenhorn producer, who had just sacked the most successful star on ITV, midway through filming a series. Thankfully, Central's top brass had recently visited the set and had picked up that all was not well. I rang Ted Childs and said I'd done a terrible thing and he said I should have done it months

before. Peter Crouch finally recognised the seriousness of it and together we planned a strategy to get Mike looked after as well and as soon as we could. I contacted as many people that I knew who could give advice for high-profile people dealing with AA. Jimmy Greaves was very helpful. The late Gordon Flemyng, father of Jason Flemyng, was wonderful in taking time to get us organised. He was the one who phoned Mike who agreed to meet him at the Holiday Inn. They talked and talked and Mike agreed to go to The Priory in Edgbaston. However, the night before he was due to go, he was once again legless at the hotel bar, pointing an accusing index finger at me and saying, 'Why should I go, just because she wants to make me?' We threw everything at him: Julia, Kate, his mother, his reputation, the love of his friends, you name it ... I said that the series would continue on his return; that we were busy re-scheduling everything, which was true. He went to bed, and next day he went to The Priory, where he stayed for two months.

The stay at The Priory was normally considered useful when it was three months or more, but Dad did brilliantly and was fighting fit by the time he left. He said later, 'I think I was too numb to be frightened about the effect of drinking, but I was shocked after I'd been in the clinic to learn what a state I was in.' A couple of years later he was approached by a probation officer to see if he could talk to drink-addicted teenagers in remand centres, to see if he could give them any advice that might help them out. He held nothing back in sharing with these lads what had happened to him:

Towards the end, it was accelerating very rapidly. I was drinking two bottles of vodka a day. My work on *Boon* was suffering disastrously. It culminated with an unholy row with the producer. I once smashed my fist into the metal side of my dressing-room caravan on location. I hit it so hard it made a dent. I thought drink helped to calm me. Now I realise it brought a whole sea of troubles in its wake.

14

Hi Ho Silver

I've said before that memories of my early childhood were rosy. I obviously felt settled, loved, secure – totally at ease, and unaware of anything in my parents' lives that had the potential to threaten the idyll. Around the time that we moved from our quirky little flat in West Hampstead to Willesden Green, Dad was becoming more famous. I can remember being very resistant to the move – I was about to turn eight, and was upset to be leaving our lovely basement home, and could see no reason to do it. But of course Dad was now earning good money as a recognised talent and we could afford a beautiful Edwardian four-bedroom house with a spacious garden. I was also now starting to experience what it was going to be like to have an instantly recognised father. One day I went with him to a record shop on West End Lane, to buy Mum an Everley Brothers album for her birthday; immediately I noticed how they greeted Dad differently from other customers – how 'chuffed' they seemed to have us there and how they fussed around us during our stay. When we went to pay, the guy behind the counter asked us *both* for an autograph. I felt a frisson of excitement.

It was a novelty at first: as Dad's fame on television spread, so did the acknowledgement at school. More and more children would come up to me in the playground, saying that they'd seen him on TV or carrying an article from a magazine. Parents on the school run would shout out cheerily about Dad's performances. I understood that somehow I had become the daughter of a famous person and, at that time, the spotlight on me felt benign.

But I suppose it would be about this time when it began to dawn that my parents were not the close loving couple that they had always appeared to be. Conversation was beginning to dry up, and my mother would often abruptly leave the room when my dad was in the middle of speaking. She sometimes just stood up and stared at him or rolled her eyes and picked up her book. I know that they rarely went to bed at the same time, and Dad would sit up into the night 'finishing the bottle'.

It was a wet, dark morning as we sat in unmoving traffic on the Salisbury Road, on the school run. The car was quiet, save for the noise of the windscreen wipers clearing the constant blur of our vision. I was gazing out of my window watching all the local mums with their brollies, ushering wet children along the pavement to school, but thinking about my dad: 'Mummy, what's an alcoholic?' Drawn abruptly from her own thoughts she took a long breath, her eyes fixed on the rear lights of the car in front. I turned to face her but she didn't meet my eyes. I must have thought that the question was significant because I can remember that I wasn't surprised at how long it was taking her to reply. The windscreen wipers began to grate every other arc and I started to count. After about five or six of these, she replied: 'An alcoholic is somebody who needs to drink every day.'

She didn't enquire further. No questions. No 'Why do you ask?' No probing. A simple, single-sentence answer and that was the end of it. It wasn't exactly a conversation but it confirmed to me that my dad had this problem, and it confirmed to her that I knew.

The first series of *Boon* came out in 1986, the same year that I moved up to Hampstead Comprehensive. By the time I left my cosy junior school and started secondary school in September, Dad was quite a big name. Hampstead Comprehensive sounded to me terribly exclusive then. It wasn't. Hampstead Girls was. My school was basically in Cricklewood, rather than Hampstead, and had over 1,200 students at the time – a whole world away from my little junior school. Mum had done some asking around of local friends and neighbours, to see if there were any over-11-year-olds starting that September with whom I could walk to school.

We found Hannah, and before the first day at the new school, Mum drove my new friend and I along the mile-long route as a practice run. This was known as the 'Walm Lane way'. Walm Lane was a quiet, wide, tree-lined avenue that constituted half the journey to school: St Gabrielle's Church was at one end and Hampstead School at the other. 'The Cricklewood way' we were to discover later in our school careers. It was actually quicker but meant walking through the noise and dirt of the busy High Road. There was a lingering smell of takeaways, and you had to negotiate your way through numerous drunks even at that early hour. As I progressed into my teenage years we would always walk that way, lured by the shops that sold cigarettes as 'singles', and then by the McDonald's, which was later to open on our route.

The school seemed massive in comparison to the Juniors. The buildings were tall, in huge imposing blocks, and my sense of adventure was really satisfied by discovering it, bit by bit, in playtimes. I really enjoyed the experience. It wasn't long before the kids here, too, cottoned on to who my dad was, and made a much bigger deal of it than I thought it warranted. A note of aggression underpinned enquiries about whether I was 'Boon's daughter', and I found that I was starting to lie. I began, for the first time in my life, to feel ill at ease. My clothes were uncool; my accent was wrong – I sounded middle class. I became aware of 'cool'. I couldn't define it, but I knew that I wasn't 'it'. I was 'uncool'. I was a walking target, especially so, with my newly famous dad. I wouldn't say that I was bullied, certainly not as badly as some of the other kids, but I wouldn't describe it as a walk in the park either.

Each autumn, as a new series of *Boon* would start, Dad's face would be splashed, not only across the TV magazines, looking happy and handsome, a real household name, but also across the tabloids, looking drunk and often demented, portrayed as either a womanising monster, a gun-wielding loony or something equally embarrassing. More than once, as I entered my tutorial room, I would see newspaper articles stuck to the blackboard, obviously for my attention. I always remember one morning, when the lad who sat next to me – a cheeky, lively little fellow who always seemed to sport the most fashionable gear – decided that it was time to have a word. Up to then he had verged on the cruel, with his mickey-taking of me; he'd do anything to get a laugh. Over the weekend, the press had published a particularly vicious attack on Dad, claiming that he was violent at home to Mum and me: you couldn't imagine anything that could possibly be further from the truth. My little classmate spoke, unusually quietly for him, words along the lines of: 'Don't worry, Kate, all families argue. My mum once hit my dad with a frying-pan!' There was such sympathy in his eyes that I was torn, appreciating his kind gesture, but still wanting to set the record straight. I felt that I had to assure him that what he had read was all lies. Offended that I wasn't confiding back, he snapped: 'Well, there's never smoke without fire, Kate!'

I couldn't help but see his point of view. If I'd read something similar in a newspaper about somebody else, I would probably have believed every word too. These were bad times for our family. Dad took legal advice about suing on a number of occasions, but not only were the costs prohibitive by the time any hidden clauses were investigated, such laws that restricted the invasion of privacy, the protection of the children of celebrities or even common trespass, seemed to evaporate when 'the public interest' was invoked. Even our extended family were 'fair game'. When my Uncle Robin's stepson died in a fire, Granny Joan, Dad's mother, was called at two in the morning to be asked 'if Boon knew about the tragedy'.

Back at school, the 'Boon' theme song followed me everywhere. I was no longer Kate Elphick, but always introduced as 'Boon's daughter'. Initially, I had been viewed as a 'bit of a boffin', but dropping a few grades meant that this no longer applied. This, and my newly acquired Willesden accent, made me feel much more accepted. One of the girls that Mum had found to accompany me to school was called Cathy and I developed a lasting friendship with her. She, more than anyone, got me through this difficult time, boosting my confidence and telling me that having a famous Dad didn't have to be a curse, and that I wasn't the 'un-coolest' person alive; she said that I was pretty and that any grief that I was getting were from girls who were just jealous. For the life of me, I couldn't work out why anyone would want to be jealous of me!

Boon was running for the whole of my teenage years and of course there were advantages to accrue from this as well. There was suddenly a lot more money around, so whatever negatives came with Dad's success, no one could say he wasn't bringing home the bacon. However, he wasn't allowed to spoil me. I suppose that both parents, coming from their working-class backgrounds, thought that it was essential that I understood the value of money. There had been an issue about my schooling and their socialist beliefs. When I'd gone to Hampstead, the money had been there for private education, which despite Mum's working in the state sector, she half-believed would be better for me. But she stuck to her socialist guns and, becoming a late convert to hard academic work, I was pleased to end up getting better results than most of her friends' children who had had a private education.

What I didn't realise at the time was that my mother had always ferociously held on to her independence. She insisted on halving all bills: the mortgage, utilities, rates, etc. She had her own account, and my dad had his. She set up an account for me, though, and my dad paid into it by standing order. In addition, there was a trust for me. So I benefited from the 'Boon' money; I went on all the school trips, and we could afford to go away during most school holidays. However, I had to wait for birthdays or Christmas for that important clothing upgrade and my parents would only replace my trainers – the most important part of school attire by which you were judged immediately – when the current pair were sufficiently worn out. Pat – with whom we went on holiday when I was small – remembers asking my mum what she was going to get for my approaching birthday one year. Pat knew that I was horse-mad. Riding was the hobby that had kept me out of trouble throughout my early teens. I had been taking riding lessons once a week for ages; riding was my passion. I would spend my holidays and weekends for as long as I could at the stables, working from dawn to dusk, lugging hay-bales, filling water-buckets and mucking out for the pure love of it. Mum said: 'Well, she's been asking non-stop for years for a horse of her own, so this year's no different.'

'Are you going to get her one?'

'No,' came Mum's answer, 'We're sticking to the trainers again.'

I suppose, as the years progressed, I got used to all the unwarranted attention and this ceased to be the hardest thing with which I had to cope; because as the fame increased, so did the drinking, which was affecting every area of Dad's life. Through the latter part of the 1980s he was away a lot, filming *Boon*, first in Birmingham and then in Nottingham. He would tell Mum and me how he would get lonely and bored and so would end up each evening in the bar. I could understand that, but it was obvious even to me at my age then, that we were not just dealing with an issue of social drinking. Although Dad was away for long spells due to work, he would often not make it home in between filming, and this lack of presence was noticeable but passed without comment. Mum, for her part, had told him not to come home if he was drunk, something that was becoming part of who he was, as opposed to being a lifestyle choice. As he became more famous, his lifestyle *was* changing too, which also contributed to the uncontrolled bouts of drinking. He was becoming more and more like the 'Champagne Charley' for whom he'd had some disparaging words in the past. To be fair, I'm sure at that time of his life, it was a preferable activity and much more fun than his 'normal' life waiting at home. Juggling the two was a constant battle for him and would leave him with enormous guilt, as he loved us, but knew that he was neglecting his role within our family unit.

Somehow fame brought with it greater expectations: what had once simply been 'audiences' now became 'fans'; so as Dad's work increased (which of course he welcomed) his life came under greater scrutiny. He found fame a much greater pressure than work. It's been said before that no one can know until it happens how fame is going to affect them; people make all sorts of assumptions about how wonderful it must be, but many find it's not quite what they imagined.

So many boys from working-class families in the 1960s who made it in music, acting and sport, were casualties of a system that gave them little support when fame came to call. Dad used to put on disguises of scarves, hats and glasses, if he had to go out in the evening, to get us fish-and-chips, and even then he would be recognised and find himself stopping and chatting a few times, there and back. He'd take me with him, so we could talk to each other and then people would be less likely to interrupt us on the way. Then, of course, there would be the benefit of a little 'Dutch courage'; for a person who could seem so amazingly self-confident, the idea that a 'glass of the usual' might be essential for him to be a man among equals now seems to me to be ridiculous. It may have been that the fact that he had left school early concerned him, but he was a self-taught student of PPE and psychology, as anyone who crossed swords with him on these subjects would attest to.

Mum wanted no part of Dad's new life – one I'm sure other women could only dream about. She dreaded film premieres and high-powered social events, complaining that she'd have to find a new 'posh frock'. She hated the role of support act, knowing that everyone would want a piece of Dad. Her chosen life was so different, working hard as an infant-school teacher and parenting me. The orbits of my parents' two detached worlds were spiralling apart, with me in the middle, feeling that I was the only reason that they didn't separate completely. I know now that it wasn't as simple as that: they did continue to love and care about each other, but sometimes in a very perverse way. My dad imagined that Mum was on some sort of pedestal from which he was excluded through his lifestyle choices; the short-term pleasures of drugs, drink and other women would sentence him to a lifetime of guilt and exile from his home. My mother was pragmatic. Her partner had gone and she accepted her new status as a single mother with what looked like equanimity. Close friends, at different stages of my life, were approached and asked whether, were she to succumb finally to cancer, they might consider including me within their family. Each one agreed. It was understood that Dad would not be able to undertake the role of single father for a number of reasons. I'm sure to the rest of the world my dad, with a drink inside him, was the best company you could wish for; never one for being grumpy or aggressive on the booze, he'd be generous, fascinating and hilarious.

Although I really loved my dad and was proud of his success, I must say, personally, I became grateful for his absences; the atmosphere at home when he was there was just awful. Neither of my parents shouted so there would be this tense quiet engulfing Mum. I would see the way she'd look at him, as he tried to make us laugh, pretending everything was normal. Hurt and angry myself, and probably a little disgusted at what I was witnessing, I would chatter away at the dinner table, desperate to fill the uncomfortable silence as Dad gave up trying. The whole thing was very cringe-making and we all felt it. Later Dad would slide away into his study, leaving Mum in the living-room. Feeling sorry for him, I would follow, a little of me always feeling at the time that Mum wasn't being fair to him. Dad would then get emotional; he was always a sentimental drunk. He'd play me The Dubliners with tears in his eyes and repeatedly apologise for his behaviour; the guilt and self-criticism would come pouring out. I knew that he wouldn't stop drinking. As a teenager I actually got a bit bored with it all, this endless cycle. Then I hated myself for that. When I became an adult and was living with my dad by myself, it was very different. We would discuss his drinking and could be so open about it that it wouldn't affect our relationship, but as a teenager it was hard. I didn't understand the whole situation properly and I wasn't able to communicate what I felt to anyone I knew. I never wanted my friends to come back to my house after school, if he was there. But as I was 'Boon's daughter' they all wanted to come back for a nose. I felt as if it was my dirty secret, with the whole world assuming that I had this amazing life with a film-star dad. At this time Mum had other worries too. Her cancer had returned; I think that I was about 12. Again, I was much protected from it all, as Mum never showed any concern, and played it all down. In fact, I remember very little about it, except that she had started to experience pain in her arm as she brushed my hair each morning in the hallway, before school. She would wince, as she dragged through the knots, to put my mop up into a ponytail for me, before we rushed out of the door. A visit to the doctor, followed by a number of tests, showed that the cancer was back. When I think about it now, as an adult with my own family, I am in awe of her quiet strength; I really had no idea of how she must have been feeling then, as life continued so normally. The one change I remember at home was that Mum went on a salt-free diet and suddenly the kitchen was full of rice-cakes. Presumably, the ball-and-chain that was Dad's institutional guilt grew tenfold, as Mum was once again 'battling the Big C.', as he saw it. He drank more and came home less; it was a vicious circle. He was very scared: he adored Mum and wanted to support her, but the drinking meant that he just wasn't able to, in the way that she wanted. She had to rely on her female friends for emotional support. Chief among these at the time was Elizabeth.

Mum would go off for mammoth walks every day with our lurcher Flossie, either round the local Gladstone Park or across the heath. She told Elizabeth that it was how she coped, 'It stops me going mad,' she'd say. The plan had been that while Dad was away, filming *Boon*, he would try to get back for the weekends. It was always: 'He might be coming back; he might not.' From my recollection, it was usually 'not'. Often Elizabeth would go walking with Mum, who would ask her best friend for advice on how to handle Dad: 'So, if he comes home this Friday, and he's drunk, should I let him in or send him away?' Mum would ask, 'Should I be understanding and not spoil the night? Or should I put my foot down and make another stand? If I send him away, will that make him worse? What should I do for the best for *him?*' Elizabeth says she knew at the time that Mum would do what she thought was best, regardless of any advice that she might offer. She made me chuckle recently, when she relayed, from over the years, Mum's following observation: 'If he saw my pursed lips when I opened the door, he knew he would not be coming in.' It was a look that she had perfected; I knew it well. As Elizabeth says, the shame is that she resented what she had become: his drinking had made her a bitter, joyless nag. Mum could only look at Dad in a critical fashion, and she felt that this was counter to her natural disposition.

Another consequence of this unpredictable lifestyle was Mum's constant need to revise her weekend plans; she was never confident how things were going to turn out. So, with Dad only appearing home for sporadic dates, she started a regular Friday night cinema ritual with Elizabeth. She would go out unless Dad had definitely confirmed he would be back in good order. If she knew this, she would stay in. Elizabeth says that however frustrated Mum might be with her situation, she was always prepared to understand and forgive Dad, if she felt he was making an effort, adding that Mum could become very concerned about how she came across to Dad. She says that one Friday, when Dad was definitely due home, she had the need to pop over to our house for something. She says that Mum opened the door, expecting Dad, and looked absolutely exquisite; how depressed she would have been if he never turned up. The truth is that everyone who knew my parents well could see that they cared enormously for each other, and that Dad's alcoholism was preventing them having the relationship that was their due. One incident struck me particularly. Jimmy Nail also lived in a house in Willesden Green. Dad and he were old mates, having acted together in *Auf Wiedersehen Pet*. He was having a day-time party at his place. The sun was shining and my parents were looking gorgeous and happy. At some point Mum realised that she'd left her handbag in the car. 'Don't worry. I'll go and get it for you, love.' Somehow, that tiny comment, that little gesture brought Mum into floods of tears, not a common sight for me. It was so incongruous, but something had snapped and she'd seen again the partner she'd chosen and how alone she had become.

Things changed for a while in 1988, after the shock of nearly being fired from *Boon*, as it would, after an ultimatum like that. He was on the wagon for nearly four years. He looked great. He even looked like a national heart-throb, as we went out with him drinking fizzy water. This was when I went on holiday with him to Portugal, without Mum, and had a really great time getting to know him. For my parents I think there had been too much water under the bridge for a normal relationship. Their lives continued to be pretty separate, Dad away working and Mum during the week involved with her job, yoga and taking our lurcher out for a walk; as I got older, Mum would also be away at weekends with her girlfriends. When my parents were together, though, the atmosphere in the house was definitely much easier.

During Dad's 'dry spell', I started to do more with him. Going to some of the movie premieres, of the films he had appeared in, was understandably memorable; unlike Mum, I quite enjoyed the whole scene. Like she had been, I was a bit of a tomboy at this age, so I wasn't one really for getting dressed up, but events like these were too much fun to be missed. The one I most remember was *The Krays*. We were sitting directly behind Charlie Kray, although I had no idea at the time. Apparently I made a joke about his hair and Dad, in an attempt to hush me up, just couldn't stop giggling. I will never forget the reception waiting for us, as we left the cinema, experiencing the blinding flashes, from what seemed like a thousand photographers outside. It was like diving into a surreal sea of them: it was as if I had landed up *in* a movie, myself. I froze. I just couldn't move. Dad, ever the professional, gripped my arm and smilingly ushered us through. There was a picture of both of us, alongside the review, in the paper the next day. I was sixteen. Another premier that I remember as being amazing was the one for the film *Let Him Have It*. We were introduced to Derek Bentley's sister, Iris, whom you couldn't help but feel desperately sorry for, knowing what her family had been through: her whole life spent fighting for a posthumous pardon for her brother. And she had died, by the time it happened.

Just as I was getting used to a new way of life, it happened. Dad fell off the wagon and my world fell apart again. It was the circumstances in which it happened that was so shocking, as much as his return to the old way of life. We were holidaying in Portugal: Mum and her friend, Elizabeth, me and my oldest friend, Rosie, from infant-school days, Elizabeth's children Sara and Christoff, and his mate Tom. Rosie had recently moved back again to London from Brighton, as her father was an alcoholic, and her parents had recently split up. She and her mum had moved near to us, so Rosie could go to my secondary school; I was thrilled. We children were having a great holiday together ... until that day. The five of us had been hanging out in the village and were heading up the hill, back towards home on this sunny afternoon, when I saw a man leaning heavily on the wall as he tried to walk. I stopped and stared, while my brain took time to register slowly that it was Dad. I didn't even know that he was in Portugal. Where was he staying? Why was he so obviously drunk? He saw me and his face crumpled, and he began to apologise. I just stared at him. I couldn't speak. I wouldn't have known what to say. He scrambled off in the opposite direction, and I just burst into tears. My friends, I suspect, were more shocked by seeing me cry for the first time, a *very* unusual occurrence, than by Dad's bizarre appearance. They were really supportive. I was so embarrassed that they had seen him like that. I was left confused and gutted that all the good work that had gone into his rehabilitation had been wasted.

It turned out that Mum had found out that Dad was drinking again and that he was proposing to go to Portugal at the same time as us. She had strongly advised him to stay in a hotel, out of our way. However, it would only have been a matter of time before I found out. Children or partners of alcoholics develop a sixth-sense: they only need to hear the voice, and it can be on the phone, to know what they must have been up to. Rosie was the one friend, with whom I'd grown up, who knew what it was like to have a parent who was an alcoholic. Perhaps her being there made it a little easier for me. Her father, like mine, was a sweet man, kind and gentle, and like mine a very mellow drunk, with not a nasty bone in his body. There was a difference, however, in how Rosie reacted to her dad's condition. She was, in contrast to me, a very quiet child. She would be painfully shy in company, finding talking to adults, apart from her parents, quite taxing. However, to her father, when he was drunk, it was a different matter. She would get really angry with him, shouting at him and uncharacteristically exploding over minor lapses of behaviour. She would tell me that I was being soft with Dad, and that ultimately our fathers were being selfish at our expense and didn't deserve any sympathy. For the most part we didn't talk about it at all, but I remember once going down to Brighton to stay with her, when we were about fifteen. We just happened to be in the kitchen together with a group of kids with the radio on in the background. A programme came on about alcoholism, with an adolescent describing the difficulties of living with an afflicted parent. One by one, our friends left the room, leaving just Rosie and me at the end, sitting silently, with tears in our eyes, staring straight ahead. Rosie's lovely dad, Ron, died in 1995.

I would never convince Rosie that she should feel sorry for him, just as she could never dissuade me that Dad needed sympathy for his unhappiness. I am forever indebted to Mum for providing me with the way that I viewed my father's alcoholism. Although it must have been hard for her not to talk to me the way that Rosie did, to vent her own frustration, she never did. She never let me know how let down and hurt she must have felt. She never let me feel as if he was choosing drink over me; so I grew up without feeling unloved or rejected by him. She just explained to me from an early age that he was sick, that he had a disease and his behaviour was not to do with how he felt about me. Such a non-judgemental view, I'm sure, impacted not just on my attitude to Dad but had a major influence on my all-round character building. I think lots of men, over the years, would have liked to have lured Mum away. They saw that she was a special person, a beautiful woman to whom Dad was not able to be a proper partner. I always felt that the men in our lives felt overtly protective towards her, that she was wasting her time on a relationship that was going nowhere. Mum knew about Dad's other women, his affairs, although not always who they were, unless they turned up at her work, as one did, or if the press decided to enlighten us, particularly if the lady in question was famous. She knew, but it seemed as if she felt that she could accept it, as she also knew that he would never leave her.

15

The White Swan

The first I heard about it, I was being doorstepped by a journalist outside the school gates: 'Is it true your dad's left your mum and is living with another woman in Warwickshire? What do you feel about it?' Whatever I felt about it and whatever grain of truth was not in it, the story duly appeared that Sunday. For 'another woman' they might have written 'Peter and Sheila Vandrill', as the former was to be Dad's collaborator in the project. The 'love-nest' was The White Swan Inn, in Henley-in-Arden, which they had both bought. The White Swan had been trading as an inn, according to records, as far back as 1350. It had been a well-known coaching stop with at least seven coaches a day stopping there to change horses. Over the years many famous people had stayed there. Doctor Samuel Johnson was a regular visitor, stopping overnight on his way back to his home in Staffordshire, and Dad named one bedroom, in consequence, the Samuel Johnson Room, and put a four-poster bed in it. Dr Johnson's friend and diarist, Boswell, also stayed there and the poet, William Shenstone, whose works include *Poem written at the Inn in Henley-in-Arden*:

> Whoe'er has travelled life's dull round,
> Where'er his stages may have been,
> May sigh to think he still has found
> The warmest welcome at an inn.

Obviously, to discover that your father had deserted the family home for another would have been devastating news, but discovering that he has just bought 'One of the Oldest Inns in the World' was still quite a shock. He had talked about buying a pub in the past, 'The Burgundian'. Indeed, some of the later reports on his choice of purchase suggested he had considered it seriously before taking on The Swan, but that it was too expensive. I find this hard to believe. Dad's partner in the venture was a chef, who was looking for a catering and hotel outlet, which was hardly 'The Burgundian's' strength. Also the words 'too expensive' don't chime with my memory of my dad's vocabulary.

He certainly threw himself into the whole promotional circus for The Swan. The *TV Times* shared with its readers that while Dad was asleep in his four-poster in the hotel, there was an uninvited nocturnal guest:

> She is called Mary Black, so the story goes [Dad is reported as saying], and several people who have stayed in our top bedroom have experienced her strange presence. Legend has it that Mary was a local dignitary who was having an affair with a stable boy. One night in 1860 they had a bust up and he pushed her down the stairs to her death. The ghost appears as a black shape with a woman's face and hovers over beds. One woman was terrified, very distressed indeed. She wasn't play-acting; she didn't even know we were supposed to have a ghost.

You do wonder how many people might be encouraged to stay after that; but not content with it, another mass magazine readership was informed:

The first time I saw its old leaded windows, I joked that it looked as though it should have a resident ghost. Little did I know. She's usually seen late at night, in a tiny bedroom at the top of the stairs. I didn't take much notice at first, but there were so many sightings, I began to wonder if there was something in it after all. Then one night, something extremely weird happened. A couple staying in the room woke up to see a young girl in white, with beautiful long red hair, gliding through their room. After a while, she disappeared. They went back to sleep again but later the woman woke up to find her husband thrashing around and yelling 'Go away!' The terrified couple told me that the husband had seen the pale face of a girl close to him and had been trying hard to push her away. But the ordeal didn't stop there. Later that night, unseen hands kept trying to rip their bed-clothes off and they really had to fight to keep them on.

According to Dad in this report, a psychic investigator was called in to unravel the mystery. He told Dad that the ghost was the tragic spirit of Virginia Black, an 18-year-old, who'd lived and worked at the inn in the 1800s. 'Apparently, Virginia had rowed with her boyfriend and in a scuffle, accidentally slipped down the stairs which lead from the attic bedroom,' said Dad, 'Her boyfriend panicked and fled the scene, leaving her to drag herself back up the stairs, where she died, her neck broken in the fall. Her boyfriend was later tried and hanged for her murder. Perhaps she just wanted people to know what had really happened to her, and that her boyfriend wasn't to blame for her death.' And then, probably to deter would-be visitors who enjoy being frightened out of their skins or those who felt that having one's bedclothes dragged off by unseen hands wasn't such a bad thing, he added, 'Since the story of her death was discovered, Virginia's ghost hasn't been seen around the inn.'

To *TV Times* readers, Dad continued that the history of the place was really the game-changer when it came to buying the place:

That's why I chose it. It's one of the oldest coaching inns in Europe and was very much the centre of the town for hundreds of years. The market was held in the courtyard at the back of the pub; the outbuildings were used as the fire station; and the court was set up in what is now our function room. I love old places; I love the country, and I also love pubs and this gives me all three in one.

House Beautiful provided very complimentary coverage of the hotel's features:

> The Tudor-style hotel is full of character and stands proudly in the middle of the main street. It's divided into two distinct halves, joined by an attractive archway which straddles the old coachmen's entrance. Inside the original features have thankfully been retained, with old wooden beams, narrow winding passages and leaded windows.

Dad told them that 'many of the beams came from an old fort nearby which belonged to the de Montforts, who owned most of the county, but a huge fire destroyed it and much of the remaining timber was used for buildings round here.' The magazine reports that 'the windows look out on to the main street in Henley-in-Arden and high above them a Union Jack flutters from a flagpole. In summer, hanging baskets burst with geraniums and trailing lobelia.' When they also say, 'Regulars at The White Swan are used to seeing Michael in the bar where he can enjoy the company and the friendly atmosphere,' you could believe that this is a bit of fanciful writing to please an absentee landlord. It couldn't be further from the truth. Simon Birch, a reader of the local *Henley News*, shares his recollections of Dad's tenure of The Swan:

> I used to work in the office building next door, Herring House, 1986–89. Myself and colleagues (*sic*) regularly patronised The White Swan at lunchtime. It was not unusual to have our empty glasses and plates collected by Michael himself. I recognised him from the series *Private Schultz*. If you didn't know who he was, you would never glean any such celebrity pretensions from him, contrary to the awful 'sleb' culture we suffer nowadays. That's not to say he wouldn't pose, empty glasses in hand, for photographs with people who wanted one. I also recall an occasion when I spotted his *Boon* co-star, Neil Morrissey, sat at the bar with a group of others.

I suppose that if you're wondering why one of the top-earning television stars of this particular decade, in leading programmes on BBC and ITV at the same time, had chosen to be collecting glasses, as he did as a student in The Burgundian years before, it's best to listen to Peter Vandrill's story:

I met Mike in *Schultz.* I was a film and television location caterer working mostly for the BBC then. He was in every episode and I was catering throughout, so we got to know each other quite well. We kept in touch, but didn't meet again till he was working on *Boon* in Birmingham. I never worked on it myself, but I was with a film unit in Nottingham, when some guys came from Birmingham to do some technical work, who were working on it and suggested I give him a call. I duly did and he insisted that I went over to the Holiday Inn straight away. I drove from Nottingham and when I got there, he was well ensconced in the bar with Meatloaf, who was playing locally, and his retinue. Mike was so welcoming, as he always was, 'How're you getting on? What are you doing?' I told him that I was getting out of the film-catering game. I'd had enough. Twenty years of that, and the army, had meant I'd never seen my family. I was a pretty good chef. I felt that I wanted to settle down somewhere, with my wife, in a pub, say. I felt the time had come. 'Your own pub,' said Mike, 'I'd like some of that. No, really.'

'Look,' I said, 'I believe you. But,' taking a long look at the uncollected empty glasses, 'I think I'll give you a call in the morning and talk about it then.'

I little thought the next day that he'd be at all interested. 'No. Count me in. I'm really up for it,' was his reply when I phoned, and after that I realised that we would be doubling the amount of capital that I had envisaged spending on the project. We didn't limit our area of search that much, virtually half the country, Notts to Hampshire. Within about nine months of meeting at the Holiday Inn, we'd chosen The White Swan at Henley-in-Arden. It was a handy weekend retreat from Mike's *Boon* work as well. The pub/hotel was owned by Ansells and we took on the lease from the previous holders. I was there with Mike about three years in all. As everyone knows, Mike never drove, but he bought a new convertible Beetle for me to drive him round.

I drove him down to his accountant on a number of occasions. That accountant and I just didn't get on; he wasn't at all keen on the idea of the pub purchase. One person who was very encouraging was Barbara Windsor. She had her own pub near Chesham, and I drove Mike down there to see her. She gave us quite a few tips of what to do and not do. After we got started, another helpful contact was the restaurateur and TV chef, Keith Floyd. Mike invited him down and he was horrified to see his host at the end of the day, handing out free drinks to anyone gathered at the bar. 'That's exactly what I used to do,' he said, 'until a combination of my accountant and an empty cellar caused me to think otherwise. Even if *you* own the place, use money at the bar, or you'll get hopelessly out of control.' Here sounded the voice of bitter experience, as we know. Anyway, it went straight over Mike's head. The trouble was that he was generous to a fault. The local lads would hang on till closing-time, knowing that a lock-in was in the offing. When the doors closed, the drinks would be on Mike, sometimes that meant until the wee small hours.

His charity didn't just stretch to free drinks. The White Swan sponsored the local football team, Arden Foresters, and other local organisations. One local youth who was an accomplished flautist was provided with funds to attend a music academy, and an international career was subsequently established. Mike was persuaded on more than one occasion to open local fetes, not always in the best of health. Local affection, however, was ever so slightly taxed, when the Midland biking community realised that biker *Boon* owned a gaff in Henley. Considering that Mike couldn't ride a bike, the loyalty was touching, but the noise was terrible, and the fumes, descending into the kitchen and restaurant, even worse. When quiet suggestions were ignored, a ban had to be introduced. Of course, there was one celebrated occasion on a Saturday night in 1988, as Mike was having a quiet evening in the bar, when forty bikers broke in and kidnapped him. The guests looked on in horror as he was dragged out and whisked away on a motorbike. They, and Mike, found out later that it was all in a good cause. He was held to ransom in the stunt that raised £1,000 for the ITV Telethon charity. It was the Alcester-based Bulldogs riding group who staged the kidnap, and they managed to pick up a police escort to help make the whole exercise legit.

There were, of course, many other *Boon* fans who came for a peek. Coaches of pensioners came, one containing Mike's mum. He was a fabulous mine host, always entertaining, always courteous, even to the occasional journalist who wandered in for a story. We would be joined sometimes by cast members of *Boon*, Neil Morrissey mostly, who was also here for the filming of *Blood Runner*; in all my years of film catering, it was great with that film, to finally get a credit at the end. So, Mike came down mostly at weekends, while I looked after the kitchen all the time; we had a manager for the bar. This can't have been the easiest of jobs, just looking after Mike. But it was only alcohol; there were no drugs around. He was still using The White Swan as his haven after he went to be dried out. We were very worried as to what our role was going to be, when he returned. We didn't have to be. Advisers came to see us and said that we should make no special arrangements and that we shouldn't mollycoddle him. If we wanted to drink alcohol near him, that would be fine and that he could enter into being part of pub life as before. He was amazing when he came back. He had lost a lot of weight and continued to get fitter and fitter. He seemed that much more relaxed. He and I went off to Portugal, to the boat, and stayed for ten days, all the while me drinking my way through bottles of wine and him sipping at a cola. Apparently there was no going back.

The downside? Of course, there was a down side. It really started as soon as we bought the place. The previous leaseholders led us to believe that many more fixtures and fittings were going to remain than were there when we moved in. A lot of the kitchen equipment was well past its sell-by date and had to be replaced. Mike's reply? It was his favourite expression: 'I got loads of dough. Don't worry.' And I didn't, because I had bigger problems. The irony of my looking forward all those years to settling down with my wife in one fixed abode, is that almost as soon as we did, she left. She went off with another pub employee, which I couldn't cope with. I stayed three years, but when she returned after our divorce to live in Henley, I felt I had to leave and return to my home roots of Berkshire. Mike bought out my share, and I think he kept it for another three years. We just went our separate ways then.

Peter Vandrill's reference to *Blood Runner* is a reminder of one of the more extraordinary consequences of Dad's time at The Swan. The film actually appeared in the UK as *I Bought a Vampire Motorcycle*. It might well have been re-christened *I Made a Phantom Film*, because a lot of the cast, crew, equipment and locations were from *Boon*, as Mycal Miller, the producer says, 'without Central Television knowing'. It's reminiscent of those old spaghetti westerns where the director is actually making two movies at once, but the unsuspecting actors, although encumbered with long shooting schedules and impenetrable scripts, don't question it, and only get paid for one. At least, this time the actors and crew knew what was going on. Dad and Neil Morrissey exchange billings for the film. Neil is the lead and Dad is in a supporting role. For a low-budget horror comedy the film received some favourable reviews. *Today* said:

> This is one of those small-budget, British, efforts that looks as if it was spliced together in the director's front room in Cricklewood. *Vampire* is Dracula meets Dick Emery reeking of bad taste. I laughed till I ached despite myself. It's basically an outing for the *Boon* TV crowd, with Michael Elphick playing a garlic-breathing, trilby-hatted police inspector spouting lines such as 'my name is Inspector Cleaver and if I don't solve this I'm for the chop.' ... The two scenes that gave me special delight are a tottering OAP who crosses the road as a dozen Hell's Angels roar by, only to be pole-axed by a coughing Ford Escort, and the final full-throttle exorcism. Wonderful stuff.

And the *Daily Mail*:

> Throttled by a Spiffing Spook Spoof – It's all there in the title – a cheap 'n' cheerful, ribald British spoof horror epic about a Norton Commando with teeth in its headlamp and an insatiable thirst for blood rather than petrol. Bikers and people who like their rubbish replete with rude bits and gleeful bad taste should have a great time. It could become a cult video. I'm well-disposed towards *Vampire Motorcycle*, if only for blowing a resounding, Birmingham-based raspberry at imported, humourlessly gruesome horror tosh.

The film premiered at Birmingham's New Street Odeon in July, 1990. Mycal Miller had worked on *Boon* as a film editor, but in 1988 he left Central to co-write and produce the film:

> We signed up Neil Morrissey. Then, Michael kindly agreed to take the part of Inspector Cleaver, the garlic-breathed cop. He was a joy to work with! Before Michael came on board, I had to negotiate with his agent Peter Crouch who I met in a pub in Soho to discuss the project. Obviously, we could not afford the sort of fee that would normally be expected. Peter (who I think also represented Glenda Jackson) was very wary of low-budget productions. In the end, Peter gave it the go-ahead and also suggested to Michael that he became an investor! We also used Mike's pub, The White Swan in Henley-in-Arden as a production office and the location for the interior pub fight sequence. Michael's business partner also provided location catering. The Pub Landlord was played by Ed Devereaux (formerly The Ranger in *Skippy*), who was also recommended by Peter Crouch. The desk-sergeant at the police station was played by David Daker, who was Harry Crawford in *Boon*. Michael filled the role brilliantly; it was his suggestion to wear glasses which we had specially fitted with non-magnifying lenses. The Cleaver character was supposed to have foul garlic breath. As a Method actor, Michael actually munched raw garlic throughout filming – so the watering eyes of the other cast members was quite genuine! Of course, it was his bad breath that saved him from the vampire in the end ...

Other cast members included Anthony Daniels, who had played C-3PO in *Star Wars*, Dad's driver Midge Taylor, and Burt Kwouk, who he had worked with on *Pink Panther*, as the proprietor of a Chinese take-away. The music was composed by Dean Friedman, the composer of the music from ... *Boon*. The film's meandering storyline, about a possessed motorcycle ('She Runs on Blood ... She Don't Run on Gasoline') inflicting damage on the world at large and bikers in particular, is secondary to the ghoulish characters and gory special effects; one delight is to see a 'talking turd' leap from the pan into the mouth of a surprised Noddy (Neil Morrissey). What Central Television made of the film, when it came out, is not recorded. By the time it was released, Peter Vandrill and Dad had parted company.

Whether the new sobriety caused Dad to re-evaluate his role as a catering supremo, I don't know, but his later conversations about his role at the pub sound a little more jaundiced. In a promotional interview for the programme *The Absolute Beginner's Guide to Cookery* in the *Daily Mirror* in 1990, we read:

> Mike has had to learn about food to avoid landing in the financial soup when his caterer partner in The White Swan hotel-restaurant decided to quit. Until then Mike had merely been a sleeping partner – and a drinking partner. 'I never thought I was a businessman until I was forced to become one,' he says.

Again, the same year:

> Over the four years he has owned the hotel, Michael has instigated repairs to the roof and the heating, and improved the décor. He has always been happy to take advice from local experts, but he took a personal interest in the rewiring. 'I was a stage electrician for three years,' he explains, 'so that's something I've been able to do partly on my own. But there must be thousands of feet of wiring here, and there are still some wires I can't trace back because someone's built over them. Unfortunately, it's been bodged continually over the years and I know there are probably several years of hard work ahead of me to get everything just the way I want it.'

A year later, we read:

> Running a pub can have its problems. The White Swan is expensive to maintain – rewiring it will cost a hefty £40,000. But while Michael is determined to make it work as a business, he says, it's also a lot of laughs. 'When you run a small country hotel you find out how true to life *Fawlty Towers* really was.'

If the wiring system was complicated for an electrician, you can imagine the complications of running a staff for someone who had never done it before and basically had no wish to. So originally we hear:

> Michael has a staff of 12 but is always ready to help out where he can – even to the extent of waiting in the dining room. 'I have the best of both worlds living here,' says Michael contentedly, 'I can always have company whenever I need it, but if I want to be alone for a while, all I have to do is pop upstairs and close the door behind me.'

And then, a year later in *Woman's Realm* he is reported as saying:

> Nottingham is only an hour's drive to my hotel so, depending on when shooting finished, I'd either go over there on a Friday night or Saturday morning. I get up early when I'm at The White Swan – I am there to work. I don't treat it as somewhere to relax, although that was the theory to start with. But it is impossible. I have to be there to know what is happening. If everything is running smoothly, I'll go home to London on a Saturday evening, but there are often problems. The staff want to talk about personal things, like perhaps an illness in the family, and you automatically get involved. I can't do that business thing and simply treat staff as numbers. I've always been sympathetic to people – a bit too much really – you can come unstuck. At home, I can really relax. I put my feet up and don't answer the phone ...

Dad had installed a manageress, Jackie Bollard, to look after The Swan on a day-to-day basis, but he was spreading himself too thin and what had started out as a business venture had become a huge 'money pit'. The writing was on the wall and by 1992 he was out of it.

16

Go Number Two

Of all the theatrical experiences that Dad was privileged to share with an audience, there was one that I know was very close to his heart. Pantomime is a great family experience and it was certainly a great experience for our family. For nearly ten years, from 1988 to 1997, Dad was treading the boards in the five or six weeks after Christmas playing some eye-rolling villain or other. He played the Dame once but didn't take to it. So, depending where he was performing, I would see him at least once, and sometimes two or three times. When I was younger, I would be accompanied by Mum, but later I might go with a group of friends or relatives from both sides of the family. Dad relished these shows; he loved the company of children, anyway, and an audience of them to relate to, was magic. He could also ham it up to his heart's content, move off the script and develop a great rapport with his co-stars that straightforward drama didn't necessarily afford. They were a fascinating group over the years: Danny La Rue, Britt Ekland, Brian Conley, Lionel Blair, Lorraine Chase, Matthew Kelly, and Fern Britton, amongst many others. These pantomimes took Dad through the good and the bad times, his own poor health and that of Mum. January and February can be depressing enough, anyway, but not for him. When the party finished on the stage, it started backstage. I'm sure that the audience picked up the atmosphere and realised that they were joining something special. I, personally, loved the backstage parties. Once, when Dad was appearing in Southampton, we were whisked off after the show to a newly opened nightclub, because one of Dad's co-stars, Emily Symons, who was also appearing in *Home and Away*, was going out with one of Southampton's footballers, Matt Le Tissier, whose club it was.

Dad had a delightful portfolio of villains: Abanazer, Fleshcreep, and King Rat, depending on the panto. King Rat was the villain of the piece in *Dick Whittington*. One year in Southsea, Fern Britton, who coincidentally was also a Central graduate from a later time than Dad, was playing the fairy to Lorraine Chase's 'Dick'. Dad's 'King Rat' was suitably decked out in mud-streaked clobber and 'bovver boots' as befits a denizen of the sewers. Fern remembers hearing his boots striding down the corridor to her dressing room and the tentative knock at the door: 'Got something nice for my fairy,' he said, as he came in, his fist closed. 'She's got to look really good, well-dressed. Hold out your hand.' He dropped two diamante earrings into it. Fern says that she would always wear the earrings for the final 'walk down' at the end. She said that she found this part of the show quite difficult to handle, a little embarrassing, so she would do a little bob and quickly pull away to the side. Dad remembered having to have a word with her: 'You know what you must do? You've got to go down there, stand tall, take the applause and *then* walk to the side.' Fern says: 'He was a lovely, lovely man and his death at the age of fifty-five was a tragedy. I still have the earrings he gave me.'

The only bad note that came from the pantomime years was once again, through no fault of Dad, receiving the wrong type of publicity. The producers would be eager, naturally, to have their pantos promoted on the national media that Dad's 'name' at the time could achieve. It seems that no amount of pre-show agreements could prevent this happening. When you consider that the object of the exercise was to talk about shows for children, Dad found that his alcoholism and Brit Ekland's love life, for which an embargo had been asked, was not what they should have been questioned about on the *Richard and Judy Show*, when they were there to talk about *Aladdin*. An infamous studio mauling by Derek and Ellen Jameson on Radio Two about Dad's drinking, after he had been dry for three years, when he was there to promote *Jack and the Beanstalk*, was probably the final straw. It was a pattern that emerged after his treatment: parrying the constant questioning about his illness, when he clearly wanted to get on with the next stage of his life.

Dad never had much of a need to discuss his work, or more particularly, the work in hand. However, as I pointed out in the previous chapter, he was beginning to take me out to premieres and discuss a little about his chosen profession. This was helped by the fact that he was coming home more, when he could, and when filming would allow. So it was that I began to study him a little, to come to terms with what sort of man my father was. He, meanwhile, was reviewing, domestically and professionally, what he was about and where he stood in the eyes of those around him. Everybody who knew Dad talked about his charisma. 'When he engaged with you, it was as if you were the only person in the world' is a familiar description of his style – and not only said by women. 'He looked at you directly, with that twitch of the mouth, full of humour and promise, and you felt drawn in.' My mum's friend Pat once asked him how he managed to stand out from the crowd in a photograph. 'Confront the camera,' he told her. 'Most people shrink away from the camera – they're wary of it, and it shows.' He taught her what to do: 'Be quite aggressive,' he said. 'Look through the camera at the person taking the picture, and imagine that person being the most attractive, charming and generous person you've ever met.' Pat has always followed his advice; she believes she has become more photogenic as a result, and can often be heard shouting out the same advice to anyone having their photograph taken: 'Confront the camera! Confront the camera!'

This ability to 'draw in' other people, while it came naturally to Dad, was a facility he was quite aware of; it became embedded in his growing repertoire of techniques he used to full effect in his relationship with the camera. He would rarely come across anyone who was resistant to his charm, and therefore I was very interested to observe his response to our cat, Toby, who seemed deliberately indifferent.

This cat, black, long-haired, of indeterminate breed, was extremely affectionate, a real people pleaser. As soon as we sat down, with a paper or book, or to watch TV, the cat would jump into a lap, demand cuddles, and generally luxuriate. Strangely, though, he ignored Dad, seeming not to hear his cajoling attempts to entice him onto his own lap, and often leaving the room when Dad came in. Dad, only half joking, would grumble about this and appeal to me and Mum: 'What's the matter with that cat? Why doesn't it like me? Does it think it's the man of the house?' I always thought that the cat was giving him the silent treatment because Dad was so infrequently home. Mum would do her eye-rolling – she was beginning to treat Dad as if he had learning difficulties – and say 'Don't be so ridiculous; you're paranoid.' But it didn't stop him moaning on about the bad attitude of the cat.

It was during this time, when Dad was filming, that Mum was woken in the middle of the night by the familiar chug chug of the black cab drawing up outside, and the sound of the key in the lock. She waited, half dozing, for him to come upstairs, but he didn't appear. She could hear vague noises, and his voice, coming from downstairs, and eventually she went down to investigate. Dad was crouched in the kitchen, on all fours, eye to eye with the cat that was eating something from a proffered spoon. It was caviar. Dad, in an effort to get the cat onside, had bought several pots of the stuff.

His attempt to befriend the cat may have paid off. A few days later, Dad found himself alone in the house, with only Toby for company. He'd fallen asleep in the chair when he was woken by a persistent yowling. It took him a couple of minutes to realise that one of the gas knobs was still fully on, without its flame, and that the kitchen was stinking of gas. He liked to draw attention to the fact that the cat had saved his life, but my mother cruelly pointed out that the cat was more interested in saving his own.

Back on the set of *Boon*, there was a new businesslike air. According to the terms of Dad's rehabilitation contract with AA, he was doing the rounds of admission: 'Hey Rocky, I hope I didn't piss you off too much before.' He was similarly engaged with the rest of the crew. Where it wasn't necessary, as many are apt to forget, is with the viewing public. No one had noticed anything untoward. No critic had drawn the public's eye to a lack of form. Acres of print had been written in the 'news' pages, about Dad's illness, as a duty to keep the public informed, but curiously what he was there for, and why the public chose to watch him, was interestingly unaffected. A new, slimmed-down 'Boon' was evidently one of the consequences of his treatment. There was a flurry of articles about his new 'health' regime, suitably illustrated with photographs of Dad in swimming pools or on exercise bikes. He was even persuaded to make the odd 'fashion shoot', not, I have to say, looking perfectly at ease. Neil Morrissey says that the 'new' Dad, on set, was a little more discerning of the direction and the script in hand. As things had deteriorated before, Dad had been very unquestioning about both, but without playing his 'star-rating' card, he would now make constructive suggestions, which would be readily received.

The show continued to receive some outstanding plaudits. Brian Sewell, the art critic, given the television reviewing detail in the *Evening Standard*:

The opening titles to *Boon* are irrelevant and misleading. The series may have started long ago with Michael Elphick as a valetudinarian despatch rider rumbling round the Midland streets of Dottygam, dreaming that he was some latterday Paul Revere, but the quality of the writing, narrative and production that inspire the present series have removed Boon far from his first self-image, and further still from any dependence on early spaghetti Westerns. Indeed, in his revised role as a private detective, Boon seems a wholly original character, owing nothing, even in a general sense, to Holmes, Poirot, Wexford or Lew Archer and their ilk, all of whom are designed detectives, rigidly constrained by style, fundamentally fictional. Boon is fundamentally real, the bloke next door; grouchy and self-deprecating; his IQ is below the hundred mark, his attention span too short, his eye for the prime target too easily diverted; slow in reflex and instinctive response, he is an old dog past his prime, too obstinate for his own good. Creased and crumpled, shifting from not-quite-clown to not-quite-hero, Elphick plays Boon with bumbling neatness; I suspect that within his typecast limits he is a much more subtle underplaying actor than we realise. Ever since he played that roguish private in the German Army I have been his devotee.

By the time that Series Four was on the stocks, Central Television had moved to new studios in Nottingham. The crew and cast decamped from the Birmingham Holiday Inn to the Waltons Hotel in Nottingham. Dad was now so famous that even his driver, Midge, qualified for an in-depth interview in the *News of the World* Sunday magazine, which ran:

> But though Michael was destroying his life and his career he [Midge] says, 'It wasn't all bad. Often we'd go out for a few beers and have some great laughs together. We sit and chat about the things men like to talk about – such as politics, religion, sex. We had great times.'

The author was Rebekah Wade, later to become Rebekah Brooks.

You could buy *Boon* wallpaper now, and board-games and plastic toys, whatever was merchandisable. And then there was the execrable 'Gotcha', Dad's first and only, attack on the pop music charts. For someone who loved songs and singing, this croaky offering didn't do him justice. The whole recording was rather dubious. The cover of the disc showed the silhouette of the lower half of what looks like a young mini-skirted woman; to the side are the silhouettes of a couple of male hands reaching out to her. With lyrics like 'Look out for me, I'm behind that tree,' it was probably best that it was never performed in public. Some headlines at the time, intimated that Dad wasn't beyond the occasional miracle: 'Boon Saves Dying Fish – TV actor Michael Elphick yesterday saved thousands of fish from boiling alive. The star of *Boon* was filming at Newstead Abbey, near Mansfield, when he saw the fish dying as water evaporated from a pond. Firemen pumped the level back to normal.'

As a series finished, Dad would immediately involve himself again in film work. Ray Burdis from *Three Up, Two Down* had moved into film production, and his first film was the biopic *The Krays*, starring the Kemp brothers, Gary and Martin. Dad was very happy to accept a cameo role in that, and Ray said that his ex-screen father was now a transformed man and how wonderful it was to see that. However, one concerned newspaper reported, 'Michael's role in *The Krays* film has angered some of his fans, who don't believe it fits his lovable, easy-going Boon image. He reveals: "I appear in just one scene but I've already received letters complaining about it."'

Dad made another film at this time called *Buddy's Song*, in which he co-starred with Roger Daltrey, who produced it. Daltrey plays a reformed teddy-boy crook, whose son wants to become a rock-star. Dad plays a small-time villain called Des King, who has a knack of getting the Daltrey character into trouble. The boy was played by Chesney Hawkes, who I had a bit of a crush on at the time. Dad was particularly enamoured of a lovely, faux leopard-skin jacket that he had to wear for his part. He insisted that when the time came he should be buried in it. A third film, a little later, was *Let Him Have It*, the story of the trial of Derek Bentley. Dad played prison officer Jack, and Christopher Ecclestone had the leading role. My dad raved about this young actor and said that it was one of the finest performances that he had ever seen on film. He hated the part that he was playing:

> In this film I played the warder who spent his last hours with the condemned kid and I had to write his last letter home to his parents for him. Now, I have nothing against prison-warders in real life, or even this one in the film, who was quite compassionate, but I had a burning hatred of that character and everyone else who had any part in sending young Bentley to the gallows.

As the ubiquitous voice of a number of television series, Dad was also getting more and more voice-over work: B&Q, Nescafé and 'I Can't Believe It's Not Butter' were all given an Elphick nudge. It was becoming impossible not to hear his voice at some time during any given day. There was a lot of talk in interviews at this time about him being insured for a million pounds, mostly in terms of his past injuries and the prevention of future ones, through various forms of dare-devilry. Nevertheless, all his stunts, even the simple motor-bike riding, were undertaken by stunt men, principally his look-alike Scott Hammond. Insurance cover of this magnitude was actually required for any exigencies where the show could not proceed, and that I suspect had more to do with Dad's health and ability to fulfil his contract – what Liz, his later companion, referred to as 'the liver clause'. There was some talk that one Harley Street consultant, 'who had helped out Burton', could be relied upon to sign the appropriate papers. Luckily, no call was made for any such undertaking and Dad was around for all the future *Boon* series.

There was a troubling new development in the sort of parts that Dad was being touted for; at one time it was the 'hard case' that inevitably came to be viewed as ideal for him. But now his agent was being offered scripts, with parts underlined, that were either alcoholics or recovering alcoholics, as if life and art were indivisible. Central Television were responsible for Kingsley Amis's *Stanley and the Women*, in which Dad played a drunk. John Thaw was the 'Stanley' of the title and Dad played his best friend in this four-part series, 'The character is a top TV commercial-maker. The dialogue drives home forcibly why people like him drink. He simply can't cope with his success and wealth.' By way of relaxing, Dad took refuge in a totally undemanding television show with his great friend Don Henderson. He'd known Don for years as the two had often been chasing the same part and were sometimes mistaken for brothers. Don had guested on *Boon* and the two old friends had got together with actor-writers Gawn Grainger and Paul Angelis to set up a production company called AGHE Ltd. From this company was born *The Absolute Beginner's Guide to Cookery*. It was a simple enough format: two culinary ingénues choosing their ingredients, then setting about producing simple but interesting recipes, with a booklet available by post from the television company. It wasn't going to storm the ratings, but it was good fun for both of them and ran for twenty-six weeks. It was described as 'Morecambe and Wise with groceries'.

There was an item in *The Stage* at the time:

Michael Elphick has a rough-hewn but irresistible charm which has made his *Beginners Guide to Cookery* (a memorable pairing with Don Henderson) such good viewing and even enabled him to sail through those coffee commercials without grating the nerves. Now he has returned with a new series of *Boon,* as the private investigator with a tough exterior, but a very soft heart, and the format shows no sign of palling. One of the strengths of *Boon* is in its top-class casting. In this story, the fragrant Jenny Agutter wafted about, and in less time that it took to flutter her eyelashes at Boon, had uncovered the sentimental underside of the private investigator – a useful piece of character analysis for new viewers. Elphick looks very comfortable in the role of Boon, who never takes his job too seriously, frequently voicing philosophical doubts, but always staying the right side of parody. *Boon* has previously demonstrated its mass appeal; to the credit of all involved it never underestimates its audience.

It is no surprise when a series, as long-running as *Boon* was eventually, comes to an end. There were ninety-two episodes and a special, ninety-three in all. Every action hero has at some time to find a more comfortable way of solving life's problems than perpetually leaping onto a motorbike. What is great, in looking back, is realising how much pleasure the series gave viewers and thereafter how many people were able to let Dad know that. Looking at the old cuttings it's quite touching to come across this one from the *Sunday Express,* published a year after the one above, this time with a nice line in *mea culpa.* It refers to the penultimate series:

> There are only so many television programmes a human being can watch. At some point one just has to decide which series to be loyal to, and which to ignore. So, of the three great detective series on the air – *Morse, Taggart* and *Boon* – I have always been an admirer of the first two, while drawing a veil over the third. This, I have realised over the past couple of weeks, has been a major mistake. The first two episodes of the seventh series of *Boon* have both been excellent ... I can only apologise to Boon for having been so slow to recognise his many virtues.

As Dad was filming the final series he took time out for another project, which said much more than all the posed shots in health clubs could about his rehabilitation, and his sense of returning to his old self. Once again he found himself in *Hamlet*, his favourite play, with Kenneth Branagh in the title role, and a cast that included Richard Briers, Judi Dench, John Gielgud and Derek Jacobi – all members of the Renaissance Theatre. This time Dad was the grave-digger and the medium, for which age was immaterial, was radio. This prestige production for Radio Three presented quite new challenges for Dad: 'It's weird having somebody else actually wielding the spade for you, although I still have to mime the digging to match the words. You get right into the atmosphere with the chilling sound effects of the cawing crows.' Dad liked the idea of this man of the people having a total disregard for the importance of the nobility who wished to use his graveyard. In this backyard he was the boss and dictated who went where. Certainly, in the popular press, it was Dad, or rather, 'Boon', who was used to promote the play to a wider audience, and Dad was very pleased to oblige.

17

My Mum's Death

1994 was a very significant year for me: 'A' Levels over, I had just turned nineteen and I was travelling round Spain with three of my girlfriends: Sara, Rosie and Sam. We had a brilliant time with our little tent, having adventures from Alicante to Barcelona, which we loved and where we stayed for almost a month. When the time came to train it back to Alicante for the flight home, Rosie, Sam and I decided to spend our last few pounds on the overnight ferry to Ibiza. It was the beginning of the season and we figured it would be easy to find work. It was. We found jobs all at the same bar and had a most excellent summer. Having broken free from a horrible two-year relationship, exams behind me, and a university place secured for the autumn, the world felt like my playground. I was living away from home for the first time ever, and felt wonderfully free and incredibly happy. Luckily, I savoured every moment, as when I got back home in September, Mum's cancer had returned.

As a family we all put on our bravest faces, but typically didn't discuss what we were really thinking. Added to which, my cousin Louise, my Uncle Jim's daughter, had moved into our house with her son Harley, so it meant that even more people were not talking about it. Mum and I were very close because we had spent so much time together, just the two of us, but maybe because I had been a child for much of this, we never really spent a lot of time talking about the things that mattered to me when I was growing up. I used to feel sad sometimes that she only seemed to be interested in my studies and schoolwork. It was all courses and grades. I used to see my friends discussing boys and clothes with their parents. I guess Mum was just worried about my future, should she not be around. So we steered well clear of talking about our emotions, each trying to protect the other. On the other hand, Dad and I had become much more communicative. We found it easy to talk. So that Christmas he was in panto, as he was most Christmases; this year it was Bath. I thought that it was a good opportunity to discuss together what was going on at home: how Mum was and what proactive measures we could adopt, to help her. With my friend, Rosie, I stayed where my dad was staying, the beautiful Bath Spa Hotel. I was shocked at the time by the price of a room, £300 a night; actually, it still shocks me now and that was twenty years ago! Rosie and I loved Bath and couldn't wait to sample the nightlife after Ibiza. We were not disappointed. There were cool people, some great music and lots of quirky little bars. I was beginning to understand the pull of the nightlife for my father and this weekend I shared my first proper night out with him. I don't know who found it the most strange.

The panto that year at Bath's Theatre Royal was *Aladdin*, with Dad playing the evil Fleshcreep. As always it was great fun and even at the age of nineteen I was drawn into the magic, thoroughly enjoying myself and giving out a great cheer, when amongst the children's names shouted out by the cast, for special mention at the end, mine was included. Going backstage always gave me a buzz, and this was no exception; there were the performers, full of adrenaline, discussing the evening's performance and greeting family members, while removing the make-up and glitter from their faces. We waited for Dad to change and then, with a large group of cast, crew, dancers and the ubiquitous hangers-on, we headed off to a local club. Dad had managed to get a private room for our party, with weird glass walls and funky plastic furniture. As the night progressed, we moved outside the room into the general club area, so that Dad could position himself in his favourite stance, parked up at the bar. Rosie and I took the opportunity to join the dancing, with me occasionally feeling the need to go and have a good glower at any young woman who presumed to insinuate herself next to him.

We had a great time but it was all rather surreal in the circumstances. Dad left before us, with a backward call to indicate that the party was going to continue at our hotel. Rosie and I danced almost till we dropped and then a very charming young cast-member drove us back to the Bath Spa Hotel. We were ill-prepared for the embarrassing scene awaiting us. When I arrived in the reception area, I asked to be directed to Mr Elphick's room. My request was treated with downright rudeness:

'Mr Elphick is not receiving any visitors.'

'I'm sorry, but I am his daughter.'

There was a look of even greater intransigence, with arched eyebrows and a totally unsmiling face:

'I have to tell you that Mr Elphick arrived here, about half an hour ago *in the company of his daughter!*' This last rounded off with an air of triumphalism.

'I am his daughter,' I said, 'and I'd like you to tell him that I am here!' The possibility that Dad might have two daughters suddenly occurred to the gate-keeper and he was duly rung. Crimson-faced, the poor receptionist apologised and said that there had been a mistake. At the time I never questioned what had happened, and when Dad joined us downstairs at the bar, alone, I had no reason to delve deeper. By this time, I was quite merry, and decided to roll a joint as I had been in the habit of doing while living in Ibiza. Dad couldn't have looked more surprised. This made me laugh, which in turn made him laugh. He rolled his eyes. We had become very close in our own way, but we were never going to have the typical father-daughter relationship. I don't think he ever told me off as a child, any disciplining being Mum's province; he wasn't going to start now. We ended up crying together about Mum's cancer, but we never realised at this stage that this was a battle that she was about to lose.

As Mum's cancer returned this final time, she was not able to overcome its evil hold. As the realisation that she was not going to recover sank in, my behaviour began to change. Not consciously, but when I look back on that time now, I can see with the advantage of hindsight, just how much it affected me. The start of 1995 was a particularly bad one for me. As well as the fact that my beautiful mum was terminally ill, I had boyfriend troubles, health problems of my own, was not feeling particularly motivated at university and was desperately worried about both parents. Poor Dad was of course also battling with the prospect of having cancer looming over us all once more. He was having a miserable time filming *Harry* and getting lots of bad press. I remember him doing some promotional work for the series at this time and ending up on the *Big Breakfast Bed* for an interview with Paula Yates, whom he would end up in the Priory clinic with in some years to come.

As the year developed it was obvious I was not coping well: my studies were slipping, I was working late in various pubs most nights, and partying after work in any hours that remained. This amounted to me sleeping very little, eating very little and generally feeling very agitated most of the time. My mood swings were dramatic and usually Mum bore the brunt of them and I hated myself for taking them out on her when she needed me most. I was drinking lots, vodka mostly. I had my Ibiza training to thank for my capacity to drink more than most people twice my age or size! I was also taking drugs regularly; I was hardly ever home. As my first year at university came to an end, I knew it was the wrong thing to do, but as soon as I could I jumped on the first flight away from London straight back to where I had been happiest, Ibiza. Bless Mum, she seemed to understand. We never talked about her cancer other than what a doctor had told her at her most recent consultation. We never discussed what would happen, how we felt, how scared and sad we were. I felt useless, helpless, and so I left. I was away until my course started again, it must have been between three and four months I guess. I feel so terribly guilty when I think about it now.

Elizabeth broke my heart when she told me after Mum died that she had waited and waited for my calls, which never came. She was asking her friend why I didn't get in touch, saying she wished that I would. I did keep meaning to, but this was before the days of mobile phones, and finding a working phone box within walking distance at a time of day that was appropriate to call was not that easy there. Of course, any observer could see that I had put it all to the back of my mind, totally in denial that my mum might not be around for much longer and that, really, I should be spending this precious time with her. Also, I was working hard on the island, seven days a week and this, I'm sure, was doing me good in getting my head round the unimaginable. Once I got back I needed to be strong. Mum started having treatment that autumn and then she really did need me. I bucked up my ideas and stepped into the role of carer the best I could. The anti-cancer drugs made her feel horrendous and she was unable physically to do very much at all.

People told me after Mum died, how they were all so impressed by my strength and loving care of her at this time; I did what I could, but I will always wish that I had done more and said more. I went back to uni, dog-walked, food-shopped, cooked as best I could and tried to keep the place organised at home. I would bring up drinks of whatever she felt she could manage, fluffing up her pillows and making the bed nice whenever she got up and struggled over to the bathroom. Her friends rallied round and often came for visits, bringing food and welcome, cheerful conversation. My parents' friends Dick and Leni lived around the corner and were particularly wonderful. Leni had met Dad way back at Central; they had been great friends since my first memories and a constant in my life as I grew up. They had a son and a daughter and had moved to Willesden Green around the same time as we did. We children always seemed to be at either our house or theirs. Leni prepared little individual home-cooked dishes for Mum that I could take out for her and heat up at meal times. Dick drove Mum to the hospital for her treatments. Although I had recently passed my test, the responsibility of driving my frail, nauseous Mum through the London traffic to Charing Cross Hospital was just too much for me and I began to experience panic attacks behind the wheel. I never took up driving again. At Mum's funeral, Dick read out a poem that he'd written about this time:

TAKING JULIA TO RADIOTHERAPY

Strangers were sighted sliding through the corridors,
searchlights are being triggered along your bones
and here you are, Jules. Nausea grabs
at your throat. You are folded, snail-like, in its fist.
White-coated mercenaries slam through the double doors.

And we're thinking: to hell, we're human, we can bear
This wait with you, by you, till whatever end.
But so difficult is your hair,
the freckly lip, this dish-shine on your hands –
where is that shielded room, out of the glare?

You vanish, waving in the rear-view mirror.
At last I reach for the radio. I was not able
to touch it, when driving you here, out of dread
that something might get in that might not stop,
and might not have you much in its heart, or share
our lumping wish to see you emerge through rain
dog-damp, leafy in the afternoon,
pulling towards us in a tatty cardigan,

Which may be what will happen.
No need to worry – we even sketch a plan
Of how we will laugh about it when you are free.
Things will slip back, out of sight, the usual way,
All battered down again, good they found it quickly,
Lucky this time,
The Ode to Joy
Is darkly optimistic on Radio 3.

Mum went into hospital to have a nasty cough checked out. She never came out. That day was Friday 1 March 1995. Her cough developed into pneumonia and she died two weeks later after fighting hard, on 15 March. We had all spent most of the time with her in shifts. My Aunty Sue came to London, and her friends would turn up to see her, although often she would send them away. I don't think she wanted them to see her like that. I often slept there. Poor Dad was working but came when he could. My heart went out to him as, on top of trying to cope with all this, through the last months he had been touring with a play called *It Can Damage Your Health*, which was set on a cancer ward. Mum's two weeks in the hospital were just awful. As the infection took hold she needed this appalling contraption, secured around her face, to enable her to breathe. I learnt how to adjust it, but if it was not fitted just right she would struggle. It would be removed, if she needed to eat or drink but again, if it was not put back on quickly, she would make this desperate rasping noise from her throat, as she fought for breath, which terrified me.

Her face was swollen and her hair almost all gone. On one of the days, a nurse asked me if I had come to visit my granny. The next day I brought in from home some quite recent photographs of Mum, her auburn curls flowing and green eyes bright and sparkling, as she smiled at the camera. When she saw them the nurse gasped and began to cry, which really touched me. The day she died I had entered her room after going for a coffee and I knew something had changed. I called the nurse who confirmed that she was taking her last breaths. I fled. Elizabeth went in with her and held her hand as she passed but I just had to get out of there. All I could think of was that I didn't want to watch Mum die, to have that image stay with me, and haunt me, so I just left. I passed Leni in the corridor and blurted out what was happening. I think she gave me money to get in a cab. I just wanted to get away as quickly as possible.

18

The Great Pretender

Life after *Boon?* There really was *no* life after *Boon*. Just as I was going to be Boon's daughter, Dad would always be Boon in the public's eye, at least on television. Of course, he had taken stage roles while the series was running, and found, as indeed the producers hoped, that the one did not detract from the other, but rather promoted it. But television roles were different. Even in previews of Dad's guest appearances in other series, the papers would refer to '*Boon* actor, Michael Elphick', or sometimes something of the order of, '*Boon* appears tonight in ...' Time had to pass and sadly Dad's appearance had to change drastically before he could shed the handle. All of this meant that when eventually *Boon* did come to an end, the public were still expecting more of the same, and unfortunately, *Harry* was not that. *Harry,* which was to be the big Saturday night flagship of the BBC autumn schedules for 1993, was never going to fulfil that promise either.

The series was given prominent promotion: Dad was everywhere putting his best foot forward. I think there had been so much stuff over the preceding years about his battle with alcoholism that a character who had virtually lost his battle with it came a little too close for comfort for those looking for relaxing weekend viewing. There were quite a few complaints also about the string of profanities with which the first episode had started. The other problem was that the main character was a journalist. Intentionally sometimes, and many times unintentionally, over the years, Dad had pointed out his ongoing problems with the press: 'If my daughter, Kate, becomes a journalist, I'm going to have to lock her out of the house!' The public's perception, then, before they saw the first programme, was here was a man unhappily playing a character, whose profession and lifestyle was an anathema to him. Added to which, of course, a backlog of *Boon* episodes were still to be aired on the other side. Dad brought his usual strong characterisation to the part. 'Thanks, however,' said the reviewer Maureen Paton, 'to the plug-ugly Elphick's forceful charm – plus the moodily filmed first episode – Harry came across as a highly dramatic and extremely improbable cross between the hoaxer Rocky Ryan and the campaigner Paul Foot ... with a touch of Raymond Chandler's disillusioned knight-errant Philip Marlowe.'

But *Harry* did not get off to the best start in the ratings race. On its first night it brought in less than half of the nearly 14 million viewers glued to *Casualty,* the programme that preceded it. The BBC had made a considerable investment in the programme of £6 million: '*Harry* is a new drama and it takes time to settle down,' said a spokesman, 'After twelve weeks audiences steadied at five million. We're not about to give up. It's only by sticking with them that popularity grows.' The character was based on an actual reporter, John Merry, who ran a news agency in Darlington. Described as '18 stone, 100 fags a day', John took great pride in being, in his words, 'just an old-fashioned journalist. I met Mike Elphick.' John said. 'He came up and chatted for about ten minutes.' To play a living person is usually a challenge too far, but Dad and his director had decided to develop the character in ways that were different from the original. One way was that Dad was now bespectacled – he was never going to surrender to the vanity of contact lenses anyway – so every character he now played resembled Inspector Cleaver of *Vampire Motorcycle* fame.

Whatever his appearance, the second series of *Harry* did even worse than the first. The *Sun* said:

> Any show that chooses to take place almost entirely in Darlington in the dark is likely to have problems grabbing an audience. This ridiculous drama is more likely to have people grabbing their coats and rushing out to the pub if they are subjected to more than a minute or two. Michael Elphick is a marvellous actor but you would never guess it from his performance as a preposterous freelance journalist floundering helplessly in a half-baked plot.

Esta Charkham found herself with a small cameo in *Harry*, playing the Editor of *Hello* magazine:

> I met Mike in the hotel. We greeted each other so warmly. I was pleased that the crisis days of *Boon* seemed more or less forgotten. We arranged to meet the next day, but he never came near me. I think that he knew that I'd found out that he was drinking again.

A lovely diversion was joining 'Rocky', or rather Neil, again, in a film that they were both instrumental in financing. This was *The Ballad of Kid Divine: The Cockney Cowboy*, a low-budget spaghetti Western in which Dad played a travelling quack peddling patent medicines. Neil's future stablemate in *Men Behaving Badly*, Martin Clunes, was in it, and it starred Jesse Birdsall. The whole film was shot in about three weeks outside Monte Cassino, using the villa of the director, George Rossi, as a base. Neil says that the fifty-minute film was about as shoe-string a production that anyone could conceive, and even made the *Vampire Motorcycle* seem well funded. However, everyone had a great time and someone somewhere probably saw the film. Similarly, Dad's next filmic enterprise was one of his more bizarre undertakings. The great director and *enfant terrible*, Ken Russell, had turned in his latter years into a terrible director. He had decided to make a made-for-television version of *Treasure Island*, as a musical, and starring his wife at the time, Hetty Baines, as Long Jane Silver. Probably in consideration of the sensibilities of Robert Louis Stevenson, who would be revolving in his grave, it was called *Ken Russell's Treasure Island*. Russell apparently, told his wife that he would commit suicide if she didn't appear in it, and she, for some reason, said (the story goes) that she would only appear in it if Dad did too. So Dad duly appeared as Billy Bones, the provider of the secret map. When it came out, he was heavily disguised as Fleshcreep in Southampton.

From October 1995 until April 1996, Dad was virtually on the road all the time, apart from the break to do the pantomime at Southampton. He was on tour in the play *It Can Damage Your Health* by Eric Chappell, a spin-off from the successful television series *Only When I Laugh*. Like the series, it is set in a hospital ward, where three male patients, the medical know-all, the young ingénue and the hypochondriac, idle away their time irritating the staff. It was a punishing tour: Bromley, Chichester, Eastbourne, Bath, Stevenage, Crewe, Windsor and Sheffield. Ironically, Dad's health was beginning to suffer as, after years of self-abuse, he had succumbed to diabetes. The tragedy, however, was being enacted back home in Willesden Green. Mum had to go in to hospital for the final time. Dad relied on the understudy on a couple of occasions but basically, on non-matinee days, he would visit the hospital in the morning and return to the hospital set for the evening, depending on the distance from London. It was, sadly, when he was playing the Theatre Royal Bath that the inevitable happened. He took on no new commitments for the rest of that year. 'I had already cancelled a few tellies, but I should have given us more time together,' he told an interviewer:

> When I saw her that morning, she was on a respirator. Just in a terrible state. Our daughter, Kate, had slept in the hospital room with her for a week. When I was on the motorway on the way to the theatre, she rang to say that Julia had died. I had to do this *comedy* in a cancer ward, having just come from watching her die. Not easy.

There's a very poignant picture taken in the *Express on Sunday* magazine, of Dad sitting on a backstage props basket in December of that year at the Civic Theatre, Darlington. He has just finished the last dress rehearsal of *Jack and the Beanstalk* with the White Power Ranger and the Grumbleweeds. He's been talking about Mum:

> I was very upset when she died. That's all there was to it. Now it's the panto season. I love the response from all the kids and mums and dads. I play the giant's main man and frighten all the kids. We've only got ten days to rehearse and I've got all these rhyming couplets to learn. The Grumbleweeds keep changing all the dialogue, but they've been doing it for years and they have this kind of telepathy between them. I'm usually knackered doing two performances a day, and as we don't finish until 10.30 or 10.45, by the time you get in the pub, you're being chased out because of the stupid English licensing laws. So we go to a restaurant and have a bottle of wine.

A night out in Darlington must have resonated a bit. About this time he was visiting his old friend Oliver 'Smudger' Smith, whom Dad had been responsible for securing a long-term part as the barman in *Boon*. Smudger says that they went to his local which was suddenly invaded by a coach-load of Welsh rugby fans. 'They took one look at Mike and then they all started to sing the *Boon* theme so tunefully and beautifully. I turned to him and the tears were rolling from his eyes.'

Television was beginning to evaporate or at least Dad wasn't pitching for it. He had a guest appearance in *Dangerfield* and also a play called *The Fix*, which was well-reviewed, but had its screening delayed because it dealt with match-fixing in the world of professional football, at a time when a specific case was going through the courts. Central-casting had now designated Dad as a sober journalist whose job it was to get to the bottom of *The Fix*:

> While I was away filming *The Fix* in Sheffield with Steve Coogan, Kate reorganised the whole house. She realised I wouldn't want to sleep in the bedroom I'd shared with Julia. She moved the bed down to my den. So I live in a sort of granny flat on the ground floor and she and her fellow live upstairs. She sorted it all out without even asking. Wonderful.

I think he was very pleased not to be working so hard, driven on by whatever fears he'd entertained over the years. He could still pick and choose: a peach of a part, playing Barkis to Pauline Quirk's Peggotty in *David Copperfield*, where his voice was made for 'Barkis is willin''.

Peter Crouch called to say he'd been offered the part of Doolittle, starting out at Windsor, then moving to The Albery in the West End. Dad said that he was so looking forward to being in a musical. He could have saved his breath. It was Shaw's *Pygmalion* not *My Fair Lady*. By all accounts, perhaps it should have been the latter. By the time it reached The Albery, Eliza, Emily Lloyd had left the company, and it was on its third director, Ray Cooney. The frustrated tunesmith, Dad, was given some glowing reviews, but the other tele-star, Roy Marsden, as Higgins, got less-than-glowing affirmations and the poor girl who'd come straight from RADA to play Eliza, with minimal rehearsals, as Nicholas de Jongh said, 'must have left romantics hoping she would achieve the 42nd Street trick and end her first night as the theatre's latest twinkler. Sadly it was not to be.'

Then Dad was asked to tour again. He wasn't sure, but it was going to be a Chichester Festival Theatre production, in conjunction with the Yvonne Arnaud at Guildford. There was something about returning to his roots (Gran and I went to see him in Chichester), and also the play was to be Joe Orton's *Loot*, which he loved. He met Joe Orton years before in Soho, when he was a young actor, just starting out. It could have been at the Colony Club or some such place. They were introduced by Jeffrey Bernard, who seemed to know everyone in those days. His co-star in *Loot* was Letitia Dean, who had made her name in *Eastenders*. Again, it was quite a punishing undertaking: eighteen weeks in as many theatres. Letitia fell ill at one point and I think Dad began to find it hard-going himself. He followed it up at Chichester with Jeffrey Archer's *The Perfect Murder*, which may have been the final straw. In interviews, he returned again and again to the subject of the loneliness of the long-distance actor and the unwelcoming hotel room, with the ever-present temptation of alcohol. How much better to be out in Portugal or with his little family in Willesden Green! He had also linked up with Liz Summers, who he'd first met in *Boon*, and the pair really enjoyed each other's company. I felt that it was alright to leave him now for an extended holiday.

Dad was getting the odd voice-over now, but not much else. Paul Knight, who hadn't seen him since producing him in *Holding On* all those years before, met him in one of their old drinking haunts from way-back-when:

> I was quite taken aback by how much he'd aged. We all had, but the fates appeared to be particularly unkind to him. He was shaking his head ruefully, regretting the fact that he'd just broken a tooth, and whistled when he spoke, thus preventing him from doing the voice-over that he was scheduled to do that afternoon. I cheered him up by telling him that many years before, Esta Charkham and I had thought about opening a wine-bar called 'Elphicks', but that probably common-sense prevailed.

Dad got home that night and Peter Crouch had called again. Dad had been offered a part on *Eastenders*. He wasn't sure, but he thought it could be Peggy Mitchell's 'love interest'. I think Dad told as many people as he could, including, I'm sure, a few journalists. When he found out in due course what the actual part entailed, he was horrified. He knew as anyone would that a storyline about a paedophile was bound to be short, as would be the contract, but obviously that was the least of his concerns. In the autumn of your acting years to be playing a part like that seemed totally unacceptable. Later all the talk that followed about his contract being foreshortened because of drunkenness on set could not be further from the truth. He never was. He drank a lot in the BBC bar and at home in Willesden Green, but never when he was working. When he next saw Liz he was in a terrible state. How could he play a part like that? Then again, how couldn't he? He was a professional actor. He kept changing his mind. He had given his life to his craft, often to the detriment of everything else in his life. He had to do it, if it was the last thing he did.

19

Be Lucky

Mum died on the Friday before Mother's day, which fell on Sunday 17 March that year. During the next few weeks I was also to 'celebrate' my 21st birthday. Dad, being his usual generous self, wanted to make sure it would be a birthday for me to remember. He paid for me to hire the cosy Bunker Bar by Bagleys, the London club where my friends and I chose to spend most Saturday nights. He made me laugh; he really didn't know one nightclub from another and kept boasting to his friends that he'd hired me the Camden Palace! This was substantially bigger, with a capacity of about 2,500, which would have bankrupted us! He also paid for the hire of a limousine to collect eight of us and take us for drinks in the West End, before we headed to the club. Everybody made a huge fuss of me, not just because it was my birthday, as you can imagine; but I did really enjoy my birthday, as my mum would have wanted me to do.

Being April, I had the Easter holidays off from university. Dad, again wanting to make my life as joyful as he could, helped financially, to enable six of us to go out to Portugal for a break; three boys and three girls. It was that holiday that taught me how grief can creep up on you. I felt as if I was being very strong, not giving way to tears and plastering on a smile for the world. However, the rug had been pulled out from under me: the unthinkable had happened. Subconsciously I'm sure I felt that if that can happen, anything can. Also, I started to doubt my friendships: *the* most important part of my life. It took me a long time to realise that my friends just didn't know how to behave. Should they breezily ignore the elephant in the room and pretend nothing had happened, or should they recognise my loss, and then be in danger of dragging me down further? Later, my lovely friend Felix confided:

We didn't know how to be. None of us knew what you were going through. Your mum is probably the closest person to me who's ever died. You seemed to be coping so well. We didn't want to rock the boat, to upset you. Every time you left the room we would all discuss how we thought you were, and what we could do for you. We wanted to be there for you.

I felt stupid then. I knew how much my friends loved me. It was all down to me; I had isolated myself mentally. I wondered who Dad was able to speak to and if he felt the same. The words of 'The Great Pretender' came to mind.

I returned to university but I had no energy or interest. I skipped lectures, fell behind with assignments and inevitably felt control and personal responsibility slipping away. There was no one at home to chivvy me – and, indeed, there was no one at home inside me. I somehow was missing. There was a sense of not waving, but drowning, as the poet Stevie Smith had said forty years before. Fortunately, my tutors were able to recognise the symptoms of bereavement and suggested a year's compassionate leave. I sold my Mum's burgundy Golf car, having developed that driving phobia during her illness, and spent the money so I could go back to Ibiza.

At the start of 1997, back in North London, Dad, unusually, was at home. He called me into the living room and gestured for me to sit down. Something told me not to speak, and I waited for him to begin, 'I've been doing a lot of thinking, Kate. My 50th birthday is coming up, in September ...' I wondered if he was going to suggest a party, '... and I feel as though I've had a good life. I've made a decision – hear me out – which I've come to over some considerable time. On my birthday, I am going to kill myself.' Before I could draw breath, he continued, 'I have a gun, and that's what I intend to do. It will be far better for you. You'll be sad, but you'll get over it – and you'll have the house in Portugal and the land, this ...' and he swept his arm around the room expansively, like an enthusiastic estate agent, '... property. You'll be well taken care of.' He nodded, encouragingly, convinced, I'm quite sure, that he had done enough to persuade me of his unassailable logic.

I should have gone to him and put my arms round him. I should have reassured him that I couldn't possibly bear to lose him. I could have, for a moment, stopped thinking of myself, and spent a minute or two imagining what it was like to be him, and what had brought him to this dark conclusion. But, of course, I did none of those things. I shot to my feet and glared down at him. What kind of reaction was he seriously expecting from this audience? Gratitude? I'd just lost my mum and now my remaining parent was calmly informing me that he was planning on leaving me orphaned in a few months.

'If you think I'd rather have property than my father alive then you obviously don't think very much of me as a person.' I hissed. I turned round and walked to the door, controlling my rage. How selfish he was. And before I disappeared, I flung one more parting shot in his direction, this time delivered in a sort of strangled shriek: 'Go on then – DO IT!'

We didn't speak of it again. But that summer, in Ibiza, the story appeared in one of the tabloids – Michael Elphick's planned suicide had provided colourful fodder for its readers. Needless to say I made pretty sure that I was back in Blighty by Dad's birthday on 19 September and was determined not to let him out of my sight all day. The plan was to go and see Clive Dunn's daughter Jessica's art exhibition at the Princess Arcade, Piccadilly, then onto the Albery

Theatre to watch Dad in *Pygmalion*. My boyfriend at the time, Sean, lived at our house and got on very well with Dad. He accompanied us, sticking to his side like glue as we kept him out of the house and surrounded by people. I am quite sure that the likelihood of the role of Alfred Doolittle having to be taken by an understudy was remote – but we gave him no opportunity to carry out his threat.

Dad was outstanding as Eliza's father, and I was buzzing with pride. The magical atmosphere created by the energy there, by the building, the make-up and costume, created a world of fantasy for us all; it was a welcome escape. When we got to Dad's dressing room Neil Morrissey was already there. The two of them laughed so easily together, over a drink, as Dad took off his make-up. The performance had left a real sparkle in his eyes. We four made our way through the hubbub of the West End, over to the renowned Gerry's Club. Dad seemed so at home in the bustle of the area, walking confidently through the streets that he obviously knew like the back of his hand. Our little party arrived at Gerry's, where again, I could see how totally at ease my father was. Greeting everyone as if they were family, he soon had everyone engaged and laughing.

My dad was in his element, relaxed and entertaining his friends. Everywhere he went people liked him enormously and this evening everyone made a huge fuss of him for his birthday. This was the night that I met Liz for the first time. I knew she was his girlfriend and I was pleased that he had found someone. It was comforting to me that there was someone else to look out for him and care for him. He had so far managed to keep us apart. He had his reasons: being the astute man he was he had realised that letting us join forces could mean a powerful amount of nagging against his drinking and other health issues. He was right. By the end of the night we had discreetly exchanged numbers; we would meet in the near future to work out how to confront his alcoholism. What a relief it was to share a view, talk to a sympathetic friend; we could together come to the same conclusion. Something needed to be done, and now.

Liz and I spoke often over the following weeks and developed a friendship which is still strong today. We contacted The Priory, Roehampton, and organised a consultation for Dad. We now just had to get him there.

On the corner of Station Parade in Willesden Green, a stone's throw from Sparkles, was a wonderful Greek restaurant. The building had a huge glass front facing out to the street, opposite the Tube. Greek food was pretty much our favourite food so it was easy for Liz to persuade him that the two of them should go in for a nice lunch. Our ingenious plan was that I would coincidently stroll past while they were there, and feigning surprise, pop in to join them. Faced with an array of mouth-watering meze, he would be less likely, we thought, to walk out, and readier to listen, than if we'd tackled him in a bar.

He seemed to accept my surprise appearance and, after the usual niceties, we admitted that we'd been in regular contact because we were worried about him. The crux of our conversation was that we wanted him to attend a meeting just 'to have a chat' with someone at The Priory; and, by the way, could it be the following morning? Understandably he was pretty cross. He felt we had been sneaky and underhand and ganged up on him. Well, we had; but his grumpiness was shortlived, even if he was a bit sullen for the rest of our lunch. 'It's just a talk,' we assured him.

'I'll think about it,' he grumbled. He must have realised that our intentions were good because by mid-morning the next day, the three of us were in the taxi.

Dad went into a room while Liz and I sat in apprehensive silence, waiting with hope that this man could convince Dad that he needed treatment. I wasn't very hopeful, knowing Dad's reluctance to face the fact that he had a problem and having witnessed before how he would brush away the idea of needing help. After what seemed an age, Dad emerged, a deflated, resigned expression on his face. 'He's staying,' the doctor informed us. It took a moment for those words to sink in. Liz actually went over and kissed the poor man, as if he had performed a miracle. After an emotional goodbye, just the two of us got in the taxi home, both feeling more positive about things than we had for months.

We couldn't go and see him for a few days as he would be under heavy sedation, but we could come for a visit and bring in his things after that. It wasn't going to be cheap; probably about £300 a day not including therapies. For him to stay the required length of time it was going to cost me my mum's inheritance money, over £12,000. But it would be worth every penny I had in the world if it would make him well again.

I liked the journey by train to Roehampton and went there as often as I could during the following couple of months. It was a lovely place to spend the afternoon, more like a beautiful hotel really. Dad said the food was great; he had a comfortable room and on a sunny day, there would often be a game of rounders or some such fun on the lawn, with visitors joining in. I worried it was all a bit *too* comfortable in fact. I hated the group therapy sessions. The therapists would encourage me to be hard on Dad, telling me it was essential I made him realise all the negative effects his drinking had had on me ... but I couldn't do it. Perhaps if it had just been the two of us, it would have been different, but I felt all eyes were always on Dad – I was not about to abuse him, embarrass and hurt him in front of strangers, especially as he was a really recognisable face in the group. Looking back, I probably should have done as I was told, but I'd always felt so protective of my gentle father. I explained to the group that I had always understood my dad's addiction was an illness and I didn't blame him. I don't think the therapists were very impressed. There were two other 'names' in the Priory with Dad at that time. One was *The Royle Family's* Caroline Aherne, whom Dad befriended and whom I liked very much. The other was Paula Yates, whom I saw but never spoke to. Dad spoke about her sympathetically; I could see he felt very sorry for her. She looked lost and sad, nothing like the sexy, plucky, young presenter who had interviewed him all those years before.

Liz and I would joke about the fact that Dad almost immediately claimed a chair in the TV room there. It was a running joke that this would happen whenever Dad spent a significant amount of time anywhere. In Sparkles everyone knew 'Mike's chair' and always left it free for him. It was the same in his favourite Boliqueime bar in Portugal, the Fantasia. Of course at home he had 'his' chair and now he'd adopted one for himself here, in his temporary living space. Before long Dad's skin was smooth and healthy looking: a normal complexion returned thanks to the high quantities of vitamins he was taking each day, replacing alcohol. The weight was falling off him and his eyes, now clear, resumed their twinkle. He looked and sounded great. It was wonderful to have my sober dad back. He remained 'on the wagon' for two months.

In the September of 1998 I found out that I was pregnant. At that time, Dad was living something of a 'normal' life. He was working sporadically – his very obvious ill health limiting casting opportunities. He would go to bed at a reasonable time – around eleven – and get up at the start of the day. He'd sit in the living room with a coffee and a cigarette, French doors open (weather permitting), and look over lines or open mail. The news, always on in the background, kept him in touch with the world. He'd get dressed and head up the road. I cherished these morning times. Sparkles opened at midday. Late afternoon, he'd amble home after stopping at 'Sunrise', the supermarket, and sometimes the fish-and-chip shop, walking slowly, round-shouldered, a blue carrier bag in each hand.

Liz would come round later, after work, and they'd cook together, watch TV, or pop out for dinner or a drink. I liked to see them doing what regular couples do, something that he and Mum had not done when I was growing up. They had made local friends – mainly the Sparkles crowd – who were invited round, even spending Christmas Day with us, one year. I was seeing a new side of Dad.

Having Liz around meant that I had some support looking after Dad, so Sean and I decided to do some travelling. We booked a round-the-world ticket, including stops in Africa and the Himalayas. We bought rucksacks and mosquito nets, had the necessary jabs and were ready to go. I was ignoring the growing nausea, which seemed to last throughout the day. But the inevitable was confirmed: I was pregnant. Shocked and pleased in equal measures, we cancelled the trip, but vowed to visit the places that we could take a baby to in the future. Dad was excited. Liz was too, although she playfully threatened that 'If anyone refers to me as Granny, there'll be trouble.'

My early pregnancy was problematic – sickness, lethargy, depression and dehydration prevented me from moving far from the sofa. Everyone rallied round, conscious, I'm sure, that I was missing my mother's support. After three months, I began to feel better, and we were able to go to Portugal for a pre-baby holiday. Precious times. Dad took Sean and me for lunch one day, to his favourite restaurant on the beach. I was still picking at my food – trying to avoid the last traces of the omnipresent nausea. We went off by taxi to Olhos d'Agua. Hidden from the road, it nestles in a little, deserted cove, with beautiful views of the sea. As I sat there, relaxed, the sun on my face, watching the water sparkling and breathing in the salty sea air, I was suddenly starving. For the first time in months, I was really hungry. Dad ordered his usual prawns; I plumped for calamari. The waiter asked '*Quanto lula senhor?*' and my dad said, predictably, 'All of it!' and so, of course, I was faced with a huge sea creature occupying a whole huge plate, its tentacles spread, fan-like over the edge. Sean and Dad looked apprehensively from the squid to my face, waiting for the usual response of revulsion. It was delicious; I slowly and steadily devoured the lot. To this day I can recreate its flavour and texture. Divine.

Dad did what he always did with the prawns' heads after he'd eaten the bodies. He created finger puppets, which performed a sketch, their little prawny faces peeking out above the table. I'd seen it several times since he'd first done it years ago, for the benefit of my 13-year-old self. My mother would always roll her eyes in a kind of 'not again' way. But Sean, watching the act for the first time, was an enthusiastic audience. He laughed delightedly and Dad relished the response.

We were to return to Portugal one last time, as a family. Jasmine Julia Elphick-Ross had joined us and Sean, Liz, Dad and I took her to the villa and showed her Dad's home from home.

Back in London, Dad loved being a granddad and a 'family' man, at last. He'd look after Jasmine, who was soon to call him 'Poppy' at his own request – it was what he and Robin had called their own granddad. The name stuck and he became 'Poppy' to everyone. He and I were probably the closest we've ever been during those last few years.

Over-ordering fish was to be repeated – spectacularly. I was upstairs in our living-room in Willesden one afternoon – its window overlooked the road. The doorbell rang and I stuck my head out of the window. A cheeky young face grinned up at me: 'Do you want any fish, love?'

'Hang on a sec – I'll ask my Dad.'

I went downstairs and asked Dad and Liz, both big fish eaters, what they would like. 'Salmon, haddock, trout, prawns ...?'

'Yes' said Dad.

'Well which, then? What shall I buy?'

'All of it' he replied, never taking his eyes off the news. He was serious. The lad unloaded his van. We filled our freezer, our next-door neighbour's freezer and spent the next hour ringing round the friends to find space in theirs.

We lived on fish for some time. Liz made a mean fish pie, and Dad would make his favourite – grilled rainbow trout. How sad that all this healthy eating was unable to undo the vicious damage that would kill him.

In the autumn of 2000, when Jasmine was one-and-a-half, Sean and I were ready to set off on our travels. Our little blonde daughter accompanied us across Australia for nine months, then on to Thailand. We were living on the very beautiful and, at that time, remote beach of Thong Nai Pan when, after a night out with friends at a full-moon party, Sean was drugged and robbed. Someone had spiked his drink, and when friends eventually brought him back to our beach, he was disoriented and confused. He had lost everything. We had a bag containing bank cards in storage on Samui, and we immediately set off there, intending to ask Dad to wire us some money. The boat journey was a nightmare. Halfway across to the island, a storm hit. Two-metre waves rocked the boat and the noise of the wind and rain was deafening. There was no cover on the top deck, and we huddled together in the centre, clutching our bags and each other for support. Leaving me to throw up violently over the side, Sean staggered below deck, carrying Jasmine to some sort of shelter, only to be faced by a raging fire. The engine had caught alight, and the crew were battling to control flames as tall as themselves. Sean wheeled around and struggled back to the sodden, gale-ridden upper deck.

By the time we finally got to Samui and had our feet on terra firma, I was traumatised. Still nauseous and unable to walk without swaying from side to side, we carried Jasmine to the nearest café to call Dad and gather our wits. He responded instantly and calmly – he would wire the money forthwith. He interrupted my emotional thanks with, 'Oh, by the way, I've bagged myself a part in *Eastenders!*' The trauma of the day instantly left me, and I shrieked with delight. *Eastenders*! My favourite soap! And this would surely provide Dad with guaranteed work, routine and security. He would be able to work towards regaining his health, maybe drop some weight, and recreate some of the old charm, as Peggy Mitchell's love interest. It was the best news.

*   *   *

Epilogue

I wake up in Robin and Janie's house in Bognor. My uncle is cooking breakfast and the smell of bacon wakes me. My uncle, Dad's brother, is cooking breakfast on a Sunday morning, just like Dad did. I smile into my duvet. I flew into Southampton from France yesterday and will later fly home to Faro. The book deadline is ten days away now and my part is done, bar this epilogue. Over the last year, I have had stirred up many recollections from the past. However, our two-day trip away in France has brought strongly to the forefront of my mind more memories of both my parents. Firstly, just being back in France – hearing the hum of the French accent everywhere, the strings of sweets for sale in the tobacconists, even the atmosphere – reminds me of being a child on our annual holidays years ago. Just being there again, I can hear Mum talking in a language I couldn't understand, smiling, holding my hand, spending all day on the beach and in the dunes.

We were there to speak with Neil Morrissey. He and his lovely girlfriend have been the perfect hosts, picking us up from the airport, cooking for us and making us laugh. We talked for hours. Neil's memory is excellent and I revel in hearing new stories about 'Elphisms'. He completely engages us and I am so proud of how much love and respect Neil expresses when he talks about my father. It's the perfect way he can 'do' my Dad that has brought his memory so close to me over these last few days. Its truly amazing how he can bring him into the room with his voice and gestures: the gift of a skilled actor. He has made me miss him more than I have in years.

Having had these few days away from Portugal, from work, from my family, has given me the space to reflect on the last year and writing this book. It has been a wonderful journey, travelling down memory lane, but yet bittersweet, of course. I have loved reconnecting with so many people from my past, and especially spending time with my extended family.

Today, I travel home to my partner Luke and my beautiful children, Jasmine and Jude. It's time to step out of the past and look with them to the future.

I would like to finally end with a huge thank you to Nigel, without whom none of this would have been possible. The time and energy he has given to this project and the love and support he and his family have given me always.

Acknowledgements

This is a book that would never have happened without the time and memories of others. We hope that we have done justice to their spoken words.

First, to the siblings of my parents, to Auntie Sue and Uncle Robin and his wife Janie, our thanks. Likewise, to Ros, Sylvia and Peter, who shared their early days with Mum, and Bill Bray and Julian Sluggett, who grew up with my Dad. Thanks to those voices from Central: to Michael Feast, Bruce Robinson and Stephen Barnes, and for the help of 'Smudger' Smith, James Snell and Andy McCulloch from way back when.

Thank you Neil Morrissey; what a brilliant host, raconteur and star you are. Our book is defined by your Foreword.

Some of the busiest people around found time for our story: Gwen Taylor, Dame Helen Mirren, Kate Williams, Kenneth Cranham and Sir Richard Eyre. Thank you to Brian Hammond and the *Henley News* and Peter Vandrill and Mycal Miller for their 'Henley stories'. 'Thank you' is hardly appropriate for the long-term contribution of Cilla and Clive Dunn, but here it is anyway. Thank you to Dick and Leni Hill, and Elizabeth Howell, for being there then and for being there once again now.

Where would we have been without Esther Charkham? Her wonderful memories and networking led us to Tony May, Paul Knight and Ray Burdis. Thank you to them, as well.

Thank you so much to Liz.

There were also many others whose asides and anecdotes we used, to whom we are very grateful. Thanks are due to Juliet and Charmian for their valuable feedback. And finally...To Pat for her support, suggestions and subbing when they were most needed; and to Luke, who has been such a support throughout this busy year, particularly looking after the zoo and children each time there was a need to fly back to the UK.

K.E. & N.D.

Index

INDEX